STUDY AND LISTENING GUIDE

FOR

A HISTORY OF WESTERN MUSIC
FIFTH EDITION

AND

NORTON ANTHOLOGY OF WESTERN MUSIC
THIRD EDITION

STUDY AND LISTENING GUIDE

FOR

A HISTORY OF WESTERN MUSIC
FIFTH EDITION
BY DONALD JAY GROUT AND CLAUDE V. PALISCA

AND

NORTON ANTHOLOGY OF WESTERN MUSIC
THIRD EDITION
BY CLAUDE V. PALISCA

J. PETER BURKHOLDER

W. W. NORTON & COMPANY
NEW YORK LONDON

Cover art: *Lute with Molecules,* serigraph by Ben Shahn. Courtesy of the
Israel Museum, Jerusalem. © 1996 Estate of Ben Shahn / Licensed by
VAGA, New York, NY.

ISBN 0-393-96905-3

W. W. Norton & Company, Inc.
500 Fifth Avenue, New York, N.Y. 10110
http://www.wwnorton.com

W. W. Norton & Company Ltd.
10 Coptic Street, London WC1A 1PU

3 4 5 6 7 8 9 0

CONTENTS

READ THIS SECTION FIRST

The purpose of this *Study and Listening Guide* is to help you learn the material presented in *A History of Western Music,* 5th edition (HWM), by Donald Jay Grout and Claude V. Palisca, and acquaint yourself with the music in the *Norton Anthology of Western Music,* 3rd edition (NAWM), edited by Claude V. Palisca. Each chapter of the *Study and Listening Guide* is coordinated with a chapter of HWM and several pieces in NAWM.

There is much to know about the history of Western music and much to discover in the music itself. The best way to learn it is to follow some simple rules of successful learning.

1. Know your goals. It is easier to learn and to chart your progress if you know what you are trying to accomplish.
2. Proceed from the general to the specific, from the main points to the details. We learn best when what we are learning relates to what we already know. That is easiest when we start with the big picture.
3. Do not try to do everything at once. Trying to do too much, too fast makes learning difficult and frustrating. Divide the task into units small enough to grasp at one sitting. Do not cram for tests; study every day.
4. Write down what you learn. You will retain information and concepts more readily if you write them down for yourself rather than merely read them or hear them or highlight them in a book. The mental act of putting ideas into your own words and the physical act of writing out names, terms, dates, and other information create multiple pathways in your brain for recalling what you have learned.
5. Apply what you know. You learn and retain the skills and knowledge that you use.
6. Review what you know. We learn through repetition.
7. Have fun. You learn better and remember more when you are having fun. This does not mean goofing off, but means that you enjoy learning, mastering, and applying concepts and skills, whether riding a bike or discovering music history.

This study guide is designed to help you do all of these, through the following features.

Chapter Objectives

Each chapter begins with an outline of what you should learn from reading the texts and studying the music. These are the central issues confronted in the chapter. When you read the objectives before studying the material, they will pinpoint what you are trying to achieve. When you reread them after you have read the chapter, studied the music, and worked through the study questions, they can help you to evaluate your achievement. They direct you to the big picture, so you do not miss the forest for the trees.

Chapter Outline

The chapter outline shows how the corresponding chapter in HWM is divided into sections, summarizes the main points in each section, introduces important terms and names (highlighted in *italics*), and indicates which musical selections in NAWM relate to each topic. By reading the outline *first,* you begin with a general overview of the subject. Then, as you read the chapter, the details presented there will flesh out the general concepts presented in the outline. Since you have already read the main ideas in the outline, as you read the text you are beginning to review and reinforce what you have learned, while increasing the depth of your knowledge. When you have finished a section or chapter, reread the outline to make sure you grasp the main points. The outline will also be useful as you review.

Study Questions

The readings are full of information, and it may sometimes be difficult to figure out what is more and less significant. The study questions are designed to help you focus on the most important issues and concepts addressed in each section of each chapter and to apply those concepts to the music in NAWM. Material related to any of the questions may be found in a single place in HWM or scattered throughout the section. Relevant material may also be found in the analytical discussions of individual pieces in NAWM.

The questions are grouped by topic, and each question focuses on a single issue. This helps to divide each chapter into units of manageable size and allows you to proceed step by step. The questions vary in kind, from fill-in-the-blank questions to short essays that ask you to synthesize the material and apply it to the music, and even exercises that ask you to sing or play through the music. Tackling the material in small units and doing a variety of things in each section should help to make your work more fun.

Write down your answers. Space is provided to answer the study questions in this book. Writing down what you learn, rather than merely reading or highlighting the text, will help you retain it better. This is particularly helpful for recalling terms, names, and titles in foreign languages, since spelling them out for yourself will make them more familiar.

The study questions are not review questions, to be filled in after you are done reading and have closed the book. They are guides to the reading and to the music. After you have read a section of the text, or while you are reading it, work through the relevant study questions, rereading the text for answers as needed. Always respond to the questions in your own words, rather than copying directly from the text; this will help you master each concept, making it your own by phrasing it in your own way. If there is something you do not understand, return to the reading to find the missing information, or ask for help from your instructor.

Pay attention to study questions that ask you to define or to use terms that are introduced in the text. There is rote learning in every subject, and in music, much of it is of terminology. Each musical repertory has its own specialized vocabulary, often borrowed from Italian, Latin, French, or German. You cannot communicate with others about this music without mastering these terms.

Many questions ask you to apply to the pieces in NAWM concepts and terms that are presented in the text. In this way you will get to know the music better and will reinforce your grasp of the concepts and terms by applying what you know to the music itself.

The study questions on the music are set off in boxes headlined *Music to Study.* Each of these subsections begins with a list of the pieces in NAWM under consideration, indicating the location of each piece on the recordings that accompany NAWM (by number and track on the compact disks and by number and side on the cassette tapes).

You should listen to each piece in NAWM several times, including at least once before reading about it and at least once afterward. The heart of music history is the music itself, and a major part of your study should be listening to and becoming familiar with the music.

Terms and Names to Know

Near the end of each chapter is a list of important terms and names that appear in the texts and are highlighted in italics in the chapter outline. Most of these are covered in the study questions. They are listed separately here to help you review and to test your retention of what you have learned. In addition to these names, you should know the composers and titles of the pieces you studied. Use the lists in reviewing at the end of each chapter and in reviewing for examinations.

Review Questions

Each chapter ends with review questions that ask you to reflect more generally on the material you have learned. Most of them are like essay questions that you might encounter on a test. These may be used as springboards for discussion in class or with your study group, or as essay questions for practice as you study for examinations. Others are exercises that ask you to pull together information from several places in the chapter.

How to Proceed

The following procedure is recommended, but any procedure that helps you learn the most effectively and efficiently is the right one for you.

1. As you start each chapter, read the **chapter objectives** first to see what is expected of you.
2. Read through the **chapter outline.** Notice the topics that are covered, the main points that are made, and the terms that are introduced. Important new terms and names are given in italics.
3. Now work through the chapter section by section, as divided in the outline. Each section is marked with a roman numeral in the outline and starts with a heading in capital letters in HWM.
4. Start each section by listening to the pieces in NAWM that are listed in this section of the outline. Read through the text and translation before listening to vocal pieces, and listen to every piece with the score. (If you have time, you might first listen to each piece without the score, and you might also sing or play through the piece yourself.) This lets you encounter the music first, just as music. Later, you will come back to it and apply the principles you learn in reading the text.
5. Next, read the section in HWM, using the chapter outline as a guide. As the text refers you to pieces in NAWM, look again at the music and read the analytical discussion of each piece.
6. Work through the **study questions** for this section. Refer again to the music when the questions direct you to do so, and study the music or review HWM and the analytical discussions in NAWM to find the information you need to answer the questions. (Instead of reading first and then working through the study questions, you may find it more convenient to answer the study questions as you read through the text.)
7. When you are done rereading the texts and answering the study questions, review the chapter outline for this section and look over your answers to the questions. If there is anything you do not understand, refer back to the text, or make a note of it in the margin and ask your instructor for help.
8. Listen to the music again, and check your answers to the relevant study questions. Then congratulate yourself for finishing this section of the chapter. You may move on to the next section, or save it for another day.
9. At the end of the chapter, review by checking your knowledge of the terms and names to know, rereading the chapter outline, and rereading your answers to the study questions. Read the objectives again to make

sure you have accomplished them. Read the review questions and write brief answers in outline form, or use them as practice essay questions before examinations.

Note to the Instructor

This *Study and Listening Guide* is designed to walk the student through the material in HWM and NAWM step by step. Not every teacher will want to include all the content covered in the texts, and each teacher is likely to emphasize different aspects of the music and its history. Each instructor is encouraged to tailor this study guide to the needs of the individual course.

The study questions are designed to be used as guides for the student, as the basis for work in drill sessions, or as problem sets to be handed in. There are many questions, so that each significant topic can be covered. The instructor is encouraged to select which of the questions students should do on their own, which they may omit, and which should be handed in, if any. The review questions can also be useful in several ways: as guides for individual review, as model test questions, or as short writing assignments in or out of class. For courses in which this *Study and Listening Guide* is a required text, permission is granted to use any of the questions on examinations.

ACKNOWLEDGMENTS

Any book is a collaborative effort, and teaching materials are especially so. This *Study and Listening Guide* originated in a group of study questions for the first twelve chapters of *A History of Western Music,* 4th edition, by Donald Jay Grout and Claude V. Palisca, and the *Norton Anthology of Western Music,* volume 1, 2nd edition, edited by Claude V. Palisca. Questions were contributed by me and by my associate instructors for Music History and Literature I at the Indiana University School of Music in fall 1993, Brian Bourkland, Nicholas Butler, Kirk Ditzler, Gesa Kordes, and Mario Ortiz-Acuña. I am grateful for their collaboration, their suggestions, and the questions of theirs that remain here in some form. I am also grateful to my associate instructors in fall 1995, John Anderies, Nicholas Butler, Pablo Corá, David Lieberman, Felicia Miyakawa, and Patrick Warfield, who used the first draft of this study guide and offered very helpful feedback. My students for that semester, my colleague Austin B. Caswell and his students, and my colleague Thomas Noblitt provided encouragement and useful comments. Thanks also to Claude V. Palisca for helpful advice and for letting me consult materials he had developed, Michael Ochs for guidance on format and content, Gabrielle Karp for providing up-to-date drafts, galleys, and proofs of the new editions of *A History of Western Music* and the *Norton Anthology of Western Music* as they became available, and Kristine Forney for her suggestions. Thanks finally to Doug McKinney for his seemingly unlimited patience and support.

STUDY AND LISTENING GUIDE

For

A HISTORY OF WESTERN MUSIC
FIFTH EDITION

And

NORTON ANTHOLOGY OF WESTERN MUSIC
THIRD EDITION

MUSICAL LIFE AND THOUGHT IN ANCIENT GREECE AND ROME

1

CHAPTER OBJECTIVES

After you complete the reading, study of the music, and study questions for this chapter, you should be able to:

1. identify several elements of Western music and theory that derive from the music of ancient Greece, Rome, or Israel;
2. describe in general terms the musical life of ancient Greece and Rome;
3. explain why the ancient Greeks viewed music as closely connected to numbers, astronomy, and poetry, and how they thought it affected a person's character and behavior;
4. identify some basic terms of Greek music theory and some ancient writers on music;
5. name some aspects of the liturgy and music of the Western Christian Church that derive from Jewish and Byzantine practices;
6. explain how Gregorian chant came to be the standard repertory of liturgical song for the Western Church; and
7. summarize early Christian attitudes toward music, including the role of music in the church, the place of music among the liberal arts, and the relation of audible music to the mathematical proportions that govern nature and human beings, and explain how these views relate to ancient Greek views of music.

CHAPTER OUTLINE

I. The Greek and Roman Heritage (HWM 1–2)

Western culture has roots in ancient Greece and Rome. Although little ancient music survived, ancient writings about music, particularly music theory, had a strong influence on later centuries.

II. Music in Ancient Greek Life and Thought (HWM 2–7)

A. Greek Musical Life

In ancient Greece, music was linked to the gods, divine powers, and religious ceremonies. There were three main instruments, played alone or to accompany singing:

1. The *lyre,* a plucked string instrument associated with Apollo;
2. The *aulos,* a reed instrument associated with Dionysus and Greek drama;
3. The *kithara,* a larger relative of the lyre.

Music festivals and contests were an important part of Greek musical life after the 5th century B.C. About forty pieces or fragments of music survive, most of them from relatively late periods, when Greek music had become simplified after a period of greater complexity. Greek music was *monophonic,* but was often performed in *heterophony.* It was usually improvised, not read from notation.

B. Greek Musical Thought

Greek theory associated music with numbers (through the simple ratios that produced the consonant intervals) and therefore with astronomy. Music was closely tied to poetry, which was usually sung.

C. The Doctrine of *Ethos*

The Greeks held that music could directly affect character and behavior by arousing desirable or undesirable feelings. Because of this, some argued that only certain kinds of music were desirable. (*Ethos* is related to the English word "ethics" and means "character"; music was believed to convey ethical attitudes.)

III. The Greek Musical System (HWM 8–15, NAWM 1-2)

The Greek musical system shares several elements with later Western systems, such as notes, intervals (including tones, semitones, and thirds), and scales. Greek scales were constructed from *tetrachords,* groups of four notes spanning a perfect fourth. *Pythagoras* (ca. 500 B.C.) is credited with having discovered that the consonant intervals were produced by simple number ratios of 2:1 for the octave, 3:2 for the fifth, and 4:3 for the fourth.

Sidebar: Greek Music Theory in Depth

There were three *genera* (plural of *genus,* meaning type or class) of tetrachords: *diatonic, chromatic,* and *enharmonic.* Tetrachords could be arranged so that they were *conjunct* (so that the top note of one was the bottom note of the other) or *disjunct* (with a whole tone in between). The *Greater Perfect System* was an arrangement of four tetrachords covering two octaves. The scale-types used by the Greeks were called *tonoi* (plural of *tonos*); theorists differ in describing them. Cleonides and Ptolemy recognized seven different scale-types, each with a unique series of tones and semitones, like the scales that can be played on the white keys of the modern piano starting on the seven different notes.

IV. Music in Ancient Rome (HWM 15–17)

The Romans adopted many aspects of Greek musical culture, including religious and ceremonial music, music in private entertainment, and public festivals and competitions. Roman music shared most characteristics of Greek music.

V. The Early Christian Church (HWM 17–29)

A. The Decline of Rome
As the Roman Empire declined and the Western Empire collapsed in the fifth century A.D., the Christian Church became the main cultural force in Europe. It rejected pagan uses of music, while adapting music to the needs of the Church.

B. The Judaic Heritage
Although Christian worship services were not modeled directly on Jewish ceremonies, there are strong parallels, including a symbolic sacrifice, a ceremonial meal, the reading of Scripture, the singing of *psalms,* and the practice of assigning certain readings and psalms to specific days of the calendar.

C. The Spread of Christianity
As Christianity spread, the Church absorbed musical practices from many areas. Among the most important were psalm singing and *hymns* as used in the monasteries in Syria and later cultivated in Byzantium and Milan.

D. Byzantium
Each region of the church in the east developed its own *liturgy. Byzantium,* later called Constantinople after the Roman Emperor *Constantine,* was the capital of the Eastern Roman Empire from 395 to 1453, and its musical practices influenced the West.

Sidebar: Byzantine Music in Depth
Particularly important were the Byzantine hymns, of which there were several types. The *kanones* were poetic elaborations on the biblical *canticles.* Their melodies were created from melodic formulas in a process called *centonization.* Byzantine music used eight modes (called *echoi,* singular *echos*) that resemble the *modes* later adopted in Western music theory.

E. Western Liturgies
Between the fifth and eighth centuries, each region of the Western Church also developed its own liturgy and repertory of liturgical melodies, called *chants.* The Frankish king *Charlemagne,* crowned Holy Roman Emperor in 800, sought to impose the Roman liturgy and repertory of chant throughout his entire domain (modern France, Switzerland, western Germany, and northern Italy). This led to the rise throughout this region of *Gregorian chant* (named

for Pope Gregory I or II), which combined ancient, Roman, and Frankish elements and became the standard repertory of chants for the Western Church from the 9th through the 16th centuries. Modern editions of Gregorian chant, including the *Liber usualis,* were prepared in the late 19th century by monks at the Benedictine *Abbey of Solesmes* in France. The next most important chant repertory in the West is that of Milan, named *Ambrosian chant* after St. Ambrose.

F. The Dominance of Rome

Beginning in the 4th century, the bishop of Rome, also known as the *pope,* became the leader of the Western Church, and Latin its official language. Several popes sought to improve singing and standardize the chants.

G. The Church Fathers

Early Church leaders regarded music as the servant of religion, opposed listening to music for pleasure, and excluded instrumental music from church services. Christian writers passed on the music theory and philosophy of the ancient world, including the *seven liberal arts*: the three verbal arts called the *trivium* (grammar, dialectic, and rhetoric) and the four mathematical disciplines called the *quadrivium* (geometry, arithmetic, astronomy, and harmonics, or music).

H. Boethius

The heritage of Greek music theory was transmitted to the Middle Ages through *De institutione musica* (The Fundamentals of Music) by *Boethius* (ca. 480–524). He described three kinds of music: *musica mundana* (cosmic music), the orderly numerical relations that control the natural world; *musica humana* (human music), which controls the human body and soul; and *musica instrumentalis,* audible music produced by voices or instruments.

STUDY QUESTIONS

The Greek and Roman Heritage (HWM 1–2)

1. Artists and writers of the Middle Ages and later periods imitated the art and literature of ancient Greece and Rome. Why did musicians find it difficult to imitate ancient music? What aspects of ancient music did they draw on?

Music in Ancient Greek Life and Thought (HWM 2–7, NAWM 1–2)

2. What were the three main instruments used by the ancient Greeks? How was each played, and on what occasions was it used? Which instrument was associated with Apollo, and which with Dionysus?

   a. _____

   b. _____

   c. _____

3. In the Greek conception, what were the links between music, numbers, and astronomy?

4. In Greek musical life, how was music related to or dependent upon poetry?

5. According to Plato and Aristotle, how could music affect a person's character and behavior? Why was it important that certain kinds of music be promoted and other kinds suppressed? What is the relevance of this debate for our own time?

The Greek Musical System and Greek Music Theory in Depth (HWM 8–15, NAWM 1-2)

6. Who was Pythagoras, and when did he live? According to legend, what did he discover?

7. What is a *tetrachord*?

8. What are the three *genera* of tetrachord? What intervals appear in each, in order from top to bottom?

    1. _____   _____

    2. _____   _____

    3. _____   _____

9. When are two successive tetrachords *conjunct,* and when are they *disjunct?*

    conjunct: _____

    disjunct: _____

10. How are tetrachords combined in the *Greater Perfect System?*

Music to Study
>   **NAWM 1**: *Epitaph of Seikilos,* skolion or drinking song (ca. first century A.D.)
>   CD 1.1 (Concise 1.1)   Cassette 1.A (Concise 1.A)
>   **NAWM 2**: Euripides, from *Orestes,* fragment of *stasimon* chorus (408 B.C.,
>   the date of the play, or third to second century B.C., the date of the
>   papyrus on which the music is preserved)
>   CD 1.2   Cassette 1.A

11. How do the *Epitaph of Seikilos* (NAWM 1) and the *stasimon* chorus from Euripides' *Orestes* (NAWM 2) exemplify the characteristics typical of Greek music as described in HWM, pp. 2–7 and the summary on pp. 16–17? (Note: One way they are not typical is in being notated, rather than improvised or transmitted orally.)

12. What *genus* or *genera* does each work use, the diatonic, chromatic, or enharmonic? How can you tell?

  Epitaph of Seikilos:

  Chorus from *Orestes*:

13. How does rhythm work in this music? (Hint: In the line below the staff marked "Musical rhythm," "S" indicates a short note, "L" a note twice as long.) How does the rhythm of these songs differ from rhythm in the common practice of the 19th century?

Music in Ancient Rome (HWM 15–17)

14. In what ways did musical life in Rome resemble musical life in ancient Greece?

15. What are some basic characteristics of ancient Greek and Roman music (see pp. 16–17)?

The Early Christian Church (HWM 17–29)

16. How did the Christian Church become the main cultural force in Europe? What did it replace in this role?

17. What aspects of ancient Greek and Roman music did the early Church reject, and why?

18. What similarities do you notice between Jewish religious practices and the liturgy and music of early Christian worship? In particular, how are psalms used?

19. What are *hymns*? How far back do they go in Christian worship?

20. What are *canticles*?

21. What is *centonization*?

22. What role did Charlemagne play in relation to liturgy and chant? What were the sources for Gregorian chant, and what did it replace?

23. What is the significance of the Abbey of Solesmes for Gregorian chant?

24. What attitudes toward music were held by the leaders of the Church in the early Middle Ages? How do these views compare to the views of Plato and Aristotle?

25. How does music fit into the seven liberal arts? Why is music (or harmonics) grouped with the mathematical arts, rather than with the verbal arts?

26. Who was Boethius? Why was he important for music in the Middle Ages?

27. In Boethius's view, what was *musica instrumentalis,* and how did it relate to *musica mundana* and *musica humana*? How does this view compare to ancient Greek ideas about music?

TERMS TO KNOW

Terms Related to Ancient Greek Music

aulos
lyre
kithara
doctrine of ethos
tetrachord

genus (pl. genera): diatonic,
    chromatic, enharmonic
conjunct and disjunct tetrachords
Greater Perfect System
tonos (pl. tonoi)

Terms Related to Judeo-Christian Music

psalms
hymns
liturgy
canticles
kanones
centonization
echos (pl. echoi)

chant
Gregorian chant
Ambrosian chant
liberal arts, trivium, quadrivium
musica mundana, musica humana,
    musica instrumentalis

NAMES TO KNOW

Pythagoras
Plato
Aristotle
Byzantium
Constantine
Charlemagne

Liber usualis
Abbey of Solesmes
St. Ambrose
St. Augustine
Boethius
De institutione musica

REVIEW QUESTIONS

1. Why do we study ancient Greek music? What does it have to do with our music? What are some similarities between Greek music and ours? What are some similarities between Greek music theory and common-practice music theory?

2. Why are there white and black keys on the piano? Why do we use scales that span an octave and include a perfect fourth and fifth degree? How do these phenomena relate to ancient Greek music theory?

3. What are some Greek ideas about the power of music and its role in society that are still relevant today?

4. What are the sources of Gregorian chant, the repertory of melodies used in the Western Church? What were the contributions of the Judaic tradition, Syria, Byzantium, and Europe? How did Gregorian chant come to be standardized?

5. How did early Christian writers, including St. Augustine and Boethius, view music? How do their attitudes compare to those of the ancient Greeks, including Plato and Aristotle?

CHANT AND SECULAR SONG IN THE MIDDLE AGES

2

CHAPTER OBJECTIVES

After you complete the reading, study of the music, and study questions for this chapter, you should be able to:

1. describe in general terms the liturgical context for plainchant in the Roman Church, including the names of the Offices and the main outlines of the Mass;
2. read a melody in plainchant notation and briefly describe the stages through which the notation evolved;
3. describe the varieties of Roman chant and explain how the shape and manner of performance of each chant relates to its liturgical function;
4. characterize the eight Church modes by their final, tenor, and range and identify the mode of a given chant or song;
5. describe medieval solmization;
6. name the varieties of secular musicians active during the Middle Ages and the regions and social classes from which they came;
7. describe some examples of medieval secular song by troubadours, trouvères, *Minnesinger,* and *Meistersinger;*
8. describe the *estampie,* the oldest surviving form of instrumental music;
9. name and briefly describe some of the instruments played during the Middle Ages; and
10. name and briefly identify a few of the people who contributed to the repertory of medieval monophonic music.

CHAPTER OUTLINE

I. Roman Chant and Liturgy (HWM 32–42)

A. Chant

Chant was created for religious services in the Roman Church, and the shape of each chant is determined by its role in the service. Thus, our study of chant must begin with an understanding of the Roman *liturgy,* the texts and actions that make up a religious service.

B. The Roman Liturgy

There are two main types of service.

1. The *Office* or *Canonical Hours* evolved from group prayer and psalm singing. Eight Offices are celebrated at specified times each day. Offices feature the singing of *psalms* and *canticles* (poetic passages from the Bible), each with an associated chant called an *antiphon.* They also include the singing of hymns and the chanting of lessons (passages of Scripture) with musical responses called *responsories.*

2. The *Mass* is the most important service. It opens with introductory prayers and chants, continues with Bible readings, responses, and the Creed, and culminates in a symbolic reenactment of the Last Supper of Jesus and his disciples. The texts for certain parts of the Mass, called the *Proper,* change from day to day. The texts of other portions, called the *Ordinary,* are the same each time. (For this reason, the Proper chants are called by their function, such as Introit, Gospel, or Communion, while the Ordinary chants are named by their first words, such as Kyrie or Credo.)

C. Modern Plainchant Notation

Plainchant notation uses a staff of four lines, two movable clefs, and a variety of note shapes called *neumes,* which may indicate one or more notes. Before notation, chant melodies were passed down orally. Notation helped to standardize the melodies and reduced the need for memorization.

II. Classes, Forms, and Types of Chant (HWM 42–48, NAWM 3–4)

A. Classifications of Chant

Chants can be classified in several ways:

1. by the origin and nature of the text (biblical or nonbiblical, prose or poetical);
2. by the manner of performance (*antiphonal, responsorial,* or *direct*);
3. by the number of notes per syllable (*syllabic,* primarily one note per syllable; *neumatic,* 1–5 notes; or *melismatic,* with many syllables having many notes); and
4. by the form (balanced phrases, strophic form, or free form).

Different types of chant reflect the accentuation and phrasing of the words in differing ways.

B. Recitation Formulas

The simplest chants are *recitation formulas* for chanting prayers and Bible readings. *Psalm tones* are formulas for singing the psalms in the Office. There is one psalm tone for each church mode (plus one "wandering tone"). Most of the formula consists of recitation on the *tenor* or *reciting tone* of the mode, with an initial figure at the beginning of the first verse and cadential figures to mark the middle and end of each psalm verse. The *Magnificat* is sung to a similar, slightly more decorated formula.   **Music: NAWM 4a, 4c, 4e, 4g, 4i, and 4n**

C. Antiphons

Each psalm tone and canticle in the Office is paired with an *antiphon,* sung before and after the psalm or canticle. (They are called antiphons because the psalms and canticles are sung antiphonally by halves of the choir.) There are also independent antiphons used on other occasions. **Music: NAWM 4b, 4d, 4f, 4h, and 4m**

D. Responsory or Respond

A *responsory* or *respond* is a chant sung before and after a Scripture reading or prayer. (Responsories were originally sung responsorially, although this is not always true today.)   **Music: NAWM 4j**

E. Antiphonal Psalmody

In the Mass, the *Introit* and *Communion* were once full psalms with antiphons (more elaborate than Office antiphons) sung antiphonally by the choir. The Introit now has only one verse (plus the Doxology) and the Communion has none. (Note the link between antiphonal performance by the choir and the neumatic style of these chants.)   **Music: NAWM 3a and 3i**

F. Proper Chants of the Mass

The most elaborate chants of the Mass are the Graduals, Alleluias, Tracts, and Offertories. Like the Introit and Communion, they are part of the Proper.

1. *Tracts* are long, melismatic, and formulaic and evolved from direct singing of a psalm by a soloist. (Note the link between solo performance and melismatic style.) They are sung only in Advent and Lent.

2. *Graduals* are shortened responsories in terms of their texts, with a respond followed by a single psalm verse, but are long chants because they are melismatic. They are sung responsorially between a soloist and the choir. (Note again the link to melismatic style.)   **Music: NAWM 3d**

3. *Alleluias* include a refrain on the word "alleluia," closing with a long melisma called a *jubilus*; a psalm verse that usually ends with part or all of the refrain melody; and a repetition of the refrain. Alleluias are sung responsorially and are melismatic. They are omitted during Advent and Lent.   **Music: NAWM 3e**

4. *Offertories* evolved from antiphonal psalms but became very elaborate, often melismatic.   **Music: NAWM 3f**

G. Chants of the Ordinary

The chants of the Ordinary began as simple syllabic melodies sung by the congregation. Now they are sung by the choir. The *Gloria* and *Credo,* with their long texts, remain mostly syllabic, while the others are more elaborate. Because of their texts, the *Kyrie, Sanctus,* and *Agnus Dei* tend to have three-part sectional arrangements that can vary between settings.   **Music: NAWM 3b, 3c, 3g, and 3h**

III. Later Developments of the Chant (HWM 48–53, NAWM 5–7)

A. Historical conditions

Because of the rise of new cultural centers in western and central Europe and the decline of Christian influence in the south, almost all important developments in music from the 9th century to near the end of the Middle Ages took place north of the Alps.

B. Tropes

Tropes are newly composed additions to existing chants. They served as prefaces or were interpolated within a chant. There are three types: adding both text and music; adding music only; or adding text to existing melismas. Tropes flourished in the 10th and 11th centuries and then gradually disappeared. **Music: NAWM 7**

C. Sequences

Sequences were newly composed chants, usually sung after the Alleluia in the Mass. The first sequences (ca. 9th century) were melismas added to Alleluias, to which prose texts were sometimes added. Later sequences were composed independently. The genre was at its peak between the 10th and 13th centuries. The form usually consists of a series of musical phrases, of which all but the first and last are repeated to new phrases of text. Hildegard of Bingen (1098–1179), a famous abbess and mystic, composed both words and music for several sequences. All but a few sequences were eliminated from the liturgy by the Council of Trent (1545–63). **Music: NAWM 5–6**

D. Liturgical Drama

Liturgical dramas were short dialogues set to chant and performed just prior to the Mass. **Music: NAWM 7**

IV. Medieval Music Theory and Practice (HWM 53–60)

A. Treatises

Treatises from the eighth century through the late Middle Ages tend to focus on practical issues such as performance, notation, and the modes. Among the most significant is the *Micrologus* (ca. 1025–28) by *Guido of Arezzo*.

B. The Church Modes

Medieval theorists recognized *eight Church modes*, defined by their *finalis* or *final,* their *tenor* or *reciting tone,* and their *range. Authentic modes* have the final near the bottom of their range; *plagal modes* have the final near the middle. There is one plagal and one authentic mode on each of four finals: *D, E, F,* and *G.* These modes served as the foundation for music theory for centuries.

C. Solmization

The 11th-century theorist Guido of Arezzo devised a set of *solmization* syllables to help singers remember where whole tones and semitones occur. With some modifications, these same syllables are still in use. The medieval system evolved to include three *hexachords* (*natural* on *C*, *hard* on *G*, and *soft* on *F*, with a *B♭*) and the idea of changing between hexachords *(mutation)* to cover a wider range and account for both *B♭* and *B♮*. The *Guidonian hand* assigned a pitch to each joint of the left hand as a tool to teach notes and intervals.

D. Notation

Chant notation evolved from *neumes* above the words to indicate rising or falling pitches (9th century), to *heighted* or *diastematic neumes* which showed the pitches more clearly (10th century), to the inclusion of one or two lines to indicate certain relative pitches, to the invention of the four-line staff in the 11th century, which allowed precise notation of relative pitch. Durations were not indicated precisely, and we do not know what the rhythm of chant was like.

V. Nonliturgical and Secular Monody (HWM 60–67, NAWM 8–12)

A. Early Secular Genres

Early forms of secular music (from the 11th and 12th centuries) include three types of monophonic song:

1. *Goliard songs* are secular songs with Latin texts celebrating the vagabond life of students and wandering clerics called *Goliards*.
2. *Conductus* is a term used for any serious, nonliturgical Latin song, sacred or secular, with a metrical text and a newly composed melody.
3. The *chanson de geste* was an epic narrative poem in the vernacular (such as the *Song of Roland,* the French national epic), sung to melodic formulas.

B. Jongleurs

Jongleurs or *ménestrals* (minstrels) made a living as traveling musicians and performers, on the margins of society.

C. Troubadours and Trouvères

Troubadours (feminine: *trobairitz*) were poet-composers active in southern France in the 11th and 12th centuries. They wrote in the language of the region, called *Provençal* (or *langue d'oc* or *Occitan*), and were from or associated with the aristocracy. Their counterparts in northern France, called *trouvères,* wrote in the *langue d'oïl,* the ancestor of modern French, and remained active through the 13th century. Many of the troubadour and trouvère songs are about love. Some included dialogue or enacted little dramas, and others depicted a kind of love—called *courtly love*—in which a discreet, unattainable woman was adored from a distance. **Music: NAWM 8–10**

D. Troubadour and Trouvère Melodies

Troubadour and trouvère melodies are mostly syllabic with a range of about an octave or less. The rhythm of troubadour melodies is obscure, but later trouvère melodies have clear rhythms. Various patterns of repetition are used, along with free composition. Some trouvère songs feature a *refrain,* a recurring line of text with a recurring musical setting.

E. Minnesinger

The *Minnesinger* were knightly poet-composers active in German lands from the 12th through the 14th centuries. They sang of an idealized love (*Minne*), and their melodies are formed of phrases that repeat in orderly patterns. **Music: NAWM 11**

F. Meistersinger

The *Meistersinger* were German poet-composers of the 14th through 16th centuries, drawn from the urban middle class of tradesmen and artisans rather than from the aristocracy. Their songs were governed by rigid rules. A common form is the *bar form*: aab, with the b section (*Abgesang*) often repeating some or all of the a section (*Stollen*). **Music: NAWM 12**

G. Songs of Other Countries

Other types of monophonic song include religious songs not intended for use in church, such as the Spanish *cantiga,* songs of praise to the Virgin, and the Italian *lauda.*

VI. Medieval Instrumental Music and Instruments (HWM 67–70, NAWM 13)

A. Dances

Dances were accompanied both by songs and by instrumental music. The oldest surviving form of instrumental music is the *estampie,* several of which survive from the 13th and 14th centuries. Each section was played twice, first with an *open,* or incomplete, cadence and then with a *closed,* or full, cadence. **Music: NAWM 13**

B. Musical Instruments

There was a rich variety of instruments in the Middle Ages, including plucked strings such as the harp, *psaltery,* and lute; bowed strings such as the *vielle* or *Fiedel;* an ancestor of the hurdy-gurdy called the *organistrum;* wind instruments such as recorders, transverse flutes, *shawms,* and bagpipes; brass instruments such as the trumpet; and drums. There were also church organs, *portative organs,* and *positive organs.*

STUDY QUESTIONS

Roman Chant and Liturgy (HWM 32–42)

1. What was the role of chant in the medieval church? How did its role change after the *Second Vatican Council* (1962–65)? Where is chant performed today?

2. What are the *Offices* or *Canonical Hours*? From what earlier practice do they derive?

3. Fill in the names of the Offices celebrated at the following times of day. Circle the ones that are most important for music.

before sunrise	_____	about noon	_____
sunrise	_____	about 3 P.M.	_____
about 6 A.M.	_____	sunset	_____
about 9 A.M.	_____	just after the Office celebrated at sunset	_____

4. What does the *Mass* commemorate?

5. What are the three sections of the Mass liturgy? What is the main focus of each one?

   a. _____

   b. _____

   c. _____

6. What is the *Ordinary* of the Mass, and what is the *Proper*?

   Which set of chants, the Proper or the Ordinary, are called by the first word or words of the text?

   _____

7. Which of the following chants are from the Mass Ordinary, and which are from the Proper?

Introit	_____	Credo	_____
Kyrie	_____	Offertory	_____
Gloria	_____	Sanctus	_____
Gradual	_____	Agnus Dei	_____
Alleluia	_____	Communion	_____
Tract	_____	Ite missa est	_____

8. When did chant melodies begin to be written down? _____

9. How were chant melodies transmitted before notation was developed? Why was notation useful?

10. Example 2.1 in HWM (p. 39) is a transcription in modern notation of the chant on the facing page. The plainchant notation uses a staff of four lines. As in the modern five-line staff, each line stands for a pitch a third lower than the line above it, and the spaces stand for the pitches in between. The first symbol in each line is a clef; here it is a C clef on the top line, indicating that the top line stands for middle *C*. What pitch does each of the following lines and spaces stand for?

the second line from the top   _____

the space between the second and third lines   _____

the bottom line   _____

the space below the bottom line   _____

In plainchant notation, what does a dot next to a note signify? (Note: This dot is a sign introduced by modern editors, and does not appear in medieval manuscripts.)

Musical exercise in reading chant notation (**HWM 38–39**)

You do not have to know the names of the different note shapes. But with a little practice you should be able to read the chant notation. Practice in the following way:

Reading the modern notation in Example 2.1, sing (or play on your instrument) the first phrase of the chant (the top line of the example). You may omit the words if it is easier for you to do so.

Then sing (or play) the same phrase, using the plainchant notation. Go back and forth until you understand how the plainchant notation indicates the same pitches and rhythms as the modern notation. If you have trouble with any of the note shapes, check the explanation in the text on pp. 38–40 of HWM or p. 7 of NAWM.

Go through the same process for each phrase in turn: sing it first from the modern notation, then from the plainchant notation.

When you are finished, sing through the whole chant from the plainchant notation. If you get stuck, refer to the modern transcription.

Classes, Forms, and Types of Chant (HWM 42–48, NAWM 3–4)

11. What manner of performance does each of the following terms describe?

    antiphonal performance

    responsorial performance

    direct performance

Music to Study
>   **NAWM 3**: Mass for Christmas Day, in Gregorian chant

3a: Introit: *Puer natus est nobis* CD 1.3   Cassette 1.A
3b: Kyrie   CD 1.4 (Concise 1.2) Cassette 1.A (Concise 1.A)
3c: Gloria   CD 1.5   Cassette 1.A
3d: Gradual: *Viderunt omnes*   CD 1.6–7   Cassette 1.A
3e: Alleluia *Dies sanctificatus*   CD 1.8 (Concise 1.3) Cassette 1.A (Concise 1.A)
3f: Offertory: *Tui sunt caeli*   CD 1.9   Cassette 1.A
3g: Sanctus   CD 1.10   Cassette 1.A
3h: Agnus Dei   CD 1.11   Cassette 1.A
3i: Communion *Viderunt omnes* CD 1.12   Cassette 1.A

NAWM 4: Office of Second Vespers, Nativity of Our Lord (evening service on
>   Christmas Day), in Gregorian chant

4a: *Deus in adjutorium*   not on recording
4b: Antiphon for first psalm   CD 1.13 (Concise 1.4) Cassette 1.A Concise 1.A)
4c: First psalm   CD 1.14 (Concise 1.5) Cassette 1.A (Concise 1.A)
4d: Antiphon for second psalm   not on recording
4e: Second psalm   not on recording
4f: Antiphon for third psalm   not on recording
4g: Third psalm   not on recording
4h: Antiphon for fourth psalm   not on recording
4i: Fourth psalm   not on recording
4j: Short Responsory   CD 1.15   Cassette 1.A
4k: Hymn   not on recording
4l: Verse   not on recording
4m: Antiphon for Magnificat   not on recording
4n: Magnificat (Canticle of   not on recording
   the Blessed Virgin Mary)

12. Look at the chants of the Mass and Office in NAWM 3 and 4. Find three
    examples of primarily *syllabic* chants, three *neumatic* chants, and three
    melismatic chants.

syllabic	neumatic	melismatic
_____	_____	_____
_____	_____	_____
_____	_____	_____

13. What are some ways that the music of chant reflects the accentuation and phrasing of the text? For each way you mention, find an example among the chants of the Mass and Office in NAWM 3 and 4.

14. What are *psalm tones*?

How many are there? _____
Where are they used? Where do they appear in NAWM 3 or 4?

15. How are psalm tones shaped, and how do they adjust to suit the many different texts with which they are used? Give an example from NAWM 4.

16. What is the *Lesser Doxology*? What does the abbreviation "E u o u a e" indicate (as in NAWM 3a and 4c)?

17. What is an *antiphon*? How are antiphons used in connection with the psalms in the Vespers in NAWM 4?

18. What is a *responsory* or *respond*?

19. Of the chants in the Proper of the Mass for Christmas Day (NAWM 3), which ones are generally syllabic, which tend to be neumatic, and which are melismatic? Which were originally performed antiphonally, and which responsorially?

	text-setting	performance
Introit	_____	_____
Gradual	_____	_____
Alleluia	_____	_____
Offertory	_____	_____
Communion	_____	_____

20. Diagram the form of the Introit in the Mass in NAWM 3, including repetitions of music and text. Use the following letters: A for the antiphon; P for the psalm verse; D for the Doxology.

How is the form of an Introit like the combination of psalm tone with antiphon in the Vespers, and how is it different? How could you tell the two apart?

21. How is the Alleluia in NAWM 3e shaped by musical repetition?

   Which parts are sung by the soloist(s)? _____

   Which parts are sung by the choir? _____

   What is the jubilus? _____

22. Of the chants in the Ordinary of the Mass in NAWM 3, which ones are generally syllabic, which tend to be neumatic, and which are melismatic? For any of them that use musical repetition, show the pattern of repetition.

Kyrie	_____	_____
Gloria	_____	_____
Sanctus	_____	_____
Agnus Dei	_____	_____

Later Developments of the Chant (HWM 48–53, NAWM 5–7)

23. What is a *trope*? What are the three types of trope? Where do tropes fit in the Mass?

24. What is a *sequence*? Where does it occur in the Mass?

   When were sequences composed? _____

   Why are there so few sequences in the modern liturgy?

25. Who was Notker Balbulus?   Where and when did he work?   And what, according to him, was his role in inventing the sequence?

26. What is a *liturgical drama*? What makes it liturgical? To what extent is it like a modern play?

Music to Study

> **NAWM 5:** Wipo, *Victimae paschali laudes*, sequence for Mass on Easter Day (first half of the 11th century)
>
>   CD 1.16 (Concise 1.6)   Cassette 1.A (Concise 1.A)
>
> **NAWM 6:** Hildegard of Bingen, *Ordo virtutum* (The Virtues), sacred music drama, excerpt: closing chorus, *In principio omnes* (ca. 1151)
>
>   CD 1.17–18 (Concise 1.7–8)   Cassette 1.A (Concise 1.A)
>
> **NAWM 7:** *Quem quaeritis in praesepe,* trope (liturgical drama) at Mass on Christmas Day (10th century)
>
>   CD 1.19   Cassette 1.A

27. Diagram the form of the sequence *Victimae paschali laudes* by Wipo (NAWM 5).

 In addition to the repetition of complete phrases for successive verses, where else does melodic repetition appear in this sequence?

28. How is melodic repetition used in Hildegard of Bingen's *In principio omnes* (NAWM 6)? How does this song differ from liturgical chant in function and in style?

29. In what sense is *Quem quaeritis in praesepe* (NAWM 7) a trope? Where does it fit in the Mass to which it is attached?

30. What makes *Quem quaeritis in praesepe* a liturgical drama?

31. How is the music of *Quem quaeritis in praesepe* unified through melodic repetition?

Medieval Music Theory and Practice (HWM 53–60)

32. The eight church modes are labeled by number and name. Each is defined by (1) its *finalis* or *final,* (2) its *tenor* or *reciting tone,* and (3) its *range.* Give the name, final, tenor, and range for each of the church modes.

Number	Name	Final	Tenor	Range
1	_____	____	____	_____
2	_____	____	____	_____
3	_____	____	____	_____
4	_____	____	____	_____
5	_____	____	____	_____
6	_____	____	____	_____
7	_____	____	____	_____
8	_____	____	____	_____

33. What is the difference between an *authentic* mode and a *plagal* mode?

    Which modes are authentic (indicate by number)?   _____

    Which are plagal? _____

34. Using the criteria of final and range, identify the mode of each of the following chants:

        Quem quaeritis in praesepe (NAWM 7)   _____

        Alleluia Pascha nostrum (NAWM 16a)   _____

        Conditor alme siderum (NAWM 29, verse 1) _____

    What makes the mode of *Victimae paschali laudes* (NAWM 5) hard to determine?

35. What is *solmization*? Why was it useful? When did *Guido of Arezzo* live, and what role did he play in the invention of solmization? How is medieval solmization similar to modern practice, and how does it differ?

36. What are the *natural, hard,* and *soft hexachords*? Why was it necessary to have all three? What is *mutation,* and how is it useful in singing?

37. What is the *Guidonian hand,* what was it used for, and how was it used?

38. How did chant notation evolve? What stages did it go through? What is one of its limitations?

Nonliturgical and Secular Monody (HWM 60–67, NAWM 8–12)

39. Who were the *Goliards*? Who were the *jongleurs* or *minstrels*? What kinds of music did each perform, and when and where did they perform it?

40. What is a *conductus*? How does it differ from a liturgical chant?

41. What is a *troubadour*? a *trobairitz*? a *trouvère*? When were they active, and what languages did they use? From what social classes did they come?

42. What might a performance of a troubadour or trouvère song include, besides singing?

43. What are some frequent topics or themes in troubadour and trouvère poetry?

What is *courtly love*?

44. Who are the *Minnesinger*? When and where were they active? How are their songs like troubadour and trouvère songs, and how do they differ?

45. Who are the *Meistersinger*? When and where were they active?

46. What is a *cantiga,* and where is it from? What is a *lauda,* and where is it from?

Music to Study

NAWM 8: Adam de la Halle, *Robins m'aime*, rondeau or trouvère song (ca. 1284)
CD 1.20   Cassette 1.A
NAWM 9: Bernart de Ventadorn, *Can vei*, troubadour song (ca. 1170–80)
CD 1.21 (Concise 1.9)   Cassette 1.A (Concise 1.A)
NAWM 10: Beatriz de Dia, *A chantar*, canso or troubadour song (second half of 12th century)
CD 1.22   Cassette 1.A
NAWM 11: Wizlau von Rügen, *We ich han gedacht*, Minnelied (ca. 1290–1325)
CD 1.23   Cassette 1.B
NAWM 12: Hans Sachs, *Nachdem David war redlich*, Meisterlied (ca. 1520–76)
CD 1.24   Cassette 1.B

47. Describe the melodic characteristics of troubadour songs, using Bernart de Ventadorn's *Can vei* (NAWM 9) and Beatriz de Dia's *A chantar* (NAWM 10) as examples.

    How many notes are set to each syllable? _____

    How large a range does the melody typically cover? _____

    Does the notation indicate the rhythm?

    How else would you characterize the melodic style?

48. How is the trouvère song *Robins m'aime* (NAWM 8) by Adam de la Halle different in style from the troubadour songs (NAWM 9–10)?

49. How do *Can vei*, *A chantar*, and *Robins m'aime* use melodic repetition? Chart the form of each (for the first two, chart the form of a single strophe; for the third, use capital letters for repetitions of music and text, and lowercase letters for repetitions of music with new words).

    Can vei   _____

    A chantar   _____

    Robins m'aime _____

50. What is the mode of each of these songs? (Use the mode number.)

    Can vei   _____

    A chantar   _____

    Robins m'aime _____

51. How does Wizlau von Rügen's Minnelied *We ich han gedacht* (NAWM 11) use melodic repetition? Chart its form.

This melody's consistent use of *B♭* and the ending on *A* indicate a transposed mode. If you transposed this Minnelied so that it used no accidentals, where would the final note be, and what mode would you say is used? (Use the mode number.)

        final_____   mode   _____

52. What is *bar form*? How is it used in Hans Sachs's *Nachdem David war redlich* (NAWM 12)? Does the *Abgesang* repeat material from the *Stollen*?

53. Of the secular monophonic songs in NAWM 8–11, which have a form similar to bar form as used in *Nachdem David war redlich*?

Medieval Instrumental Music and Instruments (HWM 67–70, NAWM 13)

Music to Study
   NAWM 13: *Istampita Palamento*, istampita or estampie (14th century)
      First part   CD 1.25   Cassette 1.B (all five parts)
      Second part   CD 1.26
      Third part   CD 1.27
      Fourth part   CD 1.28
      Fifth part   CD 1.29

54. What is an estampie? Which of its sections were repeated? How do the "open" and "closed" cadences work in the *Istampita Palamento* (NAWM 13)? (Note: This may be easier to follow while listening to the music.)

55. Briefly describe each of the following medieval instruments, explain how each was played, and name one or more modern instruments of which it is an ancestor.

   vielle/Fiedel

   organistrum

   psaltery

   shawm

   portative organ

   positive organ

56. What other instruments were used in the Middle Ages?

TERMS TO KNOW

In part because the Middle Ages are so long ago and the culture so distant from our own, there are many unfamiliar terms that relate to the music of this period. They are listed below in three groups. The terms related to liturgy will be useful for church music of later periods as well, since the liturgy has shaped church music of every period down to our own time.

Terms Related to Liturgy

liturgy
Office
Canonical Hours
Matins
Vespers
psalm
canticle
hymn

Mass
Ordinary: Kyrie, Gloria, Credo,
    Sanctus, Agnus Dei, Ite Missa
    Est, Benedicamus Domino
Proper: Introit, Gradual, Alleluia,
    Tract, Offertory, Communion
Magnificat

Terms Related to Chant

neume
antiphonal, responsorial,
    direct performance
melisma
syllabic, neumatic, melismatic
recitation formula
psalm tone
Lesser Doxology (Gloria Patri)
antiphon
responsory or respond
jubilus

trope
sequence
liturgical drama
mode: the eight church modes
authentic, plagal mode
final (finalis)
tenor or reciting tone
solmization
hard, soft, natural hexachords
mutation (of hexachords)
Guidonian hand

Terms Related to Other Monophonic Music

Goliard song
conductus
chanson de geste
jongleur or ménestral or minstrel
troubadour, trobairitz
trouvère
courtly love
refrain
Minnesinger
Meistersinger

bar form: Stollen, Abgesang
cantiga
lauda
estampie
open and closed cadences
vielle or Fiedel
organistrum
psaltery
shawm
portative organ, positive organ

NAMES TO KNOW

Monastery of St. Gall	Hildegard of Bingen
Notker Balbulus	Guido of Arezzo
Wipo	*Micrologus*

REVIEW QUESTIONS

1. Make a time-line from 800 to 1600 and locate on it the pieces in NAWM 5–13, their composers, and these other people and events: Charlemagne, Notker Balbulus, the Council of Trent, and Guido of Arezzo. (The chants in NAWM 3–4 come from many centuries and most cannot be dated accurately, so they cannot be fixed on your time-line.)

2. Why was notation devised, and how was it useful? How would your life as a musician be different if there were no notation?

3. How has the music of chant been shaped by its role in the ceremonies and liturgy of the Roman Church, by the texts, and by the manner in which it has been performed? Use as examples at least three individual chants of varying types, and show in what ways the musical characteristics of each are appropriate for its liturgical role, its text, and its manner of performance.

4. Write a chant melody to the text of the Kyrie, Sanctus, or Agnus Dei from the Mass in NAWM 3. Use the original chant as a model for the form, including repetition of words and of music. Use any of the eight Church modes *except* the mode of the original chant or its corresponding plagal or authentic mode. (For instance, since the Kyrie is in mode 1, do not use mode 1 or mode 2 to write your Kyrie.) Try to follow the style of chant as you have come to know it, including melodic contour, phrasing, and accentuation. You may use either modern or chant notation.

5. What practical contributions to the theory and performance of monophonic music were made between the seventh and the twelfth centuries?

6. Trace the history of monophonic secular song from the Goliards to the Meistersinger. For each group of poet-composers, note their region, language, place in society, and time of activity, and briefly describe their music.

7. In what ways are instrumental music and the use of instruments in accompanying singing similar in the Middle Ages and the present time, and in what ways do they most differ?

THE BEGINNINGS OF POLYPHONY AND THE MUSIC OF THE THIRTEENTH CENTURY

3

CHAPTER OBJECTIVES

After you complete the reading, study of the music, and study questions for this chapter, you should be able to:

1. name the new trends in 11th-century music that became distinguishing characteristics of Western music;
2. describe the varieties of polyphony practiced between the 9th and 13th centuries and trace their historical development;
3. define important terms and identify the people, works, and schools of composition that played a major role in the development of medieval polyphony; and
4. describe the origins and early evolution of the motet.

CHAPTER OUTLINE

I. Historical Background of Early Polyphony (HWM 73–74)

The 11th century brought prosperity and a cultural revival to much of western Europe, including the beginning of modern cities and universities and the rise of Romanesque architecture. This was also a time of change for music.

1. *Polyphony,* music of two or more independent voices, was becoming prominent in the church, starting a development unique in music history.
2. The development of precise *notation* allowed composers for the first time to fix a work in definitive form and transmit it accurately to others, so it could be performed by someone who had not already learned it by ear.
3. *Written composition* began to replace improvisation as a way to create new works.
4. Music was increasingly structured by *principles of order,* such as the eight church modes and rules governing rhythm and consonance.

II. Early Organum (HWM 74–77, NAWM 14)

A. Parallel Organum and Organum with Oblique Motion
Polyphony was probably improvised before it was written down. Motion in parallel intervals and *heterophony* appear in many musical cultures and were probably practiced in Europe. Polyphony was first unmistakably described in *Musica enchiriadis* and *Scolica enchiriadis,* a treatise and textbook from ca. 900. In this early *organum,* an added voice (organal voice or *vox organalis*) appears below a chant melody (principal voice or *vox principalis*), moving either in parallel motion at the interval of a fourth or fifth (*parallel organum*) or in a mix of parallel and oblique motion (*organum with oblique motion*).

B. Eleventh-Century Organum
In *11th-century organum* (also called *free organum* or *note-against-note organ-um*), the added voice usually sings above the chant (although the voices may cross), moving most often in contrary motion to the chant and forming consonant intervals with it (unison, fourth, fifth, and octave). Only those portions of chant that were sung by soloists were set polyphonically, so that in perform-ance sections of polyphony alternate with sections of chant. **Music: NAWM 14**

III. Florid Organum (HWM 77–79, NAWM 15)

New types of polyphony, called *Aquitanian polyphony,* appeared early in the 12th century in southern France and Spain. In *florid organum,* the chant is sustained in long notes in the lower voice (called the *tenor*), while the upper voice sings from one to many notes above each note of the tenor. This style was called *organum, organum duplum* (double organum), or *organum purum* (pure organum), and *organum* was also used to refer to a piece that used this style. When voices move in similar measured rhythm, the texture is called *discant.* Polyphonic settings of Latin poems called *versus* are the earliest polyphony not based on chant. Manuscripts for these types of polyphony use *score notation* (one part above the other, with notes that sound together aligned vertically), but do not indicate rhythm. **Music: NAWM 15**

IV. Notre Dame Organum (HWM 79–87, NAWM 16a–c, 16e, 17)

A. The Rhythmic Modes
A notation was developed during the 12th and early 13th centuries to indicate patterns of long and short notes. By about 1250, these patterns were codified as the six *rhythmic modes,* each indicated by a different succession of note groupings or *ligatures.* The modes were based on divisions of a threefold unit called a *perfection.*

B. Polyphonic Composition
From the 12th to the 14th century, polyphonic music developed primarily in northern France and disseminated from there across western Europe. The first

composers of polyphony known to us by name are *Léonin* (ca. 1135–ca. 1201) and *Pérotin* (ca. 1170–ca. 1236). They worked in Paris at the Notre Dame Cathedral, the center for a style of music called *Notre Dame polyphony.* (We know their names because of a treatise known as *Anonymous IV,* which describes their music and names some of their works.)

C. Léonin

Léonin wrote or compiled the *Magnus liber organi* (The Great Book of Organum), a cycle of organa for the solo portions of the responsorial chants of the Mass and Office (Graduals, Alleluias, and Responsories) for the entire church year. His organa are in two voices and alternate sections of organum with sections in discant style, called *clausulae* (singular *clausula*). The discant sections use the rhythmic modes. The upper voice of the organum may be in free rhythm, although some editors and performers treat it in modal rhythm. **Music: NAWM 16b–c**

D. Pérotin Organum

Pérotin and his contemporaries revised Léonin's work, writing discant clausulae to replace sections of organum and *substitute clausulae* in place of older sections of discant. The tenors often repeat rhythmic patterns and segments of melody. Pérotin also wrote new organa in three and four voices, in which the upper parts are written in the rhythmic modes and often use *voice exchange.* The new style of long notes in the tenor and measured phrases in modal rhythm in the upper parts is called *copula.* **Music: NAWM 17**

V. Polyphonic Conductus (HWM 87–89, NAWM 18)

The *polyphonic conductus* is a setting of a metrical Latin poem (like the earlier monophonic conductus and the versus). The tenor is newly written and is not based on chant. The two, three, or four voices move in similar rhythm and declaim the text together, in an almost syllabic style. This nearly homorhythmic and syllabic texture is known as *conductus style,* and works in other genres were sometimes written in this style. Some conductus feature long melismas called *caudae,* especially at the beginning or end. As in the organa and discant clausulae of Léonin and Pérotin, vertical consonances of the fifth and octave are prominent throughout and required at cadences, and the music is written in score notation. Both organum and conductus fell out of favor after 1250. **Music: NAWM 18**

VI. The Motet (HWM 89–96, NAWM 16d, 16f–g, 19)

A. Origins and General Features

Starting in the first half of the 13th century, words were often added to the upper voices of a discant clausula. This produced a new genre of independent composition, the *motet* (from the French word *mot,* for "word"). The duplum of a motet is called the *motetus.* Composers freely reworked existing clausulae and motets, adding or substituting new upper lines and texts. Motets were also newly composed, instead of being taken from existing clausulae, but still used fragments of chant in their tenors; later in the 13th century, secular tunes were also used in the tenors. Tenors were often laid out in repeating rhythmic patterns and were probably played rather than sung. Once removed from the liturgy, motets came to be sung on secular occasions. Their texts could be sacred or secular and need not relate to the text of the tenor. In three-voice motets, there were often two texts, both in Latin, both in French, or (rarely) one in each language. Although the texts differ between voices, they are usually on related subjects. A motet is identified by a compound title with the first word(s) of each text, including the tenor. Frequently, the upper voices would cadence at different places to maintain forward momentum. **Music: NAWM 16d, 16f, and 16g**

B. Motet Texts

Motet texts were often written to existing music and had to follow its shape. Frequently the same vowels or syllables appear in different texts, binding them together through sound as well as sense. Later motet texts are predominantly secular, and most are love songs.

C. The Franconian Motet

In the second half of the 13th century, composers often wrote motets in which the upper voice moved more quickly and had a longer text than the middle voice, while the tenor remained the slowest voice. This type is called the *Franconian motet,* after the composer and theorist *Franco of Cologne* (fl. ca. 1250–1280). *Petrus de Cruce* (fl. 1270–1300) used even more notes and shorter note values in the top voice in a style named *Petronian,* after him. Harmonically, these later motets were similar to the earlier ones, with perfect consonances on the main beats and free dissonance in between. Toward the end of the century, cadences began to be standardized, with the lowest voice moving down by step and the upper voices up by step to form a fifth and octave above the lowest voice. In this type of cadence, the outer voices expand from a harmonic sixth to an octave, and the bottom and middle voice move from a harmonic third to a fifth. **Music: NAWM 19**

D. Hocket

Hocket (from the French word for "hiccup") is a technique in which a melody is interrupted by rests, while the missing notes are supplied by another voice. It was used in motets and conductus in the late 13th and early 14th centuries. Works that use it extensively, whether vocal or instrumental, are called *hockets.*

E. Notation in the Thirteenth Century

The notation for the rhythmic modes depended on patterns of ligatures, but the syllabic text-setting of motets made ligatures impossible. This required a notation that indicated the duration of each note. *Franconian notation,* codified by Franco of Cologne in *Ars cantus mensurabilis* (The Art of Measurable Music, ca. 1280), solved this problem by using different note shapes for different relative values. (This same principle underlies modern notation.) With this more exact notation, polyphonic works no longer had to be written in score, and were notated instead in *choirbook format,* in which the voices all appear on the same or facing pages but are not aligned.

Sidebar: Thirteenth-Century Notation in Depth

Franconian notation used four note shapes: the *double long,* the *long,* the *breve,* and the *semibreve.* The basic time unit was the *tempus* (pl. *tempora*), the length of one unaltered breve, and there were three tempora in a *perfection,* equivalent to a modern measure of three beats. A long was either perfect (three tempora) or imperfect (two), a breve could be altered to be two tempora, and divisions of the breve were notated by semibreves. Although this notation still emphasized threefold divisions, it gave new freedom from the rhythmic modes.

VII. Summary (HWM 96–97)

Polyphony developed from the 11th through the 13th centuries as a process of elaborating on existing works. New voices were added to existing chants in note-against-note organum, florid organum, and discant. New discant clausulae substituted for older sections of organum or discant. Words added to the upper parts of clausulae—a kind of troping—produced motets. Additional voices and texts could be added in turn, and motets were also newly composed using segments of chant and other melodies. At each step, composers elaborated on existing material. New technical developments focused on rhythm and notation, from the rhythmic modes to Franconian notation. Whereas until the early 13th century almost all polyphony was sacred, by the end of the century secular texts were also being set polyphonically.

STUDY QUESTIONS

Historical Background of Early Polyphony (HWM 73–74)

1. What major changes in European music were under way in the 11th century? Which of the trends that were new then are still characteristic of music in the European tradition?

Early Organum (HWM 74–77, NAWM 14)

2. In what treatise was polyphony first clearly described? _____

   Name the textbook that accompanied this treatise. _____

   About when were they written? _____

   What two kinds of organum do they describe?

3. State the rules that govern the composition of Example 3.1 in HWM, p. 75 (parallel organum in two voices, with a modified cadence).

4. Following the model in Example 3.1, write parallel organum at the fourth below for the first verse of the sequence *Victimae paschali laudes.*

Vic - ti - mae   pa - scha - li   lau - des   im - mo - lent   Chri - sti - a - ni.

5. In Example 3.3 in HWM, p. 75, why can the chant (the upper line, marked *vox principalis*) *not* be accompanied by a voice a parallel fourth lower? What adjustments have been made to solve this problem?

6. Describe the style of organum common in the 11th century.

What is this style called? _____

Name a manuscript that contains examples of this style. _____

Name a treatise in which this style is described. _____

7. What are the main harmonic intervals of early polyphony? Why were these intervals considered consonant, while others were considered dissonant?

Music to Study

    NAWM 14: *Alleluia Justus ut palma*, organum from *Ad organum faciendum*
    (ca.1100)
    CD 1.30 (Concise 1.10)   Cassette 1.B (Concise 1.A)

8.   In the 11th-century organum *Alleluia Justus ut palma* (NAWM 14), some
    sections are not set in polyphony. Why not?

    In the sections in two-voice polyphony, which part is the original chant, and
    which is the added voice? Which of the two is more disjunct (fewer steps,
    more skips)? Why?

9.   Using *Alleluia Justus ut palma* as a model, add an organal voice in 11th-
    century style (note-against-note organum) to the first two verses of *Victimae
    paschali laudes*, given below. Here the organal voice will be above the
    chant, rather than below it (although it may cross below on occasion). Start
    the first phrase on a unison *D* with the chant, and end each verse on an
    octave *D–D*. Each vertical sonority should be a unison, a perfect fourth, a
    perfect fifth, an octave, or (rarely) a perfect eleventh, with a third or sixth
    permissible just before a unison or octave cadence. Use contrary motion
    most often and parallel and oblique motion for variety, but avoid parallel
    octaves and unisons. Make the organal voice as smooth as possible, and
    avoid leaps larger than a fifth. Do not go higher than the *A* above the staff.
    Do not use any accidental other than *B♭*, and avoid using both *B* and *B♭* in
    close proximity. Have fun with this, and try to write something you like
    while following all these rules.

Vic - ti - mae pa - scha - li lau - des im - mo - lent Chri - sti - a - ni.

A - gnus red - e - mit o - ves: Chri - stus in - no - cens Pa - tri re - con - ci - li - a - vit pec - ca - to - res.

Florid Organum (HWM 77–79, NAWM 15)

10. In florid organum, which voice has the chant?_____

    What is this voice called? _____

    Why did it receive this name?

    Describe the relationship between the parts in florid organum.

11. What is a *versus*? How does it differ from organum in respect to the derivation of its text and its music?

Music to Study
> **NAWM 15**: Magister Albertus of Paris, *Congaudeant catholici*, trope on
> *Benedicamus Domino* (ca. 1146–1177)
>   CD 1.31   Cassette 1.B

12. The *Benedicamus Domino* trope *Congaudeant catholici* (NAWM 15) is unusual for its time in having three voices, the bottom two moving in rhythmic unison and the top one more melismatic in character. In what other ways does it differ from the 11th-century organum *Alleluia Justus ut palma* (NAWM 14)?

Notre Dame Organum (HWM 79–87, NAWM 16a–c, 16e, 17)

13. Show the rhythmic pattern for each of the six rhythmic modes:

        Mode I   _____

        Mode II   _____

        Mode III   _____

        Mode IV   _____

        Mode V   _____

        Mode VI   _____

14. What is Notre Dame of Paris? When was it built? What is its importance for music in the late 12th and 13th centuries?

15. For which chants of the Mass and Office did Léonin write organa?

    Of these chants, which portions did he set in polyphony?

    What was his collection of organa called? _____

16. According to the treatise called Anonymous IV, what did Léonin do best?

    What was Pérotin noted for?

17. What is a *clausula*?

    What is a *substitute clausula*?

Music to Study

NAWM 16a–c and e: *Alleluia Pascha nostrum,* in plainchant and in Léonin's
setting (late 12th century), with later anonymous substitutions
16a: Plainchant (p. 53)   not on recording
16b: Léonin, organum duplum (pp. 53–54, 56, 58–59)
CD 1.32–34, 1.36 and 1.38–40   Cassette 1.B
16c: Anonymous discant clausula on "nostrum" (pp. 54–55)
not on recording
16e: Anonymous substitute clausula on "-la-" from "immolatus" (pp. 56–57)
not on recording

[NAWM 16 can be confusing to follow. See the explanation in NAWM and
the chart and explanation in Table 3.1, on pages 48–49.]

18.   The setting of *Alleluia Pascha nostrum* in NAWM 16b, c, and e includes
sections in both organum duplum and discant style. What are the main
features of each style?

organum duplum

discant style

19.   Which sections of *Alleluia Pascha nostrum* use organum style?

Which sections use discant style? Why is discant used in these passages?

Which sections of NAWM 16b use no polyphony? Why are these sections
not sung polyphonically?

20. In the discant clausula on the word "nostrum" (NAWM 16c), which rhythmic mode is used in the upper voice? How can you tell?

Which rhythmic mode is used in the lower voice? _____

Besides the rhythmic mode itself, what repeated rhythmic pattern is used in the lower voice?

How does the lower part compare to the chant melody on "nostrum" in NAWM 16a (other than being a fifth lower)? What happens in the lower voice at m. 19, where the editor has added a double bar and a roman numeral II?

21. In this same discant clausula on the word "nostrum," where do cadences occur?

Do the voices tend to move in parallel or in contrary motion at cadences?

What vertical sonorities appear on the cadential note?

What sonorities tend to precede cadences?

What vertical sonorities appear on the downbeats?

TABLE 3.1: Substitutions in *Alleluia Pascha nostrum,* NAWM 16

SECTION 1 ALLELUIA (RESPOND)			
Text	Alleluia.	Alleluia	(-a).
1. Chant (16a)	intonation	respond	jubilus
who sings	soloists	choir	
2. Léonin (16b)	organum	chant	chant
who sings	soloists	choir	
page	53	54	
CD track	1.32	1.33	

SECTION 2 VERSE					
Text	Pascha	nostrum	immola-	(-la)tus	(-tus) est	Christus.
1. Chant (16a)	syllabic	melismatic	syllabic	melismatic	syllabic	melismatic
who sings	soloists					choir
2. Léonin (16b)	organum	[discant]	organum	[discant]	organum	chant
who sings	soloists					choir
page	54		56		58	
CD track	1.34		1.36		1.38	
3. Substitute clausulae (16c, e)		discant (1)		discant (2)		
who sings		soloists		soloists		
page		54 (not on CD)		56 (not on CD)		

SECTION 3 ALLELUIA (RESPOND)			
Text	Alle-	lu-	(-lu-)ia	(-a).
1. Chant (16a)	syllabic	melismatic	syllabic	jubilus
who sings	soloists			choir
2. Léonin (16b)	organum	discant	organum	chant
who sings	soloists			choir
page	58			
CD track	1.39	1.40		

There are several stages of development represented in NAWM 16.

1. The original chant (16a) is in three sections, the respond ("Alleluia"), the psalm verse, and the repetition of the respond. In performing the chant, the soloists sing "Alleluia"; the choir repeats it and continues with the melismatic jubilus on "-a"; the soloists sing most of the verse; the choir joins in on the last word with the music of the entire respond; the soloists repeat the "Alleluia"; and the choir sings the jubilus to complete the respond.

2. Léonin (16b) substitutes polyphony for the portions of chant originally sung by soloists. The original chant appears in the lower voice, the tenor, notated a fifth lower to make room for the upper part. The opening solo section and several others are in organum, with long notes in the tenor and free melismas above. Where a solo section of chant is melismatic, as on the syllable "-lu-" from the last "Alleluia," he sets it in discant style, with the tenor moving in regular rhythm and the upper voice moving in modal rhythm, with one to four notes for each note of the tenor. A section of discant is called a *discant clausula.*

3. In turn, other composers substitute new sections of discant, called *substitute clausulae,* for the ones written by Léonin. These appear in 16c and 16e, replacing parts of Léonin's original polyphony on the words "nostrum" and "-latus" from "immolatus." Léonin's original settings for these sections do not appear in the manuscript from which this example is drawn, and thus are omitted from the example.

4. Finally, some of the sections of discant are given texts for the upper voices, making them into *motets* (listed below). The earliest motets have one added text, as in (1) NAWM 16d and (2) 16f, heard in the recording in place of the substitute clausulae on which they are based. A somewhat later development is the *polytextual* motet, some with Latin texts, as in (3) NAWM 16g, some with French texts, and some with one text in each language.

Motets based on discant clausulae in 16c or 16e or on same section of chant:

(1) **16d:** *Gaudeat devotio,* motet (p. 55, CD 1.35), based on the discant clausula on "nostrum" in 16c

(2) **16f:** *Ave Maria, Fons letitie—Latus,* Latin motet (p. 57, CD 1.37), based on the discant clausula on "-latus" in 16e

(3) **16g:** *Salve, salus hominum—O radians stella—Nostrum,* bitextual Latin motet (p. 59, CD 1.41) on "nostrum"

22. Using the questions in #20 above as clues, describe the use of rhythmic modes and rhythmic and melodic repetition in the discant clausula on "-lu-" in NAWM 16b (p. 58, CD 1.40).

23. What are the names for the various voices in an organum?

bottom voice   _____

second voice from the bottom   _____

third voice from the bottom (if any)   _____

fourth voice from the bottom (if any)   _____

Which voice carries the chant?   _____

Music to Study
    NAWM 17: Pérotin, *Sederunt*, organum quadruplum (late 12th or early 13th century), respond only
    CD 1.42–44 (Concise 1.11–13)   Cassette 1.B (Concise 1.A)

24. Compare the organum of Léonin in NAWM 16b with that of Pérotin in NAWM 17, an organum quadruplum on *Sederunt*. How is Pérotin's style like Léonin's, and how is it different?

25. What is *copula*? How is the opening section of *Sederunt* (mm. 1–55) typical of copula as described by Johannes de Garlandia?

26. Which rhythmic mode predominates in each of the following passages of *Sederunt*?

   the top three voices, mm. 2–10   _____

   the top voice, mm. 13–23   _____

   the top voice, mm. 35–40   _____

27. What vertical sonority is used most often at the cadences in *Sederunt*?

28. Compare the passages of Pérotin's *Sederunt* in mm. 13–23 and 24–34. How are they related?

   What is this technique called? _____

   Where else does this technique occur in this piece?

Polyphonic Conductus (HWM 87–89, NAWM 18)

29. How is a polyphonic conductus like a monophonic conductus?

   How is it like a versus?

Music to Study
     NAWM 18: *Ave virgo virginum*, conductus (13th century)
       CD 1.45   Cassette 1.B

30. In what ways is *Ave virgo virginum* (NAWM 18) typical of the polyphonic conductus, as described in HWM?

      How is it different from organum and from discant?

31. What vertical sonorities appear at the beginnings and ends of phrases in this conductus?

      On the grid below, circle those beats where only perfect intervals are sounding in the harmony and write in the lowest-sounding note at the end of each phrase.

      Measures 1–4 (mm. 5–8 repeat mm. 1–4)

        1 2 3 4 5 6 1 2 3 4 5 6 1 2 3 4 5 6 1 2 3 4 5 6
                          ——   ——

      Measures 9–12

        1 2 3 4 5 6 1 2 3 4 5 6 1 2 3 4 5 6 1 2 3 4 5 6
                          ——   ——

      Measures 13–17

  1 2 3 4 5 6 1 2 3 4 5 6 1 2 3 4 5 6 1 2 3 4 5 6 1 2 3 4 5 6
       ——   ——   ——

      What other vertical intervals are used?

32. Briefly describe the way the harmony works in this conductus, based on your findings in question #31.

The Motet (HWM 89–96, NAWM 16d, 16f–g, 19)

33. How did the motet originate, and how did it acquire its name?

34. What does the title of a motet indicate?

Music to Study

NAWM 16d: *Gaudeat devotio fidelium,* motet (13th century)
    CD 1.35   Cassette 1.B
NAWM 16f: *Ave Maria, Fons letitie—Latus,* Latin motet (13th century)
    CD 1.37   Cassette 1.B
NAWM 16g: *Salve, salus hominum—O radians stella—Nostrum,*
        bitextual Latin motet (13th century)
    CD 1.41   Cassette 1.B
NAWM 19: *Amours mi font souffrir—En mai—Flos filius eius,* motet in
        Franconian style (late 13th century)
    CD 1.46 (Concise 1.14)   Cassette 1.B (Concise 1.A)

35. How are the motets in NAWM 16d, 16f, and 16g related to the discant clausulae on *nostrum* and *-latus* in NAWM 16c and 16e? (See Table 3.1 for help.) What has been added, deleted, or changed in creating these new works? What has stayed the same?

36. In the motet *Gaudeat devotio fidelium* (NAWM 16d), the tenor is on the word "nostrum." Where in the motet text do the sounds "no-" and "-um" appear? Where else do the vowels "o" and "u" appear?

How do these similarities of sound help to bind together the tenor and the motetus?

37. How does the meaning of the motet text relate to the meaning of the original chant text, "Alleluia, Christ, our Paschal lamb, is sacrificed"? How does the motet text relate to the occasion (Easter Mass) on which this chant was originally sung?

38. What makes *Amours mi font souffrir—En mai—Flos filius eius* (NAWM 19) a *Franconian motet,* and how does it differ from earlier motets?

When were Franconian motets written? _____

After whom were they named? _____

About when was this person active? _____

39. What makes *Aucun vont—Amor qui cor—Kyrie,* shown in Example 3.13 of HWM, pp. 92–93, a *Petronian motet,* and how does it differ from earlier motets and from Franconian motets?

    When were Petronian motets written? _____

    After whom were they named? _____

    About when was this person active? _____

40. What new notational system was devised to indicate rhythm in motets? How was it different from the notation for the rhythmic modes? Why was this change necessary, and what results did it have?

    In what major treatise was this notational system codified? Who wrote it, and when?

    _____   _____   _____

Summary (HWM 96–97)

41. What are the most significant aspects of the period between about 1160 and 1300?

TERMS TO KNOW

Terms Related to Early Polphony

polyphony
heterophony
organum
vox principalis, vox organalis
parallel organum
organum with oblique motion
eleventh-century organum
   (or note-against-note organum)

Aquitanian polyphony
florid organum
organum duplum, organum purum
tenor (in florid organum, discant,
   and motet)
discant
versus
score notation

Terms Related to Notre Dame Polyphony

rhythmic modes
ligatures
perfection (Latin *perfectio*)
Notre Dame polyphony
clausula (pl. clausulae)
discant clausula
substitute clausula

duplum, triplum, quadruplum
copula
voice exchange
polyphonic conductus
cauda (pl. caudae)
conductus style

Terms Related to the 13th-Century Motet

motet
motetus
Franconian motet
Petronian motet
hocket

Franconian notation
choirbook format
double long, long, breve, semibreve
tempus
perfection

NAMES TO KNOW

Musica enchiriadis
Scolica enchiriadis
Winchester Troper
Ad organum faciendum
Abbey of St. Martial at Limoges
Notre Dame, Cathedral of Paris
Léonin
Pérotin

Magnus liber organi
Anonymous IV
Johannes de Garlandia
De mensurabili musica
Franco of Cologne
Petrus de Cruce
Ars cantus mensurabilis

REVIEW QUESTIONS

1. Take the time-line you made in chapter 2 and add the pieces in NAWM 14–15, 16b–g, and 17–19, their composers (when known), Franco of Cologne and Petrus de Cruce, and the *Ars cantus mensurabilis.*

2. Trace the evolution of polyphony from its origins in improvisation to the St. Martial repertory.

3. Describe the music of Notre Dame polyphony. Include in your discussion the major composers, the genres they cultivated, the rhythmic and harmonic style of their music, and the way new pieces used, embellished, or substituted for existing music.

4. Write a passage in Notre Dame organum, following the model of Léonin's setting of the opening "Alleluia" from *Alleluia Pascha nostrum* (NAWM 16b, p. 53). For a tenor, use the opening "Alleluia" from the *Alleluia Dies sanctificatus* (NAWM 3e) from the Mass for Christmas Day.

5. Write a passage in discant style, following the model of the two-voice discant clausulae in NAWM 16b, 16c, and 16e. For a tenor, use the seventeen notes to the word "Dies" in the *Alleluia Dies sanctificatus* (NAWM 3e) from the Mass for Christmas Day, laid out in a repeating rhythmic pattern like those in the tenors of the discant clausulae in NAWM 16b, 16c, and 16e. In the duplum, use rhythmic patterns derived from at least two of the rhythmic modes (but do not mix modes 1 and 2 in the same discant clausula).

6. Trace the history of the motet from its origins through the end of the 13th century.

7. How did changing musical styles and changing notational practices for polyphonic music interrelate during the period 900–1300?

8. In your view, what developments during the period 900–1300 were most significant for the later evolution of music? What styles, practices, techniques, attitudes, or approaches that were new in this time have continued to affect Western music in the last 700 years? In your opinion, which of these have most set music in the Western European tradition apart from music of other cultures?

FRENCH AND ITALIAN MUSIC IN THE FOURTEENTH CENTURY

4

CHAPTER OBJECTIVES

After you complete the reading, study of the music, and study questions for this chapter, you should be able to:

1. explain the increased emphasis on secular literature, art, and music in the 14th century;
2. describe the rhythmic and other stylistic features that characterize the music of the *Ars nova, Trecento*, and late-14th-century *Ars subtilior*;
3. describe isorhythm and its use in 14th-century motets and Mass movements;
4. name and describe the forms of secular song practiced in France and Italy during the 14th century;
5. identify some of the major figures, works, and terms associated with music in the 14th century.

CHAPTER OUTLINE

I. General Background (HWM 101–3)

A. The Church's Declining Authority

The 14th century was an unstable and secular age. The authority of the Church was undermined by the exile of the pope to Avignon (1305–78) and a schism between rival popes (1378–1417). Human reason became an authority in its own sphere, independent of church control.

B. Social Conditions

The growth of cities, plague (1348–50), the Hundred Years' War (1338–1453), and political changes challenged the old order. Great literary works by Dante, Boccaccio, Petrarch, and Chaucer appeared in vernacular languages, and *humanism* renewed the influence of Greek and Latin literature on Western culture.

C. Musical Background

Philippe de Vitry (1291–1361) helped to develop a new style that used duple as well as triple divisions of the long and breve and notes shorter than the semibreve. This style, known as the *Ars nova* ("new art" or "new technique"), became the reigning style in France until late in the 14th century.

II. The *Ars Nova* in France (HWM 103–11, NAWM 20–22)

A. The *Roman de Fauvel* and Vitry

The *Roman de Fauvel* (1310–14) is a satirical poem with interpolated music, including 34 motets. By this time, motet texts were usually secular and often referred to contemporary events. Five three-part motets in this work are by Vitry, considered the outstanding French poet and composer of the early 14th century. The motets of Vitry and other 14th-century composers use *isorhythm* (same rhythm).

B. The Isorhythmic Motet

The tenor in an *isorhythmic motet* is composed of a repeating series of pitches, called the *color,* and a repeating rhythmic pattern, called the *talea.* These are joined in varying ways: one may be longer than the other; their endings may coincide or overlap; when the color repeats, the talea may appear in diminished durations. Upper voices may also be isorhythmic in whole or in part, if they feature repeating rhythmic patterns coordinated with repetitions in the tenor. Isorhythm gave unity and form to motets, even when the structure was not fully audible. **Music: NAWM 20**

C. Guillaume de Machaut

The leading poet and composer of 14th-century France was *Guillaume de Machaut* (ca. 1300–1377). His isorhythmic motets are longer and more complex than Vitry's and frequently use hocket.

D. Machaut's Secular Works

Machaut wrote many secular songs: 19 monophonic and polyphonic *lais,* 25 monophonic and 8 polyphonic *virelais,* 22 polyphonic *rondeaux,* and 42 polyphonic *ballades.* The virelai, rondeau, and ballade are called *formes fixes* (fixed forms); each one features a particular pattern of rhymes and repeating lines of poetry called *refrains,* and the rhymes and refrains are coordinated with repeating segments of music.

1. The virelai has the form AbbaA, in which A is the refrain and both A and a use the same music. The b section often has open and closed endings.

2. The ballade has the form aabC and usually has three or four stanzas, each ending with the same line of text (C). Musically, the endings of the a section and the C section may be similar or identical. Ballades with two texted voices are called *double ballades.*

3. The rondeau has the form ABaAabAB, with a refrain in two parts (A and B), the first repeating in the middle of the stanza. The stanza uses the same two sections of music as the refrain, a and b, but with different words. **Music: NAWM 21**

The polyphonic songs are for one or two singers and instruments. Unlike the motet, in which the tenor was written first, in the secular songs the voice part is the principal line and was written first. This treble-dominated style of a voice and instrumental accompaniment is called *cantilena style*.

E. Machaut's Mass

The most famous musical work of the 14th century is Machaut's *Messe de Notre Dame* (Mass of Our Lady), a four-part setting of the Mass Ordinary. The Gloria and Credo are syllabic, with all four voices declaiming the text together, and end with isorhythmic Amens. The other movements are isorhythmic, often including isorhythm in all or most voices, and their tenors are drawn from plainchant melodies for the same texts from the Ordinary of the Mass. (The Mass was written or compiled ca. 1364 as a Mass to the Virgin Mary to be performed nearly weekly at an altar in the Rheims cathedral, where Machaut was a canon.)   **Music: NAWM 22**

F. Sacred Polyphony in the 14th Century

The secularization of 14th-century society led to a decline in the composition of liturgical works in France and Italy, and church criticism of complex and virtuosic music further discouraged composition of sacred polyphony, especially in Italy.

III. Italian *Trecento* Music (HWM 111–17, NAWM 23–24)

A. The *Trecento*

In Italian, the 14th century is referred to as the *Trecento* (tray-CHEN-toe), after the Italian formula for dates, 1350 being spoken as "mille trecento cinquanta" (thousand three hundred fifty). Most Italian music of the time was monophonic and unwritten, and most church polyphony was improvised. Secular polyphony was cultivated among the elite in certain cities in northern Italy, especially Florence, where the *Squarcialupi Codex,* the most important manuscript of 14th-century Italian music, was copied.

B. The Madrigal

The 14th-century *madrigal* (not to be confused with the 16th-century form) is a work for two voices without instrumental accompaniment. It uses a poem of two or three three-line stanzas followed by a couplet. The stanzas are all set to the same music, while the closing couplet, called the *ritornello,* is set to new music in a different meter.   **Music: NAWM 23**

C. The Caccia

The *caccia,* a mid-14th-century form, features two voices in canon at the unison over a free instrumental part. The texts were often about hunting or other action scenes, with the appropriate sounds imitated in the music.

D. The Ballata

The *ballata* evolved from monophonic dance songs with choral refrains (from "ballare," to dance). The polyphonic ballata of the late 14th century was a lyrical piece whose form resembles the French virelai (AbbaA).

E. Francesco Landini

Francesco Landini (ca. 1325–1397) was the most important Italian composer of the 14th century. He is best known for his ballate, and wrote no sacred works. In a ballata, a three-line *ripresa* or refrain (A) precedes and follows a seven-line stanza. The stanza's first two pairs of lines, called *piedi,* present a new phrase (b), repeated with open and closed endings, and the last three lines, the *volta,* are set to the music of the refrain (a), for an overall form of AbbaA. Landini has lent his name to the *Landini cadence,* in which the usual cadence formula of a sixth expanding to an octave between cantus and tenor is decorated by the upper voice descending a step before resolving to the octave. **Music: NAWM 24**

F. Performance

The *superius* (top part) of a secular song is vocally conceived, while the tenor and often the *contratenor* (third part, filling out the harmony) appear to have been intended for instrumental performance. However, any part could be sung or played or shared between voice and instrument. Vocal pieces were sometimes played by instruments, with embellishments added to the vocal line, and some instrumental versions were written down.

IV. French Music of the Late Fourteenth Century (HWM 117–21, NAWM 25)

A. Late Fourteenth-Century French Secular Music

In the late 14th century, many French and Italian composers were active at courts in southern France. They wrote mainly French secular song, using the formes fixes, in a style that was both refined and complex.

B. Rhythm

Rhythm in this style was especially complex, with subdivisions, syncopations, hocket, and different meters in different voices. Because of the technical complications, this style has been called the *Ars subtilior* (the subtler manner). This sophisticated style, intended for the most cultivated listeners and the most practiced performers, began to wane by the end of the 14th century. *Partial signatures,* in which the voices have different signatures (most often, the lower voice or voices have a signature of one flat while the others do not), were often used throughout the 14th and 15th centuries.

V. Musica Ficta (HWM 121–23)

Performers in the 14th century often altered notes chromatically, particularly at cadences. In cadences in which a minor sixth expanded to an octave, the top note of the sixth was often raised chromatically to make a major sixth, so that the top line resolved upward by half step, like a leading tone. A three-voice cadence in which both the octave and fifth are approached from a half step below is called a *double leading-tone cadence.* Other chromatic alterations were made to avoid tritones or to create smooth lines. Chromatic notes outside Guido's hexachord system were called *ficta* (feigned), and composers and scribes tended not to notate them, leaving it to performers to judge where they were needed. The practice of altering notes chromatically in performance is called *musica ficta.* Modern editors often suggest where musica ficta should be supplied by indicating accidentals above or below the affected notes.

Sidebar: Fourteenth-Century Notation in Depth (HWM 123–25)

Both Italian and French musicians developed notations for the new styles of music in the 14th century. In the Italian system, dots were used to mark groupings of two, three, or four semibreves. In the French system, which became standard, the long, breve, and semibreve could each be divided into either two or three of the next smaller note value. These divisions were called *mode, time,* and *prolation* respectively; triple divisions were *perfect,* and duple *imperfect* for mode and time, and *major* and *minor* for prolation. Combining time and prolation produced four possible meters, equivalent to 9/8, 6/8, 3/4, and 2/4. The *minim* and *semiminim* were introduced for notes smaller than a semibreve. About 1425, noteheads began to be left open ("white notation") instead of being filled in. The resulting note shapes evolved into modern notation (whole note, half note, etc.).

VI. Instruments (HWM 125–27)

Music manuscripts of the 14th century do not specify which parts are vocal and which are instrumental, for each piece could be performed in a variety of ways. Polyphonic music was probably most often performed with one voice or instrument on a part, usually featuring a variety of instruments rather than instruments from a single family. Instruments were classified as relatively loud (*haut* or "high") or soft (*bas* or "low"). Loud instruments such as shawms, *cornetts* (wooden instruments with cup mouthpiece and fingerholes), slide trumpets, and *sackbuts* (predecessors of the trombone) were often used outdoors; soft instruments such as the harp, vielle, lute, psaltery, portative organ, transverse flute, and recorder were used indoors, and percussion was used in both environments.

VII. Summary (HWM 127)

The 14th century is characterized by an emphasis on secular music; greater diversity and complexity in rhythm; a growing sense of harmonic organization; more use of imperfect consonances; musica ficta; cantilena style; the continuation of the motet as a secular genre; and new genres of secular polyphony.

STUDY QUESTIONS

General Background (HWM 101–3)

1. How did events in the 14th century affect the authority of the Church and the structure of society? What currents in philosophy, politics, and literature helped to make the 14th century a secular age?

2. What is the meaning of the phrase *Ars nova*? _____

   How do we use the term now?

3. Give the author and date for each of the following treatises:

   Ars nova   _____   _____

   Ars nove musice   _____   _____

   Speculum musicae   _____   _____

   What are the chief technical innovations described in the first two of these treatises?

   How is the last different from the others?

The *Ars Nova* in France (HWM 103–11, NAWM 20–22)

4. What is the *Roman de Fauvel*? When was it written? What music does it contain?

5. How is the tenor of an isorhythmic motet constructed? What are the names of the elements that repeat?

6. How does isorhythm give unity and form to motets? Can the isorhythmic structure always be heard? How did medieval musicians regard its audibility?

Music to Study

> **NAWM 20:** Philippe de Vitry, *Garrit gallus—In nova fert—Neuma,* motet from *Roman de Fauvel* (ca. 1314)
>
> CD 1.47–52   Cassette 1.B

7. What is the subject matter of the texts of Vitry's motet *Garrit gallus—In nova fert—Neuma* (NAWM 20)? How is this typical of the subject matter and function of the motet at this time?

8. Write out the color of Vitry's motet *Garrit gallus—In nova fert—Neuma* as a series of note names (that is, *F, G, A,* and so on).

    How many notes does the color contain? _____

    How many times is the color stated in the motet? _____

9. Write out the talea of this motet as a series of durations. Include the rests. To make it easier to follow the rhythm, reduce the value of each note or rest to a third of its value, so that a dotted whole note becomes a half note, a dotted half note becomes a quarter note, and so on. In this notation, the first note would be a dotted half note, the second a quarter note, and so on.

    How many notes does the talea contain? _____

    How many times is the talea stated in the motet? _____

    In this motet, how are the talea and color coordinated?

10. How does the tenor of this piece compare in its structure with those of the motets in NAWM 16d and 16f? In what ways is it structured according to similar ideas, and in what ways is it more complex?

11. In *Garrit gallus—In nova fert—Neuma,* how do the upper voices relate to the tenor?

    Are there any places in the upper voices where the rhythm is the same as in a previous parallel passage? If so, where? (This kind of repetition of rhythm is also called isorhythm, even when a repeating series of pitches is not involved.)

12. Where in this Vitry motet (that is, in what measures) can you find parallel octaves between the voices?

    Where can you find parallel fifths between the voices?

    Where can you find double leading-tone cadences (defined and illustrated on p. 121 of HWM)?

13. Briefly describe Guillaume de Machaut's career. Where did he live, whom did he serve, and what did he do?

14. Diagram the form of the three *formes fixes,* using letters to indicate musical repetitions and capital letters to show the refrains.

    virelai   _____

    rondeau   _____

    ballade   _____

15. How does the 14th-century rondeau resemble *Robins m'aime* (NAWM 8) by the 13th-century trouvère Adam de la Halle?

Music to Study

NAWM 21: Guillaume de Machaut, *Rose, liz, printemps, verdure,* rondeau
   (mid-14th century)
CD 1.53–55 (Concise 1.15–17)   Cassette 1.B (Concise 1.A)

16. Diagram the form of a rondeau as you did in question no. 14 above.

Which measures in the music of *Rose, liz, printemps, verdure* (NAWM 21)
correspond to each letter of your diagram?

How do the rhymes in the poetry coordinate with this form?

What relation does the music in mm. 32–37 have to music heard
previously?

How do cadences help delineate the form?

17. Describe the melodic and rhythmic style of the two upper parts, the triplum
and the cantus. How do these compare to the upper parts of the motets in
NAWM 19 and 20? Can you describe what is distinctive about Machaut's
style, in comparison with melodies of the late 13th and early 14th centuries?

Music to Study
> **NAWM 22:** Guillaume de Machaut, *Messe de Notre Dame,* Mass, excerpt:
> Agnus Dei (ca. 1364)
> CD 1.56–58 (Concise 1.18–22)   Cassette 1.B (Concise 1.A)

18.   What is the *Messe de Notre Dame*? What is special about it?

Which movements are isorhythmic?

What other style is used, and in what movements? Why is it appropriate for these movements?

19.   The tenor in Machaut's Agnus Dei is the second line from the bottom. It is adapted from a Gregorian chant Agnus Dei. To confirm this, sing the tenor part to the Agnus Dei text as underlaid below it, but instead of using Machaut's rhythms, sing the pitches in the unmeasured rhythm of Gregorian chant, with each note receiving an equal time value (and double value on the last note of each phrase of text).

Where are there repetitions of music in this chant melody?

How does the form of Machaut's Agnus Dei follow the form of the chant melody?

20. The isorhythm begins at the "qui tollis" after each "Agnus Dei." Each time, there is only one statement of the color, but there is more than one statement of the talea. The last note of each section follows after the last statement of the talea.

    (Note that in certain cases, some repetitions of an isorhythmic pattern will subdivide a few notes. For example, compare mm. 15–17 in all four voices with mm. 8–10, which are at the corresponding spot in the rhythmic pattern. Observe that for each voice, the rhythm is virtually the same in both passages, but in the top three voices there is one beat that is a half note in one passage and is divided into smaller note values in the other. This kind of small difference varies but does not negate the basic isorhythmic structure.)

    Write out the talea for the first "qui tollis." _____

    How many measures long (in this modern transcription) is this talea? _____

    How many times is it stated? _____

    To what extent are the other three voices isorhythmic?

    Write out the talea for the second "qui tollis." _____

    How many measures long (in this modern transcription) is this talea? _____

    How many times is it stated? _____

    To what extent are the other three voices isorhythmic?

21. How does Machaut's Agnus Dei compare to his rondeau *Rose, liz, printemps, verdure*? How do the upper two voices of each piece compare in melodic and rhythmic style? How do the two lower voices of each compare?

22. What factors led to a decline in the composition of sacred music in 14th-century France and Italy?

Italian *Trecento* Music (HWM 111–17, NAWM 23–24)

23. What is the *Squarcialupi Codex,* and why is it important?

24. Define and describe the 14th-century *caccia.*

Music to Study
> **NAWM 23:** Jacopo da Bologna, *Fenice fù,* madrigal (mid-14th century)
> CD 2.1   Cassette 2.A
> **NAWM 24:** Francesco Landini, *Non avrà ma' pietà,* ballata (second half,
> 14th century)
> CD 2.2–4 (Concise 1.21–23)   Cassette 2.A (Concise 1.A)

25. How does Jacopo da Bologna's *Fenice fù* fit the definition of a 14th-century madrigal as given in HWM (p. 112), regarding the type of poetry used, the form of the poem, the form of the piece, and the melodic style?

26. How does the melodic style of *Fenice fù* differ from that of Machaut's rondeau (NAWM 21)?

---

27. In a ballata, what is the *ripresa*? What measures of Landini's *Non avrà ma' pietà* (NAWM 24) correspond to this part of the form?

What are the *piedi* and the *volta*? Where do these appear in Landini's ballata?

How does the form of a ballata resemble that of a virelai, and how is it different?

28. What is a *Landini cadence*? Where do Landini cadences appear in Landini's ballata?

29. Compare Landini's melodic, rhythmic, and harmonic style to that of Machaut's rondeau (NAWM 21). Where do melismas occur in each one, and how is their practice similar or different in this respect? What other similarities and differences do you observe?

30. What combinations of voices and instruments were possible in performing secular polyphonic songs in the 14th century ?

French Music of the Late Fourteenth Century (HWM 117–21, NAWM 25)

31. What are the special characteristics of the late-14th-century *Ars subtilior,* particularly in the realm of rhythm?

Music to Study

NAWM 25: Baude Cordier, *Belle, bonne, sage,* rondeau (early 15th century)

CD 2.5   Cassette 2.A

32. How does Baude Cordier's *Belle, bonne, sage* (NAWM 25) resemble Machaut's rondeau (NAWM 21), and how is it different in style? What aspects of the Cordier link it to the *Ars subtilior*?

33. In what shape is Cordier's rondeau presented in the manuscript, and why?

---

34. What are *partial signatures*? Which pieces studied in this chapter use them?

Musica Ficta (HWM 121–23)

35. What is *musica ficta*? Under what circumstances is it used, and why? Why were accidentals not written down?

36. The editor has suggested where musica ficta should be applied in Jacopo da Bologna's *Fenice fù* (NAWM 23) by placing accidentals above certain notes. Using the rules given by Prosdocimo de' Beldomandi (in HWM, p. 122) and summarized in HWM (pp. 121–23), explain why the editor has suggested each of these alterations.

    m. 3   _____

    m. 15, third beat   _____

    m. 15, fourth beat _____

    m. 17   _____

    m. 19   _____

Fourteenth-Century Notation in Depth (HWM 123-25)

37. Briefly describe 14th-century French notation. What are the divisions of the long, breve, and semibreve called? What are the four prolations, and how do they correspond to modern meters?

Instruments (HWM 125–27)

38. What types of instruments were in use during the 14th century? What are *haut* (high) and *bas* (low) instruments? How were instruments used in vocal music?

Summary (HWM 127)

39. What characteristics distinguish 14th-century music from music of earlier periods?

Terms to Know

Terms Related to *Ars Nova* Music

humanism	virelai
Ars nova	rondeau
isorhythm	ballade
isorhythmic motet	formes fixes
color	refrain
talea	double ballade
lai	cantilena style

Terms Related to *Trecento* and Late-14th-Century French Music

madrigal (14th-century)	ballata
ritornello (in 14th-century madrigal)	ripresa, piedi, volta
caccia	Ars subtilior

Terms Related to Music Theory and Instruments

Landini cadence	perfect and imperfect time
superius	major and minor prolation
contratenor	minim, semiminim
partial signature	haut and bas instruments
musica ficta	cornett
double leading-tone cadence	sackbut
mode, time, prolation	

Names to Know

Ars nova	Guillaume de Machaut
Philippe de Vitry	*La Messe de Notre Dame*
Ars nove musice, by Jehan des Murs	Squarcialupi Codex
Speculum musicae, by Jacob of Liège	Jacopo da Bologna
Roman de Fauvel	Francesco Landini

Review Questions

1. Make a time-line for the pieces, composers, and treatises discussed in this chapter.

2. What is new about the *Ars nova*? How does it compare to 13th-century music? How does late-14th-century French music extend the ideas of the *Ars nova*?

3. Describe isorhythm as practiced in Vitry's motets and Machaut's Mass.

4. Write a short, textless isorhythmic piece in three voices, in 6/8, modeled on the style and procedures of Vitry's *Garrit Gallus—In nova fert—Neuma* (NAWM 20) and the Agnus Dei from Machaut's Mass (NAWM 22). Follow these steps:

    a. For the color in the tenor, use the sixteen notes on "quia hodie" in the *Alleluia Dies sanctificatus* (NAWM 3e) from the Mass for Christmas Day. Devise a talea of eight notes and one to four rests, using only notes and rests that are one or two longs (dotted half notes) in length; the 6/8 measures should be laid out in groups of two. Using this color and talea, write out the tenor on music paper, leaving plenty of room for the other two voices.

    b. Write a duplum above the tenor, using quarters, eighths, dotted quarters, and dotted half notes only. Write it as a series of phrases separated by rests, making sure that all sonorities on downbeats are consonant and that the beginnings and ends of phrases form perfect consonances with the tenor. Do not cross below the tenor. Avoid resting during rests in the tenor.

    c. Add a triplum in the same style as the duplum or slightly more florid. It can cross below the duplum but not below the tenor. Avoid resting during rests in the other voices. Make sure that all sonorities on downbeats are consonant and that phrases end on perfect consonances.

5. Name and describe the forms of secular song practiced in France and Italy during the 14th century. How are French and Italian music similar? How do they differ?

6. Describe the melodic, rhythmic, and harmonic style of Machaut. How do the works of Vitry, Jacopo da Bologna, Landini, and Cordier resemble or differ from those of Machaut in melodic, rhythmic, and harmonic style? What features do they all share?

ENGLAND AND THE BURGUNDIAN LANDS IN THE FIFTEENTH CENTURY

5

CHAPTER OBJECTIVES

After you complete the reading, study of the music, and study questions for this chapter, you should be able to:

1. name the characteristics of medieval English music that distinguished it from French and Italian styles;
2. describe the genres practiced in England during the 13th through 15th centuries;
3. explain how English music influenced music on the Continent during the 15th century;
4. describe fauxbourdon, chant paraphrase, and cantus firmus techniques;
5. explain how an international musical style developed in the mid-15th century and the historical circumstances that placed Burgundian composers at the center of these developments;
6. describe the music of Burgundian composers, particularly Dufay, and explain the differences between their musical practices and those of the 14th century;
7. name and describe the various types of polyphonic Mass cycle composed in the 15th century, particularly the cantus firmus Mass.

CHAPTER OUTLINE

I. English Music (HWM 130–37, NAWM 26–27, 29)

English music made important contributions to the development of an international style in the first half of the 15th century. The cantilena style began to be used in some motets and Masses as well as in secular music.

  A. General Features

  Medieval English music favored the major mode, homophony, fullness of sound, and much use of parallel thirds and sixths. Works of the Notre Dame school were known in Britain, and British composers of the 13th century wrote conductus and motets that use similar procedures.

B. Fourteenth Century

The main surviving sources of 14th-century English music are fragmentary manuscripts from *Worcester* Cathedral, containing works for the Mass, motets, and conductus. The English cultivated forms that resemble rounds, such as the *rota,* a canon at the unison over a repeating bass, and the *rondellus,* in which voices in the same range exchange phrases to create an effect like a round.

A frequent occurrence in English music is parallel motion in thirds and sixths, such that the interval between the outer voices is a sixth and between the bottom and middle voice is a third, resolving to an octave and fifth respectively at cadences. This style could be improvised to a given melodic line; such improvised counterpoint was known as *discanting,* and this texture of parallel sixth and third chords is sometimes called *English discant.* The late-13th-century English rules for discanting are the first to forbid parallel fifths and octaves, a rule for all subsequent counterpoint for the next six centuries.

C. Fauxbourdon

These parallel sixth-third streams of English music may have inspired the Continental technique of *fauxbourdon,* prominent ca. 1420–50. A fauxbourdon is a piece in which two notated voices, usually a paraphrased chant and the tenor below it, move mostly in parallel sixths, resolving to an octave at cadences, and a third unwritten part is sung a fourth below the superius, producing parallel thirds with the tenor. The same texture was often used in fully notated music. This led to a new style in which the principal melody was in the upper voice, the others moved in a similar rhythm and became almost equally important, and the music was suffused with imperfect consonances.   **Music: NAWM 29**

D. The Old Hall Manuscript

The main source for early-15th-century English music is the *Old Hall manuscript.* It includes motets, hymns, sequences, and Mass movements from ca. 1370–1420, in styles ranging from isorhythm and cantilena style to *cantus firmus* settings on a plainchant melody. The influence of English style on Continental composers was celebrated in a poem of about 1440 that praised the *"contenance angloise"* (English guise) of "lively consonance."

E. John Dunstable

John Dunstable (ca. 1385–1453) was the leading English composer of the first half of the 15th century. He served for a time in the English possessions in France, which helped bring his music to the Continent. He wrote in all the prevailing genres and styles of polyphony.

F. Dunstable's Three-Part Sacred Works

Dunstable is best known for his three-voice sacred works. They use a variety of techniques, including a cantus firmus in the tenor, an ornamented chant melody in the treble, and free counterpoint not based on chant.   **Music: NAWM 26**

G. The Carol

The 15th-century *carol* is a setting of a religious poem in English or Latin, often on the birth of Jesus, with a recurring *burden* or refrain and a series of verses. It evolved from an earlier form of carol, which was a monophonic dance song with a refrain.   **Music: NAWM 27**

H. The Fifteenth-Century Motet
In the 15th century, the isorhythmic motet waned in popularity. The term *motet* came to be applied to a polyphonic setting of a Latin text other than part of the Mass Ordinary.

II. Music in the Burgundian Lands (HWM 137–49, NAWM 28–30)

A. The Dukes of Burgundy
The late 14th and the 15th centuries saw a great expansion in the size and power of the duchy of Burgundy, until the death of the last duke in 1477. The dukes maintained a *chapel* that included about two dozen musicians, and they also employed a number of instrumentalists for secular music. Their lavish patronage for music helped nurture musicians, so that most of the leading composers of the 15th and early 16th centuries came from their lands, mainly from modern-day Belgium and northeastern France. Musicians traveled with their patrons or moved to new positions in other regions, and their interactions with musicians from all over Europe led to the development of an international style that blended elements of French, Italian, and English styles.

B. Dufay
Guillaume Dufay (c. 1400–1474) was educated at Cambrai in the duchy of Burgundy, served several patrons in Italy and Savoy in the 1420s and 1430s, returned to Cambrai, went back to Savoy in the 1450s, and finished his career at Cambrai, making him a truly international composer. He synthesized in his music aspects of all existing styles to create a cosmopolitan idiom.

The main genres of the period were Masses, Magnificats, motets, and secular chansons to French texts. The chansons continued the formes fixes and three-voice treble-dominated texture of the 14th century, but the melodic style was smoother and the harmony more consonant. Triple meter and compound meters were far more common than duple meter. The traditional sixth-to-octave cadence between tenor and superius was sometimes harmonized with a contratenor that leapt up an octave from a fifth below the tenor to a fifth above the tenor's note of resolution, creating a sound similar to a modern dominant-tonic cadence.

C. The Burgundian Chanson
In the 15th century, *chanson* (song) was the term for any polyphonic setting of a French secular text. Most chansons were in the form of a rondeau. **Music: NAWM 28**

D. Binchois
Gilles Binchois (c. 1400–1460) was the other major Burgundian composer of Dufay's generation. He was best known for his chansons.

E. Burgundian Motets
Motets in this period were often written in the style of the chanson, with the main melody in the treble, supported by the tenor, with the contratenor to fill

out the harmony. The superius was often paraphrased from chant. This use of chant was quite different in concept from that of the 13th- and 14th-century motet, which used the chant melody as a harmonic basis rather than as the principal melody. **Music: NAWM 29**

F. Masses

After about 1420, composers regularly set the five main texts of the Mass Ordinary (excluding the *Ite missa est*) as a musically unified polyphonic cycle, creating the genre of the polyphonic Mass.

1. Some Masses were unified simply by musical style.

2. A *plainsong Mass* based each movement on a plainchant for that text.

3. Musical means of unification involved using the same musical material in each movement. One early form was the *motto Mass,* in which each movement begins with the same music or motive, called a *head motive* or *motto.*

4. The most important form was the *cantus firmus Mass* or *tenor Mass,* which used the same cantus firmus in every movement. This form was developed by English composers and by 1450 became the predominant type of polyphonic Mass cycle throughout Europe. Cantus firmus Masses were often also unified by a head motive (but are still called cantus firmus Masses, not motto Masses).

The cantus firmus was usually placed in the tenor in long notes and treated in isorhythmic fashion. Below it was a *contratenor bassus* (low contratenor) or *bassus* (bass) to provide a harmonic foundation; above it was the *contratenor altus* (high contratenor) or *altus* (alto); the top part was called by a variety of names, including *superius* (highest part), *cantus* (melody), and *discantus* (discant). The cantus firmus could be taken from chant or from a secular song, and the Mass was named after the borrowed tune. One of the most frequently borrowed secular tunes was *L'Homme armé* (The Armed Man). Dufay and others also wrote Masses based on tenors borrowed from polyphonic chansons.

Although cantus firmus Masses used learned devices (such as extensions of isorhythm), they conformed to the style that prevailed after 1430, with careful control of dissonance, emphasis on consonance, equal importance of voices, smoothness of melody, four-voice textures, and some use of imitation.

STUDY QUESTIONS

English Music (HWM 130–37, NAWM 26–27, 29)

1. What are the characteristics of English music in the 13th through 15th centuries that set it apart from music on the continent of Europe?

2. What is a *rondellus,* and how does it work? Describe how the voices exchange phrases in *Fulget coelestis curia—O Petre flos—Roma gaudet,* discussed in HWM, pp. 131–33.

3. What is *discanting*? What important stylistic feature of English music is associated with it?

4. What is *fauxbourdon*? How does it work? How does it relate to English discant?

5. What is the Old Hall manuscript? What types of composition does it contain, and what compositional procedures does it feature?

6. What is the "contenance angloise"? What was its importance to music outside of England?

7. What historical circumstances may have led to the spread of English music and English musical style on the Continent, including the music of John Dunstable?

8. What genres of music did Dunstable compose? What compositional techniques appear in his music?

9. Describe the relationship between the Dunstable melody and the plainchant melody it paraphrases in Example 5.2 on p. 135 of HWM. How does Dunstable embellish the chant?

Music to Study
> **NAWM 26**: John Dunstable, *Quam pulchra es*, motet (first half, 15th
> century)
> > CD 2.6 (Concise 1.24)   Cassette 2.A (Concise 1.A)
> **NAWM 27**: *Salve, sancta parens*, carol (15th century)
> > CD 2.7   Cassette 2.A

10.   In what sense is *Quam pulchra es* (NAWM 26) a motet? Which part, if any, has the chant, and how are the parts related to each other? How had the definition of "motet" changed by the early 15th century to include a piece such as this?

11.   How does Dunstable shape the music of *Quam pulchra es* to reflect the divisions of the text and the rhythms of the words?

12.   Where are there passages in *Quam pulchra es* that feature parallel thirds, sixths, or tenths? (Note that the middle voice is to be performed an octave lower than written, so that all three parts begin on middle *C*.)

About how often during the work are imperfect consonances sounding?

Do imperfect consonances ever appear in the final sonority at the end of a phrase?

13. How often in *Quam pulchra es* do harmonic dissonances appear? How often do parallel unisons, fifths, or octaves occur? How does this compare with the 13th-century conductus *Ave virgo virginum* (NAWM 18) and with Machaut's 14th-century Agnus Dei (NAWM 22)?

14. Compare the melodic style of the top voice in Dunstable's motet to that of the top lines in Machaut's *Rose, liz, printemps, verdure* (NAWM 21) and Landini's *Non avrà ma' pietà* (NAWM 24). What are the main differences between the English style of the first half of the 15th century and these 14th-century styles?

15. Now do the same for the melodic style of the tenors, and for the relationship between the top part and the tenor.

16. What is a *carol*? How does *Salve, sancta parens* (NAWM 27) conform to the description of a 15th-century carol in HWM?

17. Where are there parallel sixths, thirds, or tenths between the outer voices in *Salve, sancta parens*? In the three-voice Burden II, where is there a texture like English discant, in which the outer voices move in parallel sixths and the bottom two voices in parallel thirds? (Note: Sometimes the rhythm of the parts is slightly different, as in mm. 18–19, while the voices are still essentially moving in parallel.)

18. Where are there cadences in this carol? What harmonic intervals are used at the cadences in the two-voice sections? What harmonic sonorities appear at the cadences in the three-voice sections?

19. If you had to assign the top voice of *Salve, sancta parens* to one of the church modes (not a rhythmic mode), which mode would you choose? Why?

On what notes do cadences occur at the ends of sections? _____

On what notes do cadences occur at the ends of phrases? _____

Are any of these important notes in the mode? If so, which ones?

In what ways does this show a concern for clarity of mode and for tonal planning?

20.   Where are there Landini cadences in *Salve, sancta parens*?

Where is there a Landini cadence in Dunstable's *Quam pulchra es* (NAWM 26)?

Music in the Burgundian Lands (HWM 137–49, NAWM 28–30)

21. What political conditions aided the rise of Burgundian musicians to prominence in the 15th century? What kinds of musicians were employed by the dukes of Burgundy? How did the music at the Burgundian court influence music across Europe?

22. Briefly summarize Dufay's career. How was it typical of musicians at the time?

23. How does the 15th-century cadence described on p. 137 of HWM resemble 14th-century cadences, and how is it like cadences in common-practice tonality?

Music to Study
> **NAWM 28:** Guillaume Dufay, *Resvellies vous et faites chiere lye*, ballade (1423)
> > CD 2.8–10   Cassette 2.A
> **NAWM 29**: Guillaume Dufay, *Conditor alme siderum*, motet (hymn para-
> > phrase) in alternation with chant (middle third of the 15th century)
> > CD 2.11–12   Cassette 2.A

24. In Dufay's *Resvellies vous et faites chiere lye* (NAWM 28), which parts of the upper line seem to suggest instrumental performance? Why?

25. *Resvellies vous* was composed in 1423 when Dufay was working in Italy, and it shows a strong influence from 14th-century French and Italian music. What elements in this piece resemble Machaut's rondeau (NAWM 21)? Which elements suggest the mannered, rhythmically complex late-14th-century *Ars subtilior* style? How does the melodic line in the texted portions suggest Italian rather than French influence?

26. Where are there double leading-tone cadences in *Resvellies vous*, created through musica ficta?

27. In Dufay's polyphonic setting of the even-numbered verses of the plainchant hymn *Conditor alme siderum* (NAWM 29), how is the chant melody embellished? Where in the phrase do embellishments occur? (Note that the chant melody itself is notated here in longs and breves, producing a pattern like the first rhythmic mode.)

28. How does this piece fit the description of *fauxbourdon* given in HWM, pp. 132–33?

How does this compare to the use of parallel sixth-third sonorities in the English carol *Salve, sancta parens* (NAWM 27)?   Which piece is more varied in its texture?

29. In what church mode is the chant hymn *Conditor alme siderum*? _____

How does the polyphonic setting reinforce the mode?

30. Why did composers begin to write polyphonic settings of the Ordinary of the Mass? What different ways were used to create unity among the movements?

31. What are the four voices of a 15th-century Mass called? What is the general character of each part?

top part

second part down

third part down

bottom part

32. What is a *cantus firmus Mass* or *tenor Mass*?

What kinds of borrowed melodies were used in cantus firmus Masses?

In what voice of the four-part texture does the cantus firmus normally occur in a Mass?

How is a movement of a cantus firmus Mass like an isorhythmic motet?

Music to Study
> **NAWM 30a**: Guillaume Dufay, *Se la face ay pale*, ballade (1430s)
>> CD 2.13 (Concise 1.25)   Cassette 2.A (Concise 1.B)
> **NAWM 30b**: Guillaume Dufay, *Missa Se la face ay pale*, Mass, excerpt:
>> Gloria (ca. 1450s)
>> CD 2.14–19 (Concise 1.26–31)   Cassette 2.A (Concise 1.B)

33. How does Dufay use the tenor of his chanson *Se la face ay pale* (NAWM 30a) in the tenor of the Gloria of his *Missa Se la face ay pale* (NAWM 30b)? How is this like isorhythm? How does it provide a form for the Gloria movement?

34. Where in the Gloria does Dufay borrow material from the other two voices of his chanson? What purpose might this borrowing serve?

35. How do the four voices of the Gloria differ from each other in function and style?

36. Examine the upper voices in the Gloria. How often do two successive measures have the same rhythm? How often do the top two voices move in the same rhythm at the same time? What does this suggest about Dufay's use of rhythm?

37. In the isorhythmic works of Vitry and Machaut, we can find parallel fifths and octaves and double leading-tone cadences. Can any of these be found in Dufay's Mass movement? How would you describe the harmony?

TERMS TO KNOW

Terms Related to English Music

rota

rondellus

discanting

English discant

cantus firmus

"contenance angloise"

carol

burden

motet (15th-century and later)

Terms Related to Burgundian Music

fauxbourdon

chapel

chanson

polyphonic Mass cycle

plainsong Mass

motto Mass

cantus firmus Mass

tenor Mass

bassus (contratenor bassus)

altus (contratenor altus)

superius, cantus, discantus

head motive

NAMES TO KNOW

the Worcester fragments

Sumer is icumen in

the Old Hall manuscript

John Dunstable

Burgundy

Guillaume Dufay

Gilles Binchois

L'Homme armé

REVIEW QUESTIONS

1. Make a time-line for the pieces and composers discussed in this chapter. Include dates for the poem that mentions the "contenance angloise"; dates for the end of the duchy of Burgundy and the reigns of Philip the Good and Charles the Bold; the dates and places of Dufay's birth, death, and employment; and dates for any historical events listed on p. 183 of HWM with which you are familiar, to help orient you to the 15th century.

2. What characteristics and procedures of English music set it apart from music on the Continent in the 13th, 14th, and early 15th centuries? How did the Continental style change as it absorbed the influence of English music in the first half of the 15th century?

3. What new ways of using and reworking Gregorian chant developed during the 15th century?

4. What special role did the duchy of Burgundy and Burgundian composers play in the development of music during the 15th century?

5. Describe the music of Dufay and explain how he synthesizes elements from France, Italy, and England in a cosmopolitan style.

6. Describe the varieties of polyphonic Mass cycle composed in the 15th century, and compare Dufay's *Missa Se la face ay pale* (a cantus firmus Mass) to Machaut's *Messe de Notre Dame* (a plainsong Mass).

THE AGE OF THE RENAISSANCE: MUSIC OF THE LOW COUNTRIES

6

CHAPTER OBJECTIVES

After you complete the reading, study of the music, and study questions for this chapter, you should be able to:

1. describe the influence of humanism on the culture and music of the 15th and 16th centuries;
2. name some of the most significant theorists and treatises of the time and explain their importance;
3. describe the beginnings and early development of music printing;
4. describe and explain the change from the composition of each successive line of a polyphonic work one after another to the composition of all parts simultaneously;
5. describe the music and briefly describe the careers of some of the major composers active at the end of the 15th century and the beginning of the 16th century.

CHAPTER OUTLINE

I. General Characteristics (HWM 152–63)

A. Humanism

The Renaissance was not a musical style, but a period of history marked by the rediscovery and renewed influence of ancient Greek and Roman culture, led by the movement called *humanism*. Although no ancient music was known, many ancient writings on music were rediscovered during the 15th century. Ancient writers' descriptions of the emotional effects of music caused some in the Renaissance to criticize the lack of such effects in the music of their own time. Several theorists made important contributions:

1. *Liber de arte contrapuncti* (Book on the Art of Counterpoint, 1477) by *Johannes Tinctoris* laid out strict rules for controlling dissonance.
2. *Franchino Gaffurio* incorporated ancient Greek theory into his treatises, the most influential of the late 15th and early 16th centuries.

3. The *Dodekachordon* (1547) of *Heinrich Glarean* added four new modes (authentic and plagal modes on *A* and *C*, akin to later minor and major modes) to the eight earlier modes.

4. *Le istitutioni harmoniche* (The Harmonic Foundations, 1558) by *Gioseffo Zarlino* codified the rules for dissonance treatment, counterpoint, and emotional expressivity.

B. Tuning Systems

Although thirds and sixths were treated as consonances in music, the traditional *Pythagorean tuning* system rendered them out of tune so that the perfect intervals would be pure. In the 15th and 16th centuries, new tuning systems were introduced that allowed imperfect intervals to sound well, such as *just intonation* and *mean-tone tuning.* This was in accord with the humanist insistence on pleasing the ear, rather than making it subservient to an abstract ideal such as the creation of consonance through simple ratios. Composers also began to explore accidentals beyond *G♯* and *E♭* on the circle of fifths.

C. Words and Music

Humanism encouraged composers to pay increasing attention to the meaning, sound, form, and rhythm of the texts they set. Whereas text underlay had often been left to the singers, 16th-century composers sought to fix it precisely, for good accentuation. There was not one musical style in the Renaissance, but a general search for means to please the human senses and express human emotions.

D. Italy

Humanism and the arts thrived particularly in Italy, where rulers of small city-states and principalities sought to outdo each other in their patronage of literature and the arts. Many of the composers they employed were from France, Flanders, and the Netherlands, particularly from the former Burgundian lands. These composers were influenced by the simple popular music of Italy, and the combination of northern and Italian elements helped to produce the international style of the 16th century.

E. Music Printing

Johann Gutenberg developed the art of printing words from movable type in 1450, and by 1473 books of chant were being printed the same way. *Ottaviano de' Petrucci* (1466–1539) of Venice was the first to print polyphonic music from movable type, using three impressions (for the staff lines, for the notes, and for the text) to create beautiful and clear books. *Pierre Attaingnant* (ca. 1494–ca. 1551) of Paris was another well-known printer, who used a more complex type that allowed printing in a single impression. Most works were published as *partbooks,* one book for each voice or part (superius, altus, tenor, and bassus). Printing allowed wider distribution of music at a lower cost and less time spent recopying by hand, creating the first real market for music as a commodity.

F. Simultaneous Composition

In a style that demanded full harmony and careful treatment of dissonance, and especially when working with imitative counterpoint, it became difficult to keep to the old method of writing a complete superius or tenor, then adding the second part, then the bassus, and finally the altus. Instead, composers in the 16th century began to work out all the voices simultaneously, sometimes using a score to see all the parts at once. (This practice is known as *simultaneous composition,* in contrast to the *successive composition* of voices one after another in music of the 15th century and before.)

II. Northern Composers and Their Music (HWM 163–73, NAWM 31–32)

Most prominent composers in the period 1450–1550 came from France, Flanders, or the Netherlands. Many of them served at least some of their career in Italy.

A. Johannes Ockeghem

Johannes Ockeghem (ca. 1420–1497) was born in the north and spent most of his career in the service of the kings of France. He was famous as a composer and as a teacher of many of the leading composers of the next generation. He wrote 13 Masses, 10 motets, and about 20 chansons. He extended the range of the bassus down to low *F,* giving a fuller and darker sound, and all four voices tend to be equally active. His melodic lines are long and sinuous, with varied rhythms and many changes of direction as they wind to their goal. They often overlap to create a continuous flow with few pauses. Ockeghem creates contrasts of light and dark by varying the texture, setting some passages for only two or three voices and sometimes alternating between high and low pairs of voices.

B. Canon

Ockeghem seldom uses imitation in his Masses, but does use *canon,* which at this time meant a procedure for deriving more than one voice from a notated voice. His *Missa prolationum* uses *mensuration canons,* in which one notated line generates two voices through a different mensuration sign. Ockeghem's *Missa cuiusvis toni* (Mass in any mode) can be read in any of four clef combinations, each resulting in music in a different authentic mode. These arcane procedures demonstrated the composer's skill, but were often inaudible and did not interfere with the appealing surface of the music.

C. The Generation after Ockeghem

Many composers of the next generation were taught or influenced by Ockeghem. They worked in Italy as well as the north and blended Ockeghem's style of long-breathed overlapping melodies in intricate polyphony with the Italian style's less serious mood, simpler texture, greater interest in homophony, more distinct rhythms, and more frequent phrase articulations.

D. Jacob Obrecht

Jacob Obrecht (ca. 1452–1505) was trained in the Low Countries and worked there and in Italy. His works include 29 Masses, 28 motets, and numerous songs and instrumental works. His treatment of the cantus firmus in his Masses is quite varied and shows considerable originality. Like others of his generation, Obrecht uses imitative counterpoint frequently.

E. The Chanson

Composers of Ockeghem's generation introduced more imitation into the chanson, but continued to use the old formes fixes. *Antoine Busnois* (d. 1492) was one of the best-known chanson composers of the late 15th century. Some chansons were very popular, being recopied and published repeatedly. Chansons were freely altered, arranged, and transcribed for instruments, and either the superius or the tenor of a chanson could be borrowed to serve as a cantus firmus for a Mass. **Music: NAWM 31**

F. The *Odhecaton*

The first volume of polyphonic music printed from movable type was the *Harmonice musices odhecaton A,* published by Petrucci in Venice in 1501. This was an anthology of chansons from ca. 1470–1500 in both older and newer styles. The newer style favored a four-voice texture instead of three voices; more imitation between the voices; greater equality of the voices; and a clearer harmonic structure. By the early 16th century, composers abandoned the formes fixes for more varied poetic and musical forms. They also began to conceive all voices simultaneously rather than one after another. Many chansons were settings of popular tunes, treating the borrowed tune like a cantus firmus or in paraphrase. **Music: NAWM 32**

III. Josquin des Prez (HWM 173–79, NAWM 33–34)

A. Career

Josquin des Prez (ca. 1440–1521) was considered the best composer of his time and is one of the greatest of all time. He was born in north-central France and served patrons in Italy and France. His works, which include about 18 Masses, 100 motets, and 70 secular vocal works, were published and recopied more widely than any other composer of his day.

B. Masses

Most of Josquin's Masses use a secular tune as a cantus firmus. One Mass uses a *soggetto cavato* to honor his patron, the duke of Ferrara. An *imitation Mass* (also called *parody Mass*) is based, not on a monophonic tune, but on all the parts of a polyphonic work. This is not a *contrafactum* (in which a new text replaces the original words, without changing the music). Rather, the entire polyphonic texture is reworked to create something new, and each movement of the Mass reworks the chanson or motet in a different way.

C. Text Setting

Most manuscripts and printed books of the 15th and early 16th centuries do not specify precisely which syllables of the text go with which notes of the music. The influence of humanism and of Italian popular songs (which were mostly syllabic) led Josquin and others to match the music more carefully to the accents and rhythms of the words. One Italian technique was *falsobordone,* in which root-position triads harmonize a recitation formula in the upper voice; some of Josquin's early motets use a similar texture. Josquin was renowned for suiting the music to the text, and in his late motets sought to depict the meaning of the text as well. **Music: NAWM 33**

D. Musica Reservata

Some 16th-century writers use the term *musica reservata* for music that reflects the meaning and emotions of the words. Josquin may have originated this practice. His music may be the first to be expressive of the emotions suggested by its text. In a Josquin motet, each phrase of text receives its own musical figure, which is usually treated in a point of imitation, with the full four-voice texture reserved until the drive to the cadence at the end of a musical sentence. **Music: NAWM 34**

IV. Some Contemporaries of Obrecht and Josquin (HWM 180–82, NAWM 35)

A. Heinrich Isaac

Heinrich Isaac (ca. 1450–1517) was born in Flanders and served patrons in Italy, Austria, and elsewhere. He wrote a great many chansons, about 30 Masses, and the three-volume *Choralis Constantinus,* a cycle of motets based on the texts and melodies for the Proper of the Mass for most of the church year. His later music was influenced by the style of Italian popular music. **Music: NAWM 35**

B. Other Contemporaries

Other significant composers of this generation were Pierre de la Rue (ca. 1460–1518) and *Jean Mouton* (1459–1522), who served the kings of France.

V. Summary (HWM 182)

The international style of the early 16th century featured a four-voice texture with independent, singable lines of nearly equal importance, composed simultaneously rather than line by line around a cantus firmus. The Mass, motet, and chanson were the preferred genres, and all used phrases in imitation interspersed with homophonic textures.

STUDY QUESTIONS

General Characteristics (HWM 152–63)

1. What is *humanism*? What was its role in Renaissance intellectual life? What aspects of music did it influence, and when?

2. Compare and contrast the comments of Cirillo and Zarlino in the vignettes on pp. 153 and 155 of HWM. Which side does each take in the argument about polyphony? How do they relate their understanding of music to humanistic concepts and to ancient Greek writings on music?

3. Who were the most important theorists of the late 15th and 16th centuries, and what were their contributions?

4. Why was the traditional Pythagorean tuning no longer ideal for Renaissance music? What other kinds of tuning systems were introduced?

5. How did humanism influence the relation between music and text in vocal pieces? How did the new understanding of text setting relate to ancient Greek ideas?

6. Why did Italy provide an ideal ground for Renaissance humanism as a movement and for the development of the international musical styles of the late 15th and 16th centuries?

7. When did printing of polyphonic music from movable type begin? Who was the first printer to use this technique, and where was he active?

Who was Pierre Attaingnant, and what did he contribute to music printing?

What was the usual format for printing polyphonic music in the 16th century?

What impact did printing have on the dissemination of musical works?

8. Why did Pietro Aron consider it important to compose all the parts at once (see vignette, p. 162 of HWM)?   How does this practice differ from that of composers in the 14th or mid-15th centuries, such as Machaut or Dufay?

Northern Composers and Their Music (HWM 163–73, NAWM 31–32)

9. Summarize Ockeghem's career and reputation.

10. What is a *retrograde canon* or *cancrizans canon*?

What is a *mensuration canon,* and how does it work in Ockeghem's *Missa prolationum*?

What is special about Ockeghem's *Missa cuiusvis toni* (Mass in any mode)?

What is the attitude of Ockeghem and his contemporaries toward such ingenious compositional techniques?

11. Where and when did Jacob Obrecht live and work?

12. How is imitation used in the opening of the Agnus Dei from Obrecht's *Missa Caput* (shown in HWM, p. 171, Example 6.5)? How does this compare to the opening of the Agnus Dei from Ockeghem's *Missa Caput* (shown in HWM, p. 165, Example 6.2)?

Music to Study

   NAWM 31: Johannes Ockeghem, *D'ung aultre amer,* chanson (second half of the 15th century)

   CD 2.20 (Concise 1.32)   Cassette 2.A (Concise 1.B)

13. In the 14th-century rondeau *Rose, liz, printemps, verdure* (NAWM 21), the first and second sections of the music (the A and B of the refrain) are clearly articulated, with a sustained chord closing the A section in m. 25 (marked with a fermata in the modern edition). In 15th-century rondeaux, the contratenor often keeps moving through the cadence of the A section, so that there is a greater sense of continuity between the A and B sections. Look at Ockeghem's rondeau *D'ung aultre amer* (NAWM 31). The end of the A section and the beginning of the B section are not marked in the music, as they are in the other rondeau, but they can be determined from the placement of the text and the musical context. Where does the A section end? Where does the B section begin? Explain your choices.

14. The motive in mm. 1–2 of the contratenor (here, the bottom voice) of *D'ung aultre amer* is imitated in mm. 3–4 of the superius. Where else does this motive appear in the chanson?

   Where else does Ockeghem use imitation between the voices?

---

15. Note the signature of one flat in each voice of *D'ung aultre amer*. This transposes the modal system up a perfect fourth. A work that begins and ends on *G*, like this one, and has a signature of one flat is in transposed Dorian or Hypodorian mode (also called *G*-Dorian or *G*-Hypodorian mode).

Where in this rondeau are octave cadences formed between the superius and tenor (here, the middle voice)? (For the moment, ignore the contratenor.)

What notes are used for these cadences? What is the function of these notes in either the *G*-Dorian or *G*-Hypodorian mode?

Which of these cadences is or are undermined by the contratenor? How?

16. Compare the frequency of the cadences in this rondeau by Ockeghem to the frequency of cadences in Dufay's ballade *Se la face ay pale* (NAWM 30b). Which composer seems more concerned with writing short, clear phrases? Which one is more interested in long, overlapping phrases, for an effect of seamless continuity?

17. In addition to being sung as originally written, how were chansons reworked and reused by composers and performers?

18. What is *Harmonice musices odhecaton A*? Who published it, and where? Why is it important?

19. What new stylistic traits appear in the chansons of the late 15th and early 16th centuries?

Music to Study
> **NAWM 32a:** Josquin des Prez, *Mille regretz,* chanson (ca. 1520)
>   CD 2.21 (Concise 1.33)   Cassette 2.A (Concise 1.B)
> **NAWM 32b:** Luys de Narváez, Arrangement for vihuela of Josquin des
>   Prez's *Mille regretz,* chanson arrangement (ca. 1538)
>   CD 2.22 (Concise 1.34)   Cassette 2.A (Concise 1.B)

20. One could sing the superius of Ockeghem's *D'ung aultre amer* (NAWM 31), and it would make sense as a monophonic song. One could perform the superius and tenor together, without the contratenor, and it would sound well in two-part counterpoint. (Try doing this, to convince yourself this is true.)

    Neither is possible in Josquin's chanson *Mille regretz* (NAWM 32a): no voice alone makes sense as a song, and no two voices form satisfactory cadences with each other. Why not? Why are all four voices essential? (HWM provides some answers, and you can figure out others on your own.)

21. How does *Mille regretz* differ from Ockeghem's *D'ung aultre amer* or Dufay's ballade *Se la face ay pale* (NAWM 30b) in the following respects? All of these are typical of the difference between 15th-century chansons and early-16th-century chansons.

    the number of voices

    the intended performance medium of each part

    the setting of the text

    the musical and poetic form

    the final sonority at the end of the piece

22. What changes did Luys de Narváez make in arranging *Mille regretz* for vihuela (NAWM 32b)? How do these changes reflect the change of medium, from voices to plucked strings? (The vihuela is a plucked string instrument akin to the guitar.)

Josquin des Prez (HWM 173–79, NAWM 33–34)

23. Where and when did Josquin live and work? How was he regarded by his contemporaries?

24. In what genres did Josquin compose? Why did he choose to write so many motets?

> *Music to Study*
> **NAWM 33:** Josquin des Prez, *Tu solus, qui facis mirabilia,* motet (late 15th century)
>   CD 2.23–26 (Concise 1.35–38)   Cassette 2.B (Concise 1.B)
> **NAWM 34:** Josquin des Prez, *De profundis clamavi ad te,* motet (first or second decade of the 16th century)
>   CD 2.27–30   Cassette 2.B

25. What is *falsobordone*? Where in Josquin's motet *Tu solus, qui facis mirabilia* (NAWM 32) does he use a similar technique?

26. How does *Tu solus, qui facis mirabilia* use borrowed material? Why is it used?

27. In what mode is *Tu solus, qui facis mirabilia*? How can you tell? How is the mode projected in the music?

28. In what mode is Josquin's motet *De profundis clamavi ad te* (NAWM 34)? How can you tell? How is the mode projected in the music?

29. Where do cadences occur in this motet? How does the location of cadences relate to the structure of the text?

30. How does Josquin's music reflect the meaning of the opening words of *De profundis clamavi ad te*?

   How does the music reflect the natural accentuation of the words elsewhere in the motet?

31. A motet of Josquin's generation is made up of a series of phrases. Each segment of the text is given its own musical phrase, which is usually treated in a point of imitation or is presented homophonically. Most phrases are marked off with cadences, although some points of imitation overlap. One of Josquin's trademarks is his alternation of voices in pairs with each other and with the full four-voice texture. These changes of texture, along with the frequent cadences, help to make the structure clear.

   In Josquin's motet *De profundis clamavi ad te,* where do phrases begin with a point of imitation? List each instance, including the measure number it begins, the first words of the phrase of text, and the number of voices that participate in the point of imitation.

Some Contemporaries of Obrecht and Josquin (HWM 180–82, NAWM 35)

32. Where did Isaac live and work? How is his music different from that of others in his generation?

33. What is the *Choralis Constantinus*? What does it contain? In what way is it like Léonin's *Magnus liber organi*?

Music to Study
NAWM 35: Heinrich Isaac, *Innsbruck, ich muss dich lassen,* Lied (early 16th century)
CD 2.31   Cassette 2.B

34. How does Isaac's setting of *Innsbruck, ich muss dich lassen* (NAWM 35) show the influence of Italian popular music?

Summary (HWM 182)

35. Describe the musical style current in Europe around 1500–1520. How does it differ from the style of Dufay?

TERMS TO KNOW

humanism
Pythagorean tuning
just intonation
mean-tone tuning
partbooks
simultaneous composition,
    successive composition
retrograde (cancrizans) canon

mensuration canon
soggetto cavato
imitation Mass
parody Mass
contrafactum
falsobordone
canto carnascialesco

NAMES TO KNOW

Franchino Gaffurio
Liber de arte contrapuncti, by
    Johannes Tinctoris
Dodekachordon, by
    Heinrich Glarean
Le istitutioni harmoniche,
    by Gioseffo Zarlino
Ottaviano de' Petrucci
Pierre Attaingnant
Johannes Ockeghem

Missa prolationum
Missa cuiusvis toni
Jacob Obrecht
Antoine Busnois
Harmonice musices odhecaton
Josquin des Prez
Heinrich Isaac
Choralis Constantinus
Jean Mouton

REVIEW QUESTIONS

1. Make a time-line for the pieces, composers, treatises, and theorists discussed in this chapter.

2. Define humanism as a movement in the Renaissance, and explain how it was reflected in the arts and music of the time.

3. Trace the development of the motet in the 15th and early 16th centuries from Dunstable to Josquin, using the motets in NAWM as examples.

4. Write a point of imitation for two voices, about eight to fifteen measures of cut time, in the style of Josquin. Use as models the opening points of imitation in both parts of his motet *De profundis clamavi ad te* (NAWM 34). Either the upper or the lower voice may enter first, but the upper must enter a fifth higher than the lower. The first few measures should be in exact imitation; the latter part may be in freer counterpoint, ending with a cadence on an octave or unison. Follow the same rules of counterpoint and dissonance treatment that Josquin followed, and try to make your vocal lines as varied in rhythm as his, with no two successive measures having the same rhythm.

5. What are the major changes in the style of secular vocal music from Ockeghem's generation to that of Josquin?

6. Trace the early history of music printing, describing the variety of printing methods as well as the important publishers.

7. Compare the careers and music of any two of the following composers: Machaut, Dufay, Ockeghem, Josquin.

NEW CURRENTS
IN THE SIXTEENTH
CENTURY

7

CHAPTER OBJECTIVES

After you complete the reading, study of the music, and study questions for this chapter, you should be able to:

1. describe the principal styles and genres of 16th-century secular vocal music and instrumental music;
2. describe the relation of music and text in 16th-century vocal music and contrast it with earlier practices of setting texts;
3. identify some of the major composers of 16th-century music; and
4. identify the characteristics of national schools of composition in the 16th century.

CHAPTER OUTLINE

I. The Franco-Flemish Generation of 1520–1550 (HWM 187–92)

A. General

The period 1520–1550 saw a growing diversity of styles, genres, and forms in vocal music and the growing importance of instrumental music. The imitation Mass gradually replaced the cantus firmus Mass. Composers increasingly wrote for five or six voices rather than four, the standard of the previous generation.

B. Nicolas Gombert

The motets of Nicolas Gombert (ca. 1495–ca. 1556) move in a continuous texture of overlapping phrases, most of them set as points of imitation.

C. Jacobus Clemens

Jacobus Clemens ("Clemens non Papa," ca. 1510–ca. 1556) wrote numerous imitation Masses, over 200 motets, and 4 collections of psalm settings in Dutch, called Souterliedeken.

D. Ludwig Senfl

Swiss composer Ludwig Senfl (ca. 1486–ca. 1542) wrote secular songs and sacred works in German, as well as Masses and motets.

E. Adrian Willaert

Adrian Willaert (ca. 1490–1562) was one of the most important composers of his generation. Director of music at St. Mark's Church in Venice for the last 35 years of his life, he exercised a great influence through his teaching, his compositions, and his ideas for the treatment of text. Unlike earlier composers, he specified which syllable was to be sung to each note and sought to ensure that the text was correctly accented and punctuated. He marked major breaks in the text with full cadences and lesser breaks with weaker or evaded cadences.

II. The Rise of National Styles (HWM 192–93, NAWM 36)

A. Italy

The 16th century saw the rise to prominence of national styles. Italian music became particularly important. By the end of the 16th century, Italy had displaced France and the Lowlands as the center of European musical life, and it continued to dominate for the next two centuries.

B. The Frottola

The *frottola,* an Italian genre common in the late 15th and early 16th centuries, was a strophic secular song with an amorous or satirical text set in a simple, syllabic, and homophonic style. The melody in the upper voice was accompanied by diatonic harmonies in the lower parts, which were often played on instruments. **Music: NAWM 36**

C. The Lauda

The polyphonic *lauda* was a religious song, not used in the liturgy, that was similar in style to the frottola.

III. The Italian Madrigal (HWM 193–206, NAWM 37–41)

A. General

The 16th-century *madrigal* was the leading form of Italian secular music and a major influence on music throughout Europe because of its focus on the emotional expression of the text. Unlike the 14th-century madrigal or the frottola, the 16th-century madrigal did not use a refrain or a set form, but was a through-composed work that sought to capture the ideas and feelings in the words through a series of changing musical textures and images. The poems used were serious or artful and were often by a major poet. Madrigal texts were often sentimental or erotic. Madrigals were sung in courtly social gatherings and academies, usually by amateurs for their own enjoyment. They were also sung in plays and theatrical productions, and after about 1570 some patrons employed professional singers to perform madrigals. Madrigals were perhaps the first commercial popular music in the modern sense; more than 2000 madrigal collections were published and sold between 1530 and 1600, and their popularity continued into the 17th century. Madrigals of 1520–50 are usually for four voices and later ones for five or more; as always, instruments might double or substitute for one of the vocal lines.

B. Early Madrigal Composers

The leading early composers of madrigals were mainly Italians active in Florence and Rome. Their madrigals are like the frottola in featuring a mostly homophonic texture. Franco-Flemish composers of madrigals, such as *Jacob Arcadelt* (ca. 1505–ca. 1568), brought into the madrigal the imitative counterpoint, overlapping cadences, and changing textures of the motet.   **Music: NAWM 37**

C. The Petrarchan Movement

The rise of the madrigal was closely connected to renewed interest in the poetry and ideals of *Francesco Petrarca,* or *Petrarch* (1304–1374), a poet of two centuries earlier. Early madrigalists often set Petrarch's poetry, especially his sonnets; later composers set 16th-century poets influenced by Petrarch. *Pietro Bembo* (1470–1547) edited Petrarch's poems and showed that Petrarch sought to reflect the mood or imagery of the words in the sound of the language itself. Bembo identified two qualities that were often contrasted in Petrarch's poetry, *"pleasingness"* (*piacevolezza*) and *"severity"* (*gravità*). The madrigals of Adrian Willaert often exemplify this contrast, and Willaert's student Gioseffo Zarlino described the musical means for representing it in his treatise *Le istitutioni harmoniche.*   **Music: NAWM 38**

D. Cipriano de Rore

Cipriano de Rore (1516–1565), a student of Willaert's, was the leading madrigalist of his generation. His music was famed for its vivid expression of the feelings in the text.   **Music: NAWM 39**

E. Chromaticism

Composers in the middle and late 16th century began to use chromatic progressions, which had previously been forbidden. They were inspired in part by interest in reviving the ancient Greek chromatic and enharmonic genera, as in the music and writings of *Nicola Vicentino.*

F. Later Madrigalists

Among the important madrigal composers of the late 16th century were northern composers as well as native Italians.

G. Carlo Gesualdo

Carlo Gesualdo (ca. 1561–1613) is known for an extreme use of chromaticism. His vertical sonorities are mostly consonant, but the motion through successive sonorities can be quite unpredictable. The contrast between chromatic and diatonic sections to convey the changing moods of the text and the brevity of his madrigals are also hallmarks of his style.   **Music: NAWM 40**

H. Claudio Monteverdi

Claudio Monteverdi (1567–1643) was the most important Italian composer of the late 16th and early 17th centuries. He was born in Cremona, worked in Mantua, and was choirmaster at St. Mark's in Venice for the last 30 years of his life. His several books of madrigals show a variety of techniques, including increased use of unprepared dissonance, declamatory passages, and other methods of conveying the feeling of the text. He defended his unorthodox use of dissonance as a "second practice" (as distinguished from the "first practice" taught by Zarlino) in which the music was the servant of the poetry. **Music: NAWM 41**

I. Other Italian Secular Vocal Genres

In addition to madrigals, Italian composers also wrote lighter genres of secular vocal music, such as the *villanella, canzonetta,* and *balletto.*

IV. Secular Song Outside Italy (HWM 207–18, NAWM 42–45)

A. France

Composers centered in Paris in the first half of the 16th century cultivated a new type of chanson, the *Parisian chanson.* These were strophic songs in a light, fast style, mostly syllabic and homophonic, with the melody in the upper voice, occasional brief points of imitation, and short repeated sections. The main publisher of Parisian chansons was Pierre Attaingnant, and the most important composers were *Claudin de Sermisy* (ca. 1490–1562) and *Clément Jannequin* (ca. 1485–ca. 1560), who was renowned for his descriptive chansons. **Music: NAWM 42**

B. The Later Franco-Flemish Chanson

Outside of Paris, northern composers continued the older, more contrapuntal chanson tradition. In the second half of the 16th century, the French chanson continued to flourish, blending aspects of both Parisian and Franco-Flemish chansons and absorbing some elements of the madrigal. A new style of homophonic, short, strophic song, known as *vaudeville* and later *air de cour,* was usually sung as a solo with lute accompaniment.

C. Musique Mesurée

The late-16th-century poet Jean-Antoine de Baïf wrote French verse in the style of ancient Greek and Latin poetry, which used long and short syllables. This was called *vers mesurés à l'antique* (measured verse in antique style). *Claude Le Jeune* (1528–1600) and other composers set these to music, setting each long syllable to a long note and each short syllable to a note half as long. This style was called *musique mesurée* (measured music). **Music: NAWM 43**

D. Germany

Secular polyphony developed late in Germany, where the Meistersinger, writing monophonic music, were important through the 16th century.

E. The Lied

The polyphonic *lied* (song), which developed in Germany in the second half of the 15th century and continued through much of the 16th century, consists of a German tune set in a contrapuntal style derived from the Franco-Flemish tradition. Later lieder are influenced by the Italian madrigal and villanella.

F. Minor Genres

The *quodlibet* was a piece composed of numerous different songs or fragments of songs put together in counterpoint, often producing an incongruous mixture of texts. Some German composers also set classical Latin verses, such as odes. German courts and cities began from about 1550 to hire mostly Franco-Flemish or Italian musicians, who helped to create a cosmopolitan style in Germany that mixed German, Franco-Flemish, and Italian traits.

G. Major Composers

Orlando di Lasso (1532–1594), who served the Duke of Bavaria in Munich for almost 40 years, was the most important 16th-century composer active in Germany. In addition to Italian madrigals and French chansons, he wrote German lieder in madrigal style. *Hans Leo Hassler* (1564–1612) united German and Italian characteristics in his music.

H. Spain

The principal Spanish secular form in the late 15th and early 16th centuries was the *villancico,* a short strophic song with refrain. *Juan del Encina* (1469-1529) was the principal composer of villancicos.

I. Eastern Europe

Several Polish and Bohemian composers of the 15th and 16th centuries were familiar with musical trends in western Europe and participated in the same developments.

J. The English Madrigal

Nicholas Yonge's publication in 1588 of *Musica transalpina,* a collection of Italian madrigals in English translation, launched a fashion for madrigal singing and composition in England. The leading composers were *Thomas Morley* (1557–1602), *Thomas Weelkes* (ca. 1575–1623), and *John Wilbye* (1574–1638). Morley was particularly skilled in lighter forms such as the *ballett* and *canzonet* (related to the Italian balletto and canzonetta). **Music: NAWM 44**

K. English Lute Songs

Solo songs with lute accompaniment, known as *lute songs,* became popular in England after about 1600, particularly the songs or *airs* of *John Dowland.* These tended to feature less text-painting than the madrigal but carefully followed the natural declamation of the text. In addition to the lute song and madrigal, which were indebted to foreign models, there was a native tradition of *consort songs,* songs for voice accompanied by a *consort of viols.* **Music: NAWM 45**

V. Instrumental Music of the Sixteenth Century (HWM 218–32, NAWM 46–47)

A. The Rise of Instrumental Music

The period 1450–1550 saw an increase in instrumental music and the beginnings of independent styles and forms of writing for instruments. Earlier, instruments accompanied or substituted for voices in vocal works, played transcriptions of vocal works, and performed dances, fanfares, and other instrumental works from memory. But now instrumental music was written down more often, reflecting an increase in status (and perhaps in musical literacy) for instrumentalists.

B. Books on Instruments

Books on instruments were published throughout the century; these were practical manuals, describing the instruments, how to tune and play them, and how to embellish a musical line in performance. Sebastian Virdung's *Musica getutscht* (Music in German, 1511) was the first book to describe instruments and how to play them, and Michael Praetorius's *Syntagma musicum* (Treatise of Music, 1618) is one of the most important. There were many types of wind instruments, and all instruments were built in *families,* with each type of instrument built in different sizes and registers from bass to soprano, giving a homogeneous sound throughout the entire range. A complete set of a single type of instrument, often made by a single maker, was called a *chest* or *consort.*

   1. Wind instruments included recorders, shawms, *krummhorns,* transverse flutes, cornetts, trumpets, and sackbuts.

   2. The main type of bowed string instrument was the *viol,* which had frets, six strings, and a delicate tone.

   3. Keyboard instruments included the organ, the *clavichord,* and the *harpsichord.*

C. The Lute

The lute was the most popular household instrument in the Renaissance. The *vihuela* was a related instrument from Spain. Both lute and vihuela music was notated in *tablature,* which showed the player, not the pitches to play, but which string to play and where to stop the string to produce the correct pitch. (For examples of tablature, see HWM, pp. 217 and 317, and NAWM 66a.)

D. Relation of Instrumental to Vocal Music

Instruments were still often used in vocal music to double or replace voice parts. Parts of the Mass and Office were sometimes sung in alternation with *versets* played on the organ. Some instrumental works were based on a cantus firmus, such as the *In nomines* and keyboard fantasies in England.

E. Compositions on Vocal Models

Numerous works for instruments are transcriptions of madrigals, chansons, or motets, embellished in a style that is idiomatic for the instruments. The manner of embellishment in written music probably derives from improvisation.

F. The Canzona

The Italian instrumental *canzona* originated as an instrumental work in the same style as a French chanson of the mid-16th century, including a typical opening figure of a note followed by two notes of half its value (e.g., a half note and two quarter notes). The early canzonas were for organ; canzonas for instrumental ensemble began to be written after 1580 and evolved into the 17th-century sonata da chiesa. Canzonas were often based on a series of different figures, most of them treated in imitation. The result was a piece in a series of sections, sometimes overlapping.

G. Dance Music

Social dancing was important to Renaissance society, and thus a great deal of the instrumental music of the time is written for dancing or based on dance forms. Here the top melody usually dominates, and there is little contrapuntal interplay. In stylized dance pieces, an instrumental style independent of vocal models could develop. An important theatrical dance form was the *ballet*. Dances were often grouped in pairs or in threes, usually a slow dance followed by a fast one, such as a *pavane* and *galliard* or *passamezzo* and *saltarello*. The *allemande* and *courante* appeared about mid-century and would become part of the standard 17th-century dance suite. **Music: NAWM 46**

H. Improvisatory Pieces

Renaissance musicians were trained in improvisation, both in embellishing a given line and in adding contrapuntal lines to a given melody. Players of keyboards and lutes improvised polyphonic pieces, and works in the same general style were written down under names such as *prelude, fantasia,* and *ricercare*. Preludes and fantasias often served to establish the mode for a following vocal piece. The chief keyboard genre in improvisatory style in the second half of the 16th century was the *toccata* (from the Italian word for "touched").

I. The Ricercare

The *ricercare,* or *ricercar,* evolved from an early improvisatory form into a work based on a series of subjects treated in imitation, like an instrumental relative of the motet.

J. Sonata

Sonata is a term with many different meanings throughout music history. It was first used for a piece of purely instrumental music. The Venetian sonata at the end of the 16th century is more serious and motet-like than the canzona. Among the most important Venetian composers of sonatas and canzonas was *Giovanni Gabrieli* (ca. 1557–1612). His *Sonata pian' e forte,* for two instrumental choirs, was among the first instrumental ensemble pieces to designate specific instruments and dynamic markings.

K. Variations

Written sets of *variations* first appear in the early 16th century. There are both variations on tunes presented in the treble and variations over *ostinatos* in the bass. In the late 16th and early 17th centuries, the English *virginalists*— composers of music for virginal, or harpsichord—wrote many variations and other keyboard works. The most prominent of these composers included

William Byrd and *John Bull.* The most important manuscript collection is the *Fitzwilliam Virginal Book.* **Music: NAWM 47**

L. English Composers on the Continent

Several English composers were active in Denmark, the Netherlands, and Germany during the early 17th century and influenced composers in the region.

VI. Summary (HWM 232–33)

The generation after Josquin continued and extended his style. Influenced by humanism, Willaert sought to match the rhythm and meaning of the text in his music, especially in his madrigals. Later madrigalists used varied textures, chromaticism, and dissonance to express more vividly the feelings in the text. Popular styles emerged in England, France, and Germany as well as Italy, and French composers tried to revive ancient Greek meters in musique mesurée. Instrumental music rose to a new prominence in publications of dance music and in genres independent of dance or singing.

STUDY QUESTIONS

The Franco-Flemish Generation of 1520–1550 (HWM 187–92)

1. Where did Willaert live and work? Who were some of his students?

2. What principles did Willaert follow in setting words to music? How does this approach differ from earlier approaches in setting text?

3. In his motet *O crux, splendidior cunctis astris* (excerpted in HWM, pp. 190–91), what does Willaert do to project the transposed Dorian mode?

The Rise of National Styles (HWM 192–93, NAWM 36)

4. During the 16th century, what idioms coexisted with the international Franco-Flemish style? Which nation or region eventually displaced France and the Lowlands as the center of musical life in western Europe?

_____   _____

5. What is a *frottola*? What is a polyphonic *lauda*? When and where were these genres popular?

Music to Study
    NAWM 36: Marco Cara, *Io non compro più speranza*, frottola (ca. 1500)
       CD 2.32–38   Cassette 2.B

6. What characteristics of the frottola are exemplified in Cara's *Io non compro più speranza* (NAWM 36)?

The Italian Madrigal (HWM 193–206, NAWM 37–41)

7. How does the 16th-century *madrigal* differ from the 14th-century madrigal? How does it differ from the frottola?

8. In what circumstances were madrigals performed, and by whom?

Music to Study
   NAWM 37: Jacob Arcadelt, *Ahimè, dov'è 'l bel viso*, madrigal (ca. 1538)
      CD 2.39–41 (Concise 1.39–41)   Cassette 2.B (Concise 1.B)

9. In what ways does Arcadelt's madrigal *Ahimè, dov'è 'l bel viso* (NAWM 37) resemble a frottola, such as Cara's *Io non compro più speranza* (NAWM 36)?

In what ways is it different from a frottola?

10. In what ways does Arcadelt reflect in his music the feelings or the imagery of the text?

---

11. Who was Francesco Petrarch? When did he live? What was his importance for the 16th-century madrigal?

12. Who was Pietro Bembo? When did he live? What was his importance for the madrigal?

Music to Study

   NAWM 38: Adrian Willaert, *Aspro core e selvaggio e cruda voglia,*
       madrigal (ca. 1540s)
       CD 2.42–46   Cassette 2.B
   NAWM 39: Cipriano de Rore, *Datemi pace, o duri miei pensieri,* madrigal
       (ca. 1557)
       CD 2.47–50 (Concise 1.42–45)   Cassette 2.B (Concise 1.B)

13. In what ways is Willaert's *Aspro core* (NAWM 38) like a motet of the 16th
    century, such as Josquin's *De profundis clamavi ad te* (NAWM 34)?

14. According to Pietro Bembo, how did Petrarch convey "pleasingness"
    (*piacevolezza*) and "severity" (*gravità*) in his poetry?

    How is this contrast reflected in the opening 21 measures of Willaert's
    Aspro core?

    What suggestions for setting a text does Zarlino (who was Willaert's
    student) make in the passage on p. 198 of HWM? How does this reflect
    Willaert's practice in *Aspro core*?

15. In what other ways does Willaert illustrate through musical means the images in the text?

16. Willaert's madrigal is a setting of a sonnet by Petrarch. A sonnet is a poem of fourteen lines divided into an octave or ottava (the first eight lines), and a sestet, or sestina (the remaining six lines). In a Petrarchan sonnet, the usual rhyme scheme is abba abba cde cde, and the sestet introduces a new thought or feeling as well as new rhymes. How does Willaert set off the sestet from the octave? In what other ways does his setting reflect the structure of the text?

17. Rore's *Datemi pace* (NAWM 39) also uses a sonnet by Petrarch. How does Rore set off the sestet from the octave? In what other ways does his setting reflect the structure of the text?

18. In Rore's *Datemi pace,* how does the music reflect the meaning of the words?

How does the music reflect the accentuation and rhythm of the words?

19. Where in Rore's *Datemi pace* is there direct chromatic motion in a melody, for instance, from a *B♮* to *B♭* or *F♮* to *F♯* ?

    Where does direct chromatic motion occur in the madrigal by Nicola Vicentino excerpted in HWM, p. 200?

    Of all the pieces you have studied in NAWM, which earlier piece or pieces include(s) melodic movement *directly* from a note to its chromatically altered form, without other notes in between?

    What connections do you see between the musical culture that produced these madrigals by Rore and Vicentino and the musical culture(s) that produced the earlier piece or pieces?

20. What was the *concerto delle donne* (women's ensemble) at Ferrara? Who established it, and who took part? How did the formation of such ensembles affect the vocal techniques composers used in their madrigals?

Music to Study
NAWM 40: Carlo Gesualdo, *"Io parto" e non più dissi*, madrigal (ca. 1600)
CD 2.51–53   Cassette 2.B

21. How does Gesualdo use chromaticism, contrasting diatonic sections, and rhythm to reflect the emotional sense of the words in *"Io parto" e non più dissi* (NAWM 40)?

22. Briefly outline Monteverdi's career, including his date and place of birth, his early training, and his employment, including place, position, and dates of service. When and where did he write and publish his fifth book of madrigals?

Music to Study
NAWM 41: Claudio Monteverdi, *Cruda Amarilli*, madrigal (ca. 1600)
CD 2.54–58 (Concise 1.46–50)   Cassette 2.B (Concise 1.B)

23. How does Monteverdi use dissonant harmonies, and particularly unprepared dissonances, to convey the meaning of the text in *Cruda Amarilli* (NAWM 41)?

24. To what did Artusi object in Monteverdi's *Cruda Amarilli*? How might the notion that certain passages include written-out embellishments answer Artusi's objections?

Monteverdi defended himself, not with an appeal to written-out embellishments, but with the claim that he was following a "second practice." What was the basis for this second practice?

Secular Song Outside Italy (HWM 207–18, NAWM 42–45)

25. Who was the major publisher of the Parisian chanson in the early 16th century?

Who were the principal composers of these chansons?

What evidence is there for the popularity of this type of chanson?

Music to Study
> **NAWM 42:** Claudin de Sermisy, *Tant que vivray*, chanson (second quarter of
> the 16th century)
> CD 2.59–60 (Concise 1.51–52)   Cassette 2.B (Concise 1.B)

26. How does the "new" Parisian chanson, exemplified by Sermisy's *Tant que vivray* (NAWM 42), differ from the older Franco-Flemish chanson, exemplified by Josquin's *Mille regretz* (NAWM 32a)?

27. How does the Parisian chanson resemble the Italian frottola? Use Sermisy's *Tant que vivray* and Cara's frottola *Io non compro più speranza* (NAWM 36) as examples for your comparison.

---

28. What changes did the French chanson experience during the second half of the 16th century?

Music to Study
> **NAWM 43:** Claude Le Jeune, *Revecy venir du printans*, chanson (late 16th
>   century)
>   CD 2.61–69   Cassette 2.B

29.   What are the characteristics of musique mesurée? How are these qualities
      exemplified in Le Jeune's *Revecy venir du printans* (NAWM 43)?

30.   In this strophic song with refrain, how does Le Jeune vary the verses? How
      does this give shape to the whole work?

---

31. What are the characteristics of German secular polyphony in the 15th and 16th
    centuries?

32. What is a *quodlibet*?

33. Where was Orlando di Lasso trained, and where did he work for most of his career?

34. How are Lasso's lieder similar to or different from the earlier German lieder and contemporary Italian madrigals? Compare Example 7.10 on p. 212 of HWM with NAWM 35 (an Isaac lied) and 38 or 39 (madrigals by Willaert and Rore).

35. What is a *villancico*? Where and when were villancicos popular?

36. What was *Musica transalpina,* and when did it appear? What effect did it have on the development of the English madrigal?

37. Who were the leading composers of English madrigals?

Music to Study
> **NAWM 44:** Thomas Weelkes, *O Care, thou wilt despatch me*, madrigal (ca. 1600)
> > CD 3.1–4 (Concise 1.53–56)   Cassette 3.A (Concise 1.B)
> **NAWM 45:** John Dowland, *Flow my tears*, air (ca. 1600)
> > CD 3.5–7 (Concise 1.57–59)   Cassette 3.A (Concise 1.B)

38. In Weelkes's madrigal *O Care, thou wilt despatch me* (NAWM 44), how are the images and feelings in the text conveyed in the music?

39. Locate where the following unusual vertical sonorities occur in Weelkes's madrigal. (Some occur more than once.)

    a diminished seventh   _____

    an augmented triad   _____

    a diminished octave   _____

    What purposes do these dissonances serve? How can you explain their presence?

40. Thomas Morley, in the passage reprinted on p. 216 of HWM, says to would-be composers of madrigals that "the more variety you show the better shall you please." What kinds of variety does he mean (that is, variety in what aspects of the music), and how does Weelkes provide that variety in *O Care, thou wilt despatch me?*

41. Comparing Weelkes's madrigal to the madrigals in NAWM 37–41, what similarities and what differences do you notice between English and Italian madrigals?

42. What are the characteristics of an English lute song around 1600, as described in HWM? How are these exemplified in Dowland's *Flow my tears* (NAWM 45)?

43. In tonal music of the common-practice period (ca. 1670–ca. 1900), there is a strong sense of direction toward the tonic (or local tonic). In familiar tonal progressions such as I-IV-vii-iii-vi-ii-V-I or I-vi-IV-ii-V-I, there is a strong tendency for root motion to progress up by fourths (the same as down by fifths) or down by thirds, rather than in the opposite direction. Modal music does not have this strong directional quality, so that motion up by thirds or down by fourths is just as likely as the reverse.

Given this difference, is Dowland's *Flow my tears* more likely to be modal (in the Aeolian mode) or tonal (in A minor)? Can you find a passage whose harmonies progress by thirds or by fourths? Does this passage follow the expectations of tonal music, or of modal music?

Instrumental Music of the Sixteenth Century (HWM 218–32, NAWM 46–47)

44. Why do we have so little instrumental music from before 1450? How and why did this change after about 1450? What evidence is there for a rising interest in instrumental music during the Renaissance?

45. What are *Musica getutscht* and *Syntagma musicum*? Who wrote them, and when? Why are they important?

46. What is an *instrument family*? Why is it significant that instruments were built in families?

47. Which were the principal instrument families in the 16th century? How do they relate to their medieval ancestors, and how do they relate to their modern relatives?

48. What is *tablature*?

49. What kinds of instrumental pieces of the 16th century were related to vocal music?

50. What is an instrumental *canzona*? What vocal form was it related to, and what did it develop into?

51. Describe the musical characteristics of a 16th-century canzona.

52. What are some of the main characteristics of Renaissance dance music?

53. How were Renaissance dances grouped? What were the most popular combinations?

Music to Study
     NAWM 46: Pierre Attaingnant (editor and printer), Basse danse and Branle
               gay from *Danseries a 4 Parties*, second book (published 1547)
      CD 3.8–9 (Concise 1.60–61)   Cassette 3.A (Concise 1.B)

54.   How do the Basse danse and Branle gay from Pierre Attaingnant's
      Danseries a 4 Parties, second book (NAWM 46), exemplify the
      characteristics of Renaissance dance music?

---

55. What role did improvisation play in 16th-century music performance and
    education?

56. What is a *toccata*? On which instruments was it performed? What are its main
    musical characteristics, and how are they exemplified in the toccata by Claudio
    Merulo excerpted on pp. 227–29 of HWM?

57. What is a *ricercare* (or *ricercar*) of the 16th century?   What are its main characteristics? What vocal genre does the late-16th-century ricercare resemble?

58. What did the term *sonata* mean in the 16th century? How is it different from the later meaning of the term?

59. What is special about Giovanni Gabrieli's *Sonata pian' e forte*?

60. What types of variations were written in the 16th century? In the music of the English virginalists, what kinds of tunes were used as themes for variations, and how were they treated in the variations?

61. What is the *Fitzwilliam Virginal Book,* when was it compiled, and what does it contain?

Music to Study
    NAWM 47: William Byrd, *Pavana Lachrymae*, keyboard variations on
        NAWM 45, *Flow my tears* (early 17th century)
    CD 3.10–12 (Concise 2.1–3)   Cassette 3.A (Concise 2.A)

62. How is Dowland's *Flow my tears* (NAWM 45) treated in Byrd's *Pavana Lachrymae* (NAWM 102b)?

VI. Summary (HWM 232–33)

63. List the major developments in secular music between 1520 and 1600.

TERMS TO KNOW

Terms Related to 16th-Century Vocal Music

frottola
lauda
madrigal (16th-century)
"pleasingness" (*piacevolezza*)
    and "severity" (*gravità*)
villanella
canzonetta and balletto
Parisian chanson
vaudeville or air de cour

vers mesurés à l'antique
musique mesurée
lied
quodlibet
villancico
ballett and canzonet
lute song
air
consort song

Terms Related to 16th-Century Instrumental Music

instrument family
consort of viols
chest of viols
viol
krummhorn
clavichord
harpsichord
vihuela
tablature
verset
canzona
pavane and galliard

passamezzo and saltarello
allemande
courante
prelude
fantasia
ricercare
toccata
sonata (16th-century)
variations
ostinato
the English virginalists

NAMES TO KNOW

Names Related to 16th-Century Vocal Music

Nicolas Gombert
Jacobus Clemens
Ludwig Senfl
Adrian Willaert
Jacob Arcadelt
Petrarch (Francesco Petrarca)
Pietro Bembo
Cipriano de Rore
Nicola Vicentino
the *concerto delle donne* of Ferrara
Carlo Gesualdo
Claudio Monteverdi

Claudin de Sermisy
Clément Jannequin
Jean-Antoine de Baïf
Claude Le Jeune
Orlando di Lasso
Hans Leo Hassler
Juan del Encina
Musica transalpina
Thomas Morley
Thomas Weelkes
John Wilbye
John Dowland

Names Related to 16th-Century Instrumental Music

Musica getutscht und ausgezogen	*Sonata pian' e forte*
Syntagma musicum	John Bull
Giovanni Gabrieli	*The Fitzwilliam Virginal Book*

REVIEW QUESTIONS

1. Make a time-line for the 16th century and place on it the pieces, composers, and treatises discussed in this chapter. (You will add to this time-line in the next chapter.)

2. Trace the development of secular vocal music in Italy from the frottola to the madrigals of Gesualdo and Monteverdi.

3. Describe the varieties of secular vocal music practiced outside Italy during the 16th century. Which of them were influenced by the Italian madrigal, and in what ways?

4. In what ways can you compare the madrigal in England (or Italy, or both) to popular music of the present or recent past? Try to come up with as many examples as you can of parallels between the madrigal, the popular music of the 16th century, and top-40 pop music, rap, rock, or any other type of popular music current today.

5. Trace the influence of humanism and the revival of ideals associated with ancient Greek music on vocal music in Italy and France during the 16th century, focusing on the genres most affected by these influences.

6. Describe the relation of music and text in 16th-century vocal music and contrast it with earlier practices of setting texts.

7. Trace the development of notated instrumental music in the 16th century, including its relation to vocal models, to dance music, and to improvisation.

CHURCH MUSIC OF THE LATE RENAISSANCE AND REFORMATION

8

CHAPTER OBJECTIVES

After you complete the reading, study of the music, and study questions for this chapter, you should be able to:

1. describe the attitudes toward and uses of music in Protestant churches in the 16th century and the genres they used;
2. describe what is distinctive about English music in the 16th century;
3. describe the effect of the Counter-Reformation on 16th-century Catholic music;
4. describe the style of Palestrina's Masses and of motets by Lasso and Byrd; and
5. identify some of the most important composers and terms associated with these trends.

CHAPTER OUTLINE

I. The Music of the Reformation in Germany (HWM 239–43)

A. Music in the Reformation

Martin Luther, the leader of the *Reformation* in Germany, loved music and gave it a central position in the Lutheran Church. Lutheran services used parts of the Roman liturgy in Latin, parts in translation, or Luther's German version of the Mass liturgy, the *Deudsche Messe* (1526). The music used was also a mixture of plainsong, Latin polyphony, and German hymns. Luther believed that the congregation should take part in the music of the service, and so he made congregational hymn singing part of the liturgy.

B. The Lutheran Chorale

The chorale was a strophic hymn sung by the congregation in unison. Chorales later became the basis for polyphonic compositions. Luther wrote many chorale texts and perhaps some of the tunes. There were four sources for chorale tunes: newly written melodies; translations or arrangements from Gregorian chant; existing German devotional songs; and secular tunes.

C. Contrafacta

Many chorales were adapted from secular songs by revising the text to give it a spiritual meaning or by replacing it with a new sacred text. This process is called *contrafactum,* and the resulting new works are called *contrafacta.*

D. Polyphonic Chorale Settings

Composers soon began to arrange the monophonic chorales in polyphonic settings intended for the choir to sing. These settings used a variety of styles, from cantus firmus style to imitative motet style to simple chordal style. Settings in *cantional style*—simple chordal settings with the chorale in the top voice—became common in the late 16th century, and after 1600 it was customary for the organ to play all the parts while the congregation sang the tune.

E. The Chorale Motet

By the end of the 16th century, Protestant composers began to write *chorale motets,* free polyphonic elaborations of a chorale.

II. Reformation Church Music Outside Germany (HWM 244–49, NAWM 48)

A. The Psalter

Reformation movements in France, the Low Countries, and Switzerland, led by *Jean Calvin* (1509–1564) and others, rejected the Catholic liturgy, artistic trappings, and nonbiblical texts in favor of simple rhymed translations of the Psalms. These were published in *Psalters* and set to melodies, sung in unison, that were either newly composed or adapted from plainchant or secular songs. They were seldom set polyphonically, except in simple harmonizations. The main French Psalter used tunes chosen or composed by *Loys Bourgeois* (ca. 1510–ca. 1561), whose melodies were often adopted by churches in other countries, including the New England colonies (the *Bay Psalm Book* of 1640).

B. England

For reasons of war and politics, England was again relatively isolated in the second half of the 15th and first half of the 16th centuries, and the newer style of imitative counterpoint was rare before 1540. Leading composers at the beginning of the 16th century included *William Cornysh* (ca. 1465–1523), known for secular songs and motets; *Robert Fayrfax* (ca. 1464–1521), known for Masses and sacred works; and *John Taverner* (ca. 1490–1545), renowned for his Masses and Magnificats. The setting for the words "in nomine" in Taverner's *Missa Gloria tibi trinitas* was used by English composers as the cantus firmus for numerous instrumental works, known as *In nomines.* The most important mid-century English composer was *Thomas Tallis* (ca. 1505–1585), best known for his music for both the Catholic and Anglican liturgies.
Music: NAWM 48

C. Anglican Church Music

The Church of England separated from the Roman Catholic Church in 1532 for reasons that were largely political (Henry VIII wanted an annulment of his first marriage, and the pope refused to grant it). A new liturgy in English was printed in *The Book of Common Prayer* (1549), and composers wrote church music in English. The two main genres were the *service* and the *anthem.*

1. A *service* consisted of music for the Morning and Evening Prayer and for Holy Communion, and could be either a *Great Service* (contrapuntal and melismatic) or a *Short Service* (chordal and syllabic).

2. The *anthem* was the English equivalent of the motet. There were two varieties: the *full anthem,* sung by the full choir throughout, and the *verse anthem,* for solo voice or voices with organ or viol accompaniment, with brief passages for chorus.

Among the most important composers of Anglican music were *William Byrd* (1543–1623), a Catholic who also wrote Latin motets and Masses, and *Orlando Gibbons* (1583–1625).

III. The Counter-Reformation (HWM 249–64, NAWM 49–52)

The *Counter-Reformation* was the Catholic Church's own program of reform, begun in response to the Protestant Reformation.

A. The Council of Trent

The *Council of Trent* met periodically between 1545 and 1563 to reform the Catholic Church. Music was only one factor that was considered, and the Council urged very general reforms designed to ensure that the words of the liturgy were clear and the music religious in tone. There is a legend that Palestrina convinced the Council not to abolish polyphony by writing the *Pope Marcellus Mass.*

B. Palestrina

Giovanni Pierluigi da Palestrina (1525/6–1594) spent his entire career in Rome as a church musician. Most of his music was sacred, include 104 Masses and about 250 motets. He also supervised the revision of Gregorian chant to conform to the edicts of the Council of Trent.

C. The Palestrina Style

Palestrina's style became a model for later composers of polyphonic church music. His Masses use a range of techniques, from cantus firmus to imitation Masses and from paraphrase to canon. His vocal lines move mostly by step in a smooth, flexible arch. He avoids chromaticism and employs a limited harmonic vocabulary, but uses different spacings to create variety in sonority. His counterpoint is supple and mostly consonant, with dissonance restricted to *suspensions,* passing notes, and *cambiatas.* The voices move in flexible rhythms, mostly independent of each other, within a regular harmonic rhythm.
Music: NAWM 49

D. Contemporaries of Palestrina

Several other composers active in Rome presaged or carried on Palestrina's style.

E. Spain

Spanish sacred polyphony was based on the Franco-Flemish style but was marked by restrained technique and heightened devotion. *Cristóbal de Morales* (ca. 1500–1553) was one of the leading Spanish composers of sacred music.

F. Victoria

Tomás Luis de Victoria (1548–1611) was a Spanish composer active in Rome and in Spain whose music is more intense than Palestrina's in its expression of the text. **Music: NAWM 50a and 50b**

G. Lasso

Orlando di Lasso (1532–1594) is as important for his motets as Palestrina is for his Masses. His motets often use pictorial, rhetorical, and dramatic devices and are written in a variety of styles. **Music: NAWM 51**

H. Byrd

William Byrd wrote three Masses and numerous motets, in addition to secular music and music for the Anglican Church. **Music: NAWM 52**

IV. Summary (HWM 264–65)

The year 1600 is only an approximate marker for the end of the Renaissance. Some Renaissance traits continued into the 17th century, and several aspects of Baroque music are already evident before 1600. The texture of similar voices in counterpoint was characteristic of the Renaissance but was increasingly replaced by homophony during the 16th century. Rhythm became comparatively steady and predictable by 1600. Sacred polyphony was marked by smooth vocal parts, full triadic harmonies, and a strong projection of the mode.

Study Questions

The Music of the Reformation in Germany (HWM 239–43)

1. In what ways was the early Lutheran service similar to the Catholic liturgy, and how was it different? What languages were used? What further changes were made in the *Deudsche Messe*?

2. What is a *chorale*? How were they sung, and by whom?

3. What are the chief sources of tunes for chorales? What are *contrafacta*?

4. In what ways did chorales receive polyphonic treatment in the 16th and early 17th centuries? How were these polyphonic settings performed? Include in your answer descriptions of *cantional style* and the *chorale motet*.

5. In Michael Praetorius's polyphonic elaboration of the chorale *Vater unser im Himmelreich* excerpted in HWM, p. 243, the first phrase of the chorale is presented verbatim in the lower voice and then paraphrased. Later phrases are paraphrased rather than being presented exactly in either voice. Based on Praetorius's paraphrases, can you reconstruct the next three phrases of the original chorale tune? Write your answer out on the staff below, and then describe briefly the methods Praetorius uses to vary the chorale tune. Here are two hints: (1) Each phrase has the same rhythm as the first phrase. (2) The first, second, and third phrases all begin on the same note, and the fourth phrase ends on that note.

Reformation Church Music Outside Germany (HWM 244–49, NAWM 48)

6. How was music used in the Calvinist churches outside Germany? How does this differ from the Lutheran Church?

7. What is a *Psalter,* and what does it contain?

What was the first American Psalter called? _____

8. How is English polyphonic music of the late 15th and early 16th centuries different from Franco-Flemish polyphony of the same time? What types of English pieces survive from this period?

Music to Study

NAWM 48: William Cornysh, *My love she mourneth*, part-song (early 16th century)

CD 3.13   Cassette 3.A

9. How does Cornysh's part-song *My love she mourneth* (NAWM 48) exemplify the characteristic features of English polyphony of his time? How is it similar to, and how is it different from, Ockeghem's *D'ung aultre amer* (NAWM 31) and Josquin's *Mille regretz* (NAWM 32a)? (Note: Although we are encountering it a chapter later than the English madrigals of the 1590s and early 1600s, please note that this work predates those madrigals by almost a century. It is placed here as an example of the native English style of polyphony early in the 16th century.)

---

10. What are the principal forms of Anglican church music? How does a *full anthem* differ from a *verse anthem*? How does a *Great Service* differ from a *Short Service*?

The Counter-Reformation (HWM 249–64, NAWM 49–52)

11. What was the Council of Trent? When was it held, and what was its purpose? What matters relating to music were discussed, and what actions relating to music did the Council take?

12. Briefly summarize Palestrina's career. Why was his music important for later composers?

13. How many Masses did Palestrina write? _____

    What compositional techniques did he use in his Masses?

Music to Study
> **NAWM 49:** Giovanni da Palestrina, *Pope Marcellus Mass*, excerpts (1562–63)
>> 49a: Credo   CD 3.14–18   Cassette 3.A
>> 49b: Agnus Dei I   CD 3.19 (Concise 2.4)   Cassette 3.A (Concise 2.A)
>
> **NAWM 50a:** Tomás Luis de Victoria, *O magnum mysterium*, motet (published1572)
>> CD 3.20–22   Cassette 3.A
>
> **NAWM 50b:** Tomás Luis de Victoria, *Missa O magnum mysterium*, Mass, excerpt: Kyrie (published 1592)
>> CD 3.23–24   Cassette 3.A

14. Describe Palestrina's style in terms of melody, harmony, counterpoint and dissonance treatment, sonority, and rhythm, using examples from the Credo and first Agnus Dei of the *Pope Marcellus Mass* (NAWM 49a and 49b).

    melody:

    harmony:

    counterpoint and dissonance treatment:

    sonority:

    rhythm:

15. How is each phrase of text treated in Victoria's motet *O magnum mysterium* (NAWM 50a)? How does the placement of cadences help to give shape to the piece and make clear the divisions of the text?

16. In what mode is this motet? How can you tell? How is the mode made clear?

17. How does Victoria's motet compare to Josquin's *De profundis clamavi ad te* (NAWM 34) in its style and approach?

18. Compare the Kyrie of Victoria's Missa *O magnum mysterium* (NAWM 50b) to the motet on which it is based (NAWM 50a). What has Victoria borrowed from his earlier motet, and how has he varied it?

19. What is an *imitation Mass* or *parody Mass* (see the definition in HWM, p. 175)? How does Victoria's Missa *O magnum mysterium* exemplify this kind of Mass?

20. How do Orlando di Lasso's career, music, and musical output contrast with those of Palestrina? (Note: There is additional information on Lasso in chapter 7 of HWM.)

Music to Study

NAWM 51: Orlando di Lasso, *Tristis est anima mea*, motet (published 1565)
CD 3.25–28 (Concise 2.5–8)   Cassette 3.B (Concise 2.A)

21. How does Lasso use pictorial, rhetorical, or dramatic devices to convey the meaning of the words in his motet *Tristis est anima mea* (NAWM 51)?

22. Briefly recount William Byrd's career. What kinds of music did he write? How did the situation of religion in England affect his career and compositional output? (You may wish to refer back to parts of chapter 7 of HWM in answering this question.)

Music to Study
> **NAWM 52:** William Byrd, *Sing joyfully unto God*, full anthem (late 16th century)
>> CD 3.29–32 (Concise 2.9–12)   Cassette 3.B (Concise 2.A)

23. What compositional traits in *Sing joyfully unto God* (NAWM 52) mark it as a work by Byrd? (One not mentioned in NAWM is the English fondness for cross-relations in different voices, here between *A* and *A♭*.)

24. How does Byrd illustrate the text? How does he highlight the accentuation and phrasing of the text?

Summary (HWM 264–65)

25. According to the summary on pp. 264–65 of HWM, what were the general characteristics of music in the 16th century in respect to the treatment of texture, rhythm, melody, and harmony?

TERMS TO KNOW

Reformation	In nomine
chorale	service: Great Service, Short Service
contrafacta	anthem: full anthem, verse anthem
cantional style	Counter-Reformation
chorale motet	suspension
Psalter	cambiata

NAMES TO KNOW

Martin Luther	*The Book of Common Prayer*
Deudsche Messe	William Byrd
Jean Calvin	Orlando Gibbons
Loys Bourgeois	Council of Trent
Bay Psalm Book	Giovanni Pierluigi da Palestrina
William Cornysh	*Pope Marcellus Mass*
Robert Fayrfax	Cristóbal de Morales
John Taverner	Tomás Luis de Victoria
Thomas Tallis	Orlando di Lasso

REVIEW QUESTIONS

1. Add to the time-line for the 16th century that you made in chapter 7 the pieces, composers, and events discussed in this chapter.

2. How was music regarded, how was it used, and what musical genres were cultivated in the Lutheran Church and in Calvinist churches during the 16th century?

3. Many chorales were adapted from Gregorian chant. Create a chorale tune based on the Gregorian hymn *Christe Redemptor omnium* (NAWM 4k) from the Second Vespers for the Nativity of Our Lord. Use for your text the first four lines of the English translation ("Jesus! Redeemer of the world!"), which is rhymed and metrical. Since chorales are almost entirely syllabic, you will need to eliminate some of the extra notes in the Gregorian melody. (One strategy might be to match the eight syllables of each line of the English verse to the eight notes or neumes in the corresponding line of music, and then, for syllables with more than one note, choose the note you like best. Or you can follow the melody more flexibly.) Use the rhythm of *Vater unser im Himmelreich* (as given above in question #5), or any rhythm that fits the accentuation of the poetry. You might create several different chorale tunes, all based on this chant.

4. What characteristics distinguished English music in the 16th century from music on the Continent?

5. How did the Counter-Reformation affect music for the Catholic Church?

6. Describe Palestrina's style in his Masses.

7. How did composers of church music in the later 16th century treat the words they set? What are some of the various approaches to setting or expressing the text exemplified by the pieces treated in this chapter?

MUSIC OF THE EARLY BAROQUE PERIOD

9

CHAPTER OBJECTIVES

After you complete the reading, study of the music, and study questions for this chapter, you should be able to:

1. describe the characteristics that distinguish Baroque music from music of earlier periods;
2. relate music of the Baroque period to the culture and art of the time;
3. describe the various styles of music that flourished and competed in the first half of the 17th century;
4. trace the evolution of opera in Italy from its forerunners through the middle of the 17th century;
5. describe the genres and styles of secular and sacred vocal music practiced in the early 17th century;
6. explain what is distinctive about Venice and Venetian music in the late 16th and early 17th centuries; and
7. name and briefly describe the most important genres and styles of instrumental music in the early Baroque period.

CHAPTER OUTLINE

I. General Characteristics (HWM 268–76)

A. "Baroque" as Term and Period

The word *baroque* (from a Portuguese word for an irregularly shaped pearl) was first used to describe art regarded as bizarre or exaggerated. Later, it was used by art historians in a more positive way to describe the flamboyant decorative and expressive tendencies of 17th- and early-18th-century art and architecture. Music historians now use it for the period of about 1600 to 1750, which includes a variety of musical styles that share some general conventions and ideals.

B. Geographical and Cultural Background

Italy remained the most influential region, with important centers at Florence, Rome, Venice, Naples, and Bologna. French music absorbed Italian influences before an Italian, Jean-Baptiste Lully, established a French style after mid-century. German music also had Italian roots, and a native English tradition was eventually largely displaced by the Italian style. Many rulers supported music, as did the Church, many cities, and independent academies. Literature and art flourished throughout Europe in the Baroque period, from the poetry of Milton to the paintings of Rembrandt. New developments in philosophy and science were particularly spectacular, with Bacon, Descartes, Galileo, Kepler, Newton, and others who helped lay the foundations of modern thought.

C. New Musical Idiom

Musicians at the turn of the 17th century sought to give expression to a wider range of emotions and ideas than before. Their search for new methods involved considerable experimentation and led to the codification of a new musical language by the middle of the century.

D. The Two Practices

Writing in 1605, Monteverdi distinguished between the *prima prattica* (first practice), in which a composer follows the rules of dissonance treatment codified by Zarlino, and the *seconda prattica* (second practice), in which those rules could be violated in order to express better the feelings in the text. The former came to be called *stile antico* (old style), as opposed to the *stile moderno* (modern style). Others divided music into church, chamber, and theatrical styles.

E. Idiomatic Writing

Renaissance polyphony might be sung or played by various combinations of voices and instruments, but the growing importance of soloists led 17th-century composers to write with a specific medium in mind. As a result, distinctive idiomatic styles developed for the voice, violin family, viol family, wind instruments, keyboard, and other instruments.

F. The Affections

Baroque composers sought to write music that was expressive of the *affections,* or states of the soul. These are not the emotions of the composer (or anyone else), but generalized states of feeling.

G. Rhythm

Music before the 17th century was conceived primarily in terms of durations, but Baroque and later composers thought in terms of strong and weak beats grouped in *measures.* On the other hand, free and irregular rhythms were used in vocal recitative and instrumental preludes and toccatas. Some standard forms paired a relatively free section with a strictly metered section, such as a recitative and aria or a toccata and fugue.

H. The Basso Continuo

Renaissance polyphony used a texture of equal voices, but in Baroque music the melody and bass were the two essential lines. In the system of notation called *thoroughbass* or *basso continuo,* the accompaniment was not fully written out; instead, *continuo instruments* such as harpsichord, organ, or lute would play the notated bass line and fill in the appropriate chords above it, while often a sustaining instrument like a viola da gamba or bassoon would reinforce the bass.

Accidentals, nonharmonic tones, and chords other than root-position triads could be indicated by numbers and other figures; a part notated this way is called a *figured bass.* A basso continuo part can be *realized* by the performer(s) in various ways from simple chords to elaborate improvisations.

I. The New Counterpoint

Composers continued to use counterpoint. Gradually there evolved a new kind of counterpoint in which the lines had to fit the harmonies implied by the basso continuo. This marks the beginning of counterpoint governed by harmony.

J. Dissonance

The new importance of harmony led during the later 17th century to a conception of dissonance as a note outside a chord, rather than an interval between two voices, and to an increased role for dissonance in defining the tonal direction of a piece.

K. Chromaticism

Chromaticism was used in the early 17th century for expression of extreme emotions or to give harmonic interest to improvisations. Later in the century, it also gained a role in defining tonal direction.

L. Major-Minor Tonalities

These and other developments led by last third of the 17th century to *tonality,* or *the major-minor system,* which replaced the older system of modes.

II. Early Opera (HWM 276–93, NAWM 53–58)

A. Forerunners

An *opera* is a staged drama set to continuous music. The first operas were written around 1600, but many earlier forms of theater used music, including Greek tragedies, liturgical dramas, religious plays, and Renaissance theater.

B. Intermedi

Intermedi were theatrical interludes between acts of a 16th-century play, and the more elaborate intermedi often incorporated madrigals, songs, and other music. Some madrigals set scenes from dramatic poems or represented a dialogue between characters, and these approached the idea of opera.   **Music: NAWM 53**

C. Madrigal Cycles

Madrigal cycles were groups of madrigals that presented a plot or represented a series of scenes. Cycles of light madrigals are now sometimes called *madrigal comedies.*

D. The Pastoral

A *pastoral* was a poem, sometimes staged as a drama, about shepherds, nymphs, and other rural (or pastoral) subjects in an idealized setting.

E. Greek Tragedy as a Model

The ancient Greek tragedies were a model for the dramatically effective theater Renaissance dramatists sought to achieve. Some felt that only the choruses of

Greek tragedy were sung, but *Girolamo Mei* (1519–1594), a Florentine scholar, argued that the tragedies were sung throughout. This set the stage for the invention of opera.

F. The Florentine Camerata

Mei's theory that the Greeks achieved powerful emotional effects through melody that followed the inflections and rhythms of the human voice was a strong influence on the *Florentine Camerata,* an informal group that met at the house of *Giovanni Bardi* in Florence during the 1570s and 1580s. Influenced by Mei, *Vincenzo Galilei* attacked counterpoint and argued that only a single melodic line, by following the natural inflections of a good orator, could express the feelings of poetry.

G. The Earliest Operas

The poet *Ottaviano Rinuccini* (1562–1621) and singer-composer *Jacopo Peri* (1561–1633) produced *Dafne* in Florence in 1597, as the first pastoral sung throughout. The first opera was *L'Euridice* (1600) by the same pair; that same year, *Giulio Caccini* (1551–1618) also set Rinuccini's *L'Euridice* and *Emilio de' Cavalieri* (ca. 1550–1602) produced in Rome *Rappresentatione di Anima e di Corpo* (The Representation of the Soul and the Body), a religious musical play. All three composers sought a style intermediate between speaking and singing, and all three wrote *monody,* music for solo voice and accompaniment. Peri developed a new style for dialogue, known as *stile recitativo* or *recitative style.* Other kinds of monody at the time included the *air,* which was strophic, and the *solo madrigal,* which was through-composed; both are included in Caccini's collection *Le nuove musiche* (The New Music, 1602). **Music: NAWM 53–55**

H. The Recitative Style

In recitative style, Peri sought to imitate speech by allowing the natural rhythms of speech to determine the rhythm of the melodic line; harmonizing the syllables that were naturally stressed or intoned in speech; letting the bass follow these main syllables, rather than making the voice "dance to the movement of the bass"; and setting the syllables in between to notes that might be either consonant or dissonant with the bass, to resemble the continuous motions of speech. The various styles of monody—recitative, air, and solo madrigal—were used in all kinds of music in the early 17th century, and they made a dramatic musical theater possible by allowing composers to represent a great variety of situations and emotions. **Music: NAWM 55**

I. Claudio Monteverdi

Monteverdi's opera *L'Orfeo* (Mantua, 1607), to a libretto by Alessandro Striggio, is on the same subject as Peri's *Euridice* and also uses contrasting styles. The recitative is more continuous and tonally organized; there are more airs and madrigals; repeating ritornellos and choruses create large-scale form; and the orchestra is large and varied. Most of Monteverdi's next opera, *Arianna* (1608), is lost, but Arianna's widely admired lament survives. **Music: NAWM 56**

J. Francesca Caccini

Only a few more operas were staged through the 1620s. The Florentine court preferred ballets and intermedi, such as *La liberazione di Ruggiero* (1625), an opera-like blend of ballet and intermedio by *Francesca Caccini* (1587–ca. 1640). The daughter of Giulio Caccini, she was known as both a singer and a composer and was the highest-paid musician at court.

K. Rome

Opera became established in Rome in the 1620s, particularly through the sponsorship of the Barberini family. There the comic opera became established as a separate genre. Solo singing separated into two distinct types, *recitative* and *aria*. By the middle of the 17th century, operas often included comic episodes, scenic spectacle, extraneous characters, and other elements that were entertaining as theater but no longer conformed to the Florentine ideal of a unified drama akin to that of ancient Greece.

L. Venetian Opera

Opera was introduced to Venice in 1637 in a public theater; this marked the first time opera was staged for a paying public. Venice was ideal for opera, with many visitors during Carnival season (from the day after Christmas to the day before Lent), wealthy backers, and a steady audience. Plots were drawn from mythology, epics, and Roman history. Monteverdi's last two operas, *Il ritorno d'Ulisse* (The Return of Ulysses, 1641) and *L'incoronazione di Poppea* (The Coronation of Poppea, 1642), were written for Venice. *Pier Francesco Cavalli* (1602–1676) and *Marc' Antonio Cesti* (1623–1669) were also important composers of opera in Venice.   By the mid-17th century Italian opera was characterized by a focus on solo singing, with little ensemble or instrumental music; a separation of recitative and aria; and the use of distinctive types of aria. The most prominent vocal style was the *bel canto* (beautiful singing) idiom of smooth diatonic lines and easy rhythms.   **Music: NAWM 57–58**

III. Vocal Chamber Music (HWM 293–99, NAWM 59–60)

A. Strophic Forms and Bass Patterns

Most secular vocal music was chamber music. Chamber works also used monody and basso continuo. *Strophic airs* used the same music for each strophe; *strophic variations* used the same harmonic and melodic plan for each strophe, but varied the melodic details. Some composers based works on the *romanesca* and other standard patterns for singing poetry in *ottave rime* (stanzas of eight 11-syllable lines) or on a repeating bass figure called a *ground bass* or *basso ostinato*. The *chaconne* and *passacaglia* both feature a repeating bass figure in a slow triple meter and usually in the minor mode.   **Music: NAWM 59**

B. The Concertato Medium

The 17th-century *concerto* brought together contrasting sounds into a harmonious whole, in what is called the *concertato medium*. A *concertato madrigal* uses instruments as well as voices; a *sacred concerto* likewise combines a vocal setting of a sacred text with parts for instruments; and an instrumental concerto pits groups of instruments against each other, usually soloists against a larger group. Monteverdi's later books of madrigals include a number of concertato madrigals. His Book 8, *Madrigali guerrieri et amorosi* (Madrigals of War and Love, 1638), also includes two staged ballets and *Il combattimento di Tancredi e Clorinda* (The Combat of Tancred and Clorinda), a theatrical piece of 1624. The latter uses pictorial music to suggest the action and introduces a new style, *stile concitato* (excited style), to suggest warlike feelings and actions. Monteverdi and his contemporaries mixed diverse elements in order to represent a variety of emotions, situations, and characters. In arias by younger composers such as Cesti and Cavalli, the creation of a graceful melody became more important than portraying every image or feeling in the text.   **Music: NAWM 59**

C. Genres of Vocal Solo Music

Monodies were very popular in early-17th-century Italy and were published in large number. The *cantata* (a "sung" piece) was a work for solo voice and continuo; early cantatas often used strophic variations, and later ones, such as those by *Barbara Strozzi* (1619–after 1664), alternated recitatives and arias, like an operatic scene. Composers outside Italy absorbed Italian influences but also worked in native forms like the French *air de cour.*   **Music: NAWM 60**

D. Influences on Church Music

Elements of the stile moderno (modern style) such as monody, the basso continuo, and the concertato medium were used in church music as well as in secular music. But Renaissance polyphony was not abandoned; the counterpoint of Palestrina became the model for elevated church style. New pieces in Palestrina's style were said to be in stile antico (old style), codified in the treatise *Gradus ad Parnassum* (Steps to Parnassus, 1725) by *Johann Joseph Fux.*

IV. The Venetian School (HWM 299–301, NAWM 61)

A. Social Conditions in Venice

In the 16th century, Venice was an independent city-state, a major trading center, and the second most important city in Italy (after Rome). St. Mark's Church was one of the centers of Venetian music and pageantry, and some of the best composers of the time served as choirmaster (including Willaert, Rore, and Zarlino) or organist (including Andrea Gabrieli and *Giovanni Gabrieli,* ca. 1553–1612). Venetian music was often homophonic, richly textured, and varied in sonority.

B. Venetian Polychoral Motets

Many Venetian motets were written for two or more choirs, each accompanied by instruments or organ and positioned separately from the others. In these motets for *cori spezzati* (divided choirs), called *polychoral motets,* the choirs sing alone, answer each other in antiphony, and join together for large climaxes.

This use of contrasting sonorities became an important element of Baroque music. **Music: NAWM 61**

C. Venetian Influence
The Venetian style influenced many composers throughout Europe.

V. Genres of Catholic Church Music (HWM 302–4, NAWM 62–64)

A. The Grand Concerto
A *grand concerto* was a large work for singers and instruments, often arranged in two or more separate choirs.

B. The Concerto for Few Voices
More common were concertos for one, two, or three voices with organ continuo. *Lodovico Viadana* (1560–1627) was among the first composers to use this medium, publishing 100 of them in *Cento concerti ecclesiastici* (One Hundred Church Concertos) in 1602. *Alessandro Grandi* (ca. 1575–ca. 1630) was noted for his sacred works in the new style. **Music: NAWM 62–63**

C. Oratorio
An *oratorio* is a sacred drama like an opera, sung throughout with recitatives, arias, ensembles, and instrumental preludes and ritornellos, but performed without staging or costumes in a church hall called an "oratorio," from which the musical genre took its name around the middle of the 17th century. Oratorios often featured a narrator, and the chorus was much more prominent than in opera. *Giacomo Carissimi* (1605–1674) was the leading Italian composer of oratorios in the mid-17th century. **Music: NAWM 64**

VI. Lutheran Church Music (HWM 304–8, NAWM 65)

A. The New Styles
Lutheran composers in Germany in the 17th century also wrote grand concertos and concertos for few voices, along with chorale motets and madrigal-like works. An important collection of small sacred concertos was *Opella nova* (1618 and 1626) by *Johann Hermann Schein* (1586–1630).

B. Heinrich Schütz
Heinrich Schütz (1585–1672) was the leading German composer of the mid-17th century. He studied in Italy and was chapelmaster for the Elector of Saxony at Dresden for over half a century. He is renowned for his church music; he apparently wrote no independent instrumental music, and most of his secular vocal music is lost. His sacred music includes simple German psalm settings, Latin motets, polychoral works *(Psalmen Davids)*, sacred concertos for few voices *(Kleine geistliche Konzerte)*, concertato motets *(Symphoniae sacrae)*, and oratorios, such as *The Seven Last Words* (ca. 1645). **Music: NAWM 65**

VII. Instrumental Music (HWM 308–18, NAWM 66–68)

A. Types of Instrumental Music

Basso continuo and vocal styles affected instrumental music in the 17th century, particularly in the sonata for solo instrument with accompaniment. Over the first half of the century, instrumental music gradually became the equal of vocal music in quantity and content. The following major types can be distinguished, several of which carry over from the 16th century:

1. Fugal works in continuous imitative counterpoint, such as the ricercare, fantasia, *fuga,* and related genres.
2. Canzonas that feature sections of imitative counterpoint and other styles. By mid-century, the canzona is succeeded by the related form of the *sonata da chiesa* (church sonata).
3. Pieces that vary a given melody or bass, such as the *partita, passacaglia, chaconne, chorale partita,* and *chorale prelude.*
4. Dances and pieces in dance rhythms, as separate pieces and as part of dance *suites.*
5. Pieces in improvisatory style for solo keyboard or lute, called toccata, fantasia, or prelude.

B. Ricercare

Most 17th-century ricercares are short, serious pieces for keyboard that treat a single subject in imitation throughout. *Girolamo Frescobaldi* (1583–1643), organist at St. Peter's in Rome, is well known for his ricercares.

C. Fantasia

A longer imitative work on a single subject was usually called a fantasia. English composers wrote imitative fantasias or *fancies* for viol consort.

D. Canzona

Canzonas featured a series of sections, most of them in imitative counterpoint. A *variation canzona* uses variants of the same subject in each section.

E. Sonata

In the 17th century, *sonata* came to be used for works for one or two instruments with continuo. The solo writing was often idiomatic and expressive, as in solo vocal works. Sonatas tend to be sectional, with contrasting mood and figuration in each section. In violin sonatas, the idiomatic violin style includes runs, trills, double stops, and improvised embellishments called *affetti.* A common scoring for a sonata was two treble instruments and continuo, called a *trio sonata.*

F. Variations

Variations were common in the 17th century, sometimes under titles like *partite* (divisions). There were several types:

1. In *cantus firmus variations,* the melody was largely unchanged and was surrounded by other contrapuntal lines.

    2. In another type, the melody was in the top voice and was embellished differently in each variation.

    3. Other types of variations are based on a bass or harmonic plan rather than on a melody.

German composers wrote variations on chorale tunes.

G. Dance Music

In addition to music for dancing and stylized dance movements, other types of pieces also used dance rhythms.

H. Suites

German composers especially favored the dance suite, a series of dances of varied character that often were melodically related.

I. French Lute and Keyboard Music

French composers adapted to the keyboard the playing style of the lute, which played chords one note at a time (this was the *style brisé* or broken style) and used ornaments called *agréments* to highlight or prolong a note. These features became characteristic of French keyboard music. *Denis Gaultier* (1603–1672) was the most important French lute composer of the early 17th century, and *Jacques Champion de Chambonnières* (ca. 1601–1672) and *Louis Couperin* (1626–1661) the most important French keyboard composers. *Johann Jakob Froberger* (1616–1667) took the French style to Germany and standardized the sequence of dances in the suite as *allemande, courante, sarabande,* and *gigue.* **Music: NAWM 66a, 66b, and 67**

J. Improvisatory Compositions

Among the best-known toccatas of the 17th century are those by Frescobaldi, which feature a series of overlapping sections, and Froberger, who alternates free improvisation with imitative sections. **Music: NAWM 68**

STUDY QUESTIONS

General Characteristics (HWM 268–76)

1. What did the term "baroque" mean in the 18th century?

   How was it later used in writing on art history?

   How is it used now in music history? Why is it more helpful to refer to "the Baroque period" than to "Baroque style"?

2. How was music supported financially in the 17th and 18th centuries, and by whom?

3. Which famous artists, writers, philosophers, and scientists were active in the 17th century? How does music show a similar intellectual ferment?

4. What is the *seconda prattica*? How does it differ from the *prima prattica*?

   How is the *seconda prattica* reflected in Monteverdi's madrigal *Cruda Amarilli* (NAWM 41)?   (Hint: See the discussion of this piece and Monteverdi's statement about the *seconda prattica* in HWM, pp. 204–5 and 206, and your answer to question 24 in chapter 7.)

5. How did the Renaissance ideal of writing music that could be performed by any combination of voices and instruments change in the 17th century? What was the effect on composition?

6. What are the *affections*? How does the representation of affections in music differ from the later idea of expressing an individual artist's feelings?

7. What is new about rhythm and meter in 17th-century music, in contrast to earlier music?

8. How does the typical musical texture in the Baroque period differ from that of the Renaissance?

9. Define the following terms, and explain the significance of each concept:

basso continuo or thoroughbass

figured bass

continuo instruments

10. Compare the opening of Giulio Caccini's *Perfidissimo volto* as it appears in NAWM 54 with the original publication, shown in HWM, p. 274. (In the latter, note that the vocal line is notated in tenor clef.) What notes are present in the NAWM edition that are not present in the original publication?

How are these notes differentiated from the others on the page?

Why are they present in the NAWM edition? Why are they absent in the original publication?

What is the practice of supplying these notes called? _____

11. How did the emphasis on the bass and the use of basso continuo change how counterpoint was conceived and written?

12. How did the definition of dissonance and the use of chromaticism change in response to the more chordal orientation of 17th-century music?

13. What is *tonality,* or *the major-minor system*? How did it evolve?

14. Why was figured bass important in the development of tonality?

Early Opera (HWM 276–93, NAWM 53–58)

15. What forms of theater before 1600 used music? In what ways did they resemble opera?

16. What was the function of an *intermedio* (pl. *intermedi*)? How was it like and unlike an opera?

17. How did madrigals and *madrigal cycles* (also called *madrigal comedies*) anticipate opera?

18. What is a *pastoral*? What is the importance of pastoral subjects and poetry in the development of opera? In what sense is *L'Euridice* (excerpted in NAWM 55) a pastoral?

19. In what sense was Greek tragedy a model for opera? Who were Girolamo Mei, Giovanni Bardi, and Vincenzo Galilei, and what did each one do to promote the revival of Greek ideals that ultimately led to opera?

20. What was the *Florentine Camerata,* and what is its significance?

21. What were the roles of Ottavio Rinuccini, Jacopo Peri, and Giulio Caccini in the creation of the first musical dramas (what we now call operas)? What was their relationship to the Camerata?

22. What does the term *monody* mean? What different types of music does monody include? How did monody make musical theater possible?

Music to Study

   NAWM 53: Emilio de' Cavalieri, *Dalle più alte sfere,* madrigal for voice and
         instruments (1589)
      CD 3.33–34   Cassette 3.B
   NAWM 54: Giulio Caccini, *Perfidissimo volto,* madrigal for voice and
         continuo (ca.1600)
      CD 3.35–36   Cassette 3.B

23. How do Cavalieri's madrigal *Dalle più alte sfere* (NAWM 53) and Caccini's madrigal *Perfidissimo volto* (NAWM 54) differ from other madrigals we have seen?

   What traits do they share with other 16th-century Italian madrigals? Why are they madrigals, and not airs?

24. What kinds of embellishments are used in the vocal line of *Dalle più alte sfere* to decorate the melodic line written immediately below it?

---

25.   What kinds of ornaments does Caccini use in the vocal line of *Perfidissimo volto,* and where do they appear? What other ornaments might have been performed by the singer?

Music to Study
   NAWM 55: Jacopo Peri, *Le musiche sopra l'Euridice,* opera, excerpts (1600)
      55a: Prologue, *Io, che d'alti sospir,* strophic air with ritornello
         CD 3.37   Cassette 3.B
      55b: *Nel pur ardor,* canzonet (dance-song) with ritornello
         CD 3.38   Cassette 3.B
      55c: *Per quel vago boschetto,* recitative
         CD 3.39–41   Cassette 3.B
   NAWM 56: Claudio Monteverdi, *L'Orfeo,* opera, excerpts (1607)
      56a: Prologue, *Dal mio Permesso amato,* strophic variations
         CD 3.42–47   Cassette 3.B
      56b: *Vi ricorda o boschi ombrosi,* strophic canzonet (excerpt)
         CD 3.48–49 (Concise 2.13–14)   Cassette 3.B (Concise 2.A)
      56c: *In un fiorito prato,* recitative
         CD 3.50–53 (Concise 2.15–18)   Cassette 3.B (Concise 2.A)
      Tu se' morta, expressive recitative
         CD 3.54 (Concise 2.19)   Cassette 3.B (Concise 2.A)
      Ahi caso acerbo, chorus (madrigal)
         CD 3.55–56 (Concise 2.20–21)   Cassette 3.B (Concise 2.A)

26.   What is the *stile recitativo* or *recitative style*? How does Peri describe it in the preface to *L'Euridice* (excerpted in HWM, p. 283)? How does the dialogue from his setting of *L'Euridice* (NAWM 55c) reflect his conception?

27. How does Peri use harmony, dissonance, and rhythm in Orfeo's response to the death of Euridice (mm. 63–87) to convey the meaning of the words and the feelings they reflect?

28. What style of monody does Peri use in the other excerpts from *L'Euridice* (NAWM 55a and 55b)? How does this style differ from recitative style?

29. Compare and contrast Monteverdi's *L'Orfeo* with Peri's *L'Euridice,* including the excerpts in NAWM 56 and 55 respectively and the description of each in HWM. In what ways is the Monteverdi similar and in what ways is it different?

30. Monteverdi's prologue (NAWM 56a) is a *strophic variation,* in which the harmony and general melodic contour are the same for each strophe of the text, but details in the music are changed to fit the new text. How are the first two strophes different? Note the changes Monteverdi has made.

    How does the last strophe differ from the others in the way it ends, and how does that illustrate the text?

31. In what ways does Orfeo's canzonet (NAWM 56b) resemble a frottola?

32. How does Monteverdi convey the meaning of the text and the feelings it reflects in Orfeo's expressive recitative *Tu se' morta* (NAWM 56c, mm. 43–64, and Example 9.1 in HWM, p. 286)?

33. How do the music and the text of the choral madrigal that concludes excerpt 56c relate to what has preceded it?

34. In *Orfeo,* Monteverdi uses particular musical forms and styles to convey the changing dramatic situation and the feelings of the characters. What characteristics make each of the following forms and styles appropriate for the scene in which it is used?

56a: La Musica, strophic variation with ritornello

56b: Orfeo, strophic canzonet with ritornello

56c: Messenger, recitative

Orfeo, expressive recitative

Chorus, choral madrigal

35. Who was Francesca Caccini, when and where did she live and work, and for what was she renowned?

36. How was opera supported in Rome in the period 1620–50?

    How was Roman opera of this period different from earlier opera in Florence and Mantua?

37. When and where was opera first made available to the paying public?

    What made this city ideal for opera?

38. Compare the performance context of Venetian opera to that of *L'Euridice* and *L'Orfeo*. What effects did the shift in audience and performing context have on the development of opera?

39. Who were Francesco Cavalli and Marc' Antonio Cesti? When and where did each live and work, and what were their contributions?

Music to Study

> **NAWM 57**: Claudio Monteverdi, *L'incoronazione di Poppea*, opera, excerpt:
>   Act I, Scene 3 (1642)
>   CD 4.1–5   Cassette 4.A
> **NAWM 58**: Marc' Antonio Cesti, *Orontea*, opera, excerpt: *Intorno all' idol
>   mio*, aria from Act II, Scene 17 (ca. 1649)
>   CD 4.6–7   Cassette 4.A

40. Compare and contrast the scene from Monteverdi's *L'incoronazione di Poppea* in NAWM 57 with the scene from *L'Orfeo* in NAWM 56c. What devices does Monteverdi use in each case to depict the text and portray the dramatic situation?

41. In this scene from *L'incoronazione di Poppea*, the music shifts back and forth often between recitative and aria styles. Why does Monteverdi set Poppea's "Deh non dir di partir" (mm. 280–87) as recitative, and her words "Vanne, vanne ben mio" (mm. 303–9) as aria? (Hint: Don't be fooled by the notation of the latter; it is in a fast triple time.)

42. Contrast the aria from Cesti's *Orontea* (ca. 1649) in NAWM 58 with the airs from Peri's *Euridice* (1600) in NAWM 55a and 55b. How has the operatic song changed in style from the beginning to the middle of the 17th century?

43. How does the aria from *Orontea* exemplify the *bel canto* style?

44. What important operatic conventions took shape in Italy by the middle of the 17th
century? How did opera of this time differ from Florentine operas of about 1600?

Vocal Chamber Music (HWM 293–99, NAWM 59–60)

45. What is a ground bass or basso ostinato?

Why are devices like this useful for composers of secular vocal chamber music?

46. Define the following terms:

concertato medium

concertato madrigal

sacred concerto

instrumental concerto (in the 17th century)

Music to Study
> **NAWM 59**: Claudio Monteverdi, *Ohimè dov' è il mio ben*, madrigal (1610s)
> CD 4.8–11   Cassette 4.A

47.   What is the *romanesca*? How does it fit the poetry of the ottava rima?

How is each of the four parts of Monteverdi's madrigal *Ohimè dov' è il mio ben* (NAWM 59) a variant of the romanesca?

48.   In what senses is this work a strophic variation?

In what senses is this a madrigal, and how does it compare with 16th-century madrigals?

---

49. What is the title of Monteverdi's 8th book of madrigals (in either Italian or English), and what is special about the collection?

50. What is the *stile concitato*? Who first used it? When, and in what piece?

51. What is a *cantata* in the 17th century? How does it resemble opera, and how is it different?

Music to Study
   NAWM 60: Barbara Strozzi, *Lagrime mie*, cantata (published 1659)
      CD 4.12–16   Cassette 4.A

52. In her cantata *Lagrime mie* (NAWM 60), Strozzi uses sections of recitative, aria, and arioso (in between recitative and aria, usually more metric than recitative). Where is each kind of monody used? (Indicate by measure numbers.)

   recitative   _____

   aria   _____

   arioso   _____

   In what ways are the sections of text set as aria particularly appropriate for that style of music?

53. What musical devices does Strozzi use to represent the following words and the feelings or actions behind them?

   "lagrime" (tears)

   "respiro" (breath)

   "tormenti" (torments)

54. What are the *stile moderno* and *stile antico* in 17th-century church music?

55. What is *Gradus ad Parnassum*? Who wrote it, and when? What was its significance?

The Venetian School (HWM 299–301, NAWM 61)

56. What was special about Venice and its music in the 16th century?

Music to Study
> **NAWM 61**: Giovanni Gabrieli, *In ecclesiis*, motet (published 1615)
>   CD 4.17–22   Cassette 4.A

57. What are *cori spezzati*? What is a *polychoral motet*? How does Gabrieli's motet *In ecclesiis* (NAWM 61) exemplify the characteristics of the genre?

Genres of Catholic Church Music (HWM 302–4, NAWM 62–64)

58. What varieties of sacred concertos were written in the 17th century? For what circumstances and occasions was each type suited?

59. What is an *oratorio*? From what does its name derive? How is it like opera, and how does it differ?

Music to Study

NAWM 62: Lodovico Grossi da Viadana, *O Domine Jesu Christe,* sacred
  concerto (ca. 1602)
  CD 4.23   Cassette 4.A
NAWM 63: Alessandro Grandi, *O quam tu pulchra es,* motet (1625)
  CD 4.24–26   Cassette 4.A
NAWM 64: Giacomo Carissimi, *Historia di Jephte,* oratorio, excerpt (ca. 1650)
  64a: *Plorate colles,* expressive recitative
  CD 4.27   Cassette 4.B
  64b: *Plorate filii Israel,* chorus
  CD 4.28   Cassette 4.B

60. How is Viadana's *O Domine Jesu Christe* (NAWM 62) like a 16th-century
    motet, such as Victoria's *O magnum mysterium* (NAWM 50), and how is it
    different?

    How is Viadana's sacred concerto like secular monody of around the same
    time, such as Caccini's *Perfidissimo volto* (NAWM 54), and how is it
    different?

61. How is Grandi's *O quam tu pulchra es* (NAWM 63) like a 16th-century
    motet, and how is it different?

    How does Grandi's motet compare to the alternation of recitative and aria
    styles in the scene from Monteverdi's *L'incoronazione di Poppea* in
    NAWM 57? How does each work respond to the text?

62. Compare the excerpt from Carissimi's *Historia di Jephte* in NAWM 64 with the scene from Monteverdi's *Orfeo* in NAWM 56c. What elements does each use?

    How do Monteverdi and Carissimi use harmony to convey emotions?

    How does each use the chorus?

Lutheran Church Music (HWM 304–8, NAWM 65)

63. Identify each of the following publications: who wrote it, when was it published, what does it contain, and for what performing forces was it written?

    Opella nova

    Psalmen Davids

    Kleine geistliche Konzerte

    Symphoniae sacrae

64. How does Schütz's setting of *O quam tu pulchra es* (described in HWM, pp. 306–7) differ from that of Grandi (NAWM 63)? How does Schütz use rhetorical figures—unorthodox dissonances that are allowed as expressive devices?

65. How was Schütz's music affected by the Thirty Years' War?

Music to Study
   NAWM 65: Heinrich Schütz, *Saul, was verfolgst du mich* (SWV 415), grand
         concerto (ca. 1650)
   CD 4.29–30 (Concise 2.22–23)   Cassette 4.B (Concise 2.A)

66. How does Schütz use changes of texture and other musical effects to depict the events and text of *Saul, was verfolgst du mich* (NAWM 87)? What types of style and texture does he use?

Instrumental Music (HWM 308–18, NAWM 66–68)

67. What main types of instrumental music were practiced in the first half of the 17th century? How do these types compare to the forms used in the 16th century?

68. In the first half of the 17th century, what is the difference between a ricercare and a fantasia?

    What is the difference between a canzona and a sonata?

69. What kinds of variations were written in the 17th century? In each type, what stayed the same in each variation, and what changed?

70. What is a dance *suite*? What dances were included in early-17th-century suites? What dances are typically found in a suite by Froberger?

71. What is *style brisé* (broken style)?

    What are *agréments*?

    On what instrument did *style brisé* and *agréments* originate? _____

    Why were they necessary or useful on that instrument?

    To what instrument were *style brisé* and *agréments* later adapted? _____

Music to Study

> **NAWM 66a**: Ennemond Gaultier, La Poste, gigue for lute (early to mid-17th century)
> CD 4.31   Cassette 4.B
> **NAWM 66b**: Anonymous arrangement for harpsichord of Ennemond Gaultier's *La Poste* (17th century)
> CD 4.32   Cassette 4.B
> **NAWM 67**: Johann Jakob Froberger, *Lamentation on the Death of Emperor Ferdinand III* (1657)
> CD 4.33–34   Cassette 4.B
> **NAWM 68**: Girolamo Frescobaldi, Toccata No. 3 (1628)
> CD 4.35 (Concise 2.24)   Cassette 4.B (Concise 2.A)

72. Compare Gaultier's gigue for lute (NAWM 66a) with its arrangement for harpsichord (NAWM 66b). How does the keyboard version imitate the style of the lute?

73. What features of Froberger's *Lamentation on the Death of Emperor Ferdinand III* (NAWM 67) mark it as a piece in French style?

    What features are particularly appropriate to its subject?

74. How is Frescobaldi's Toccata No. 3 (NAWM 68) divided into sections? Where does the style or figuration change?

75. Frescobaldi's toccata is in the Dorian mode on *G* (i.e., transposed up a fourth). Where are the main cadences, and on what scale degrees do they occur?

TERMS TO KNOW

Terms Related to the Baroque Period

baroque
prima prattica, seconda prattica
stile antico, stile moderno
the affections
measures
thoroughbass

basso continuo
continuo instruments
figured bass
realization of a figured bass
tonality
the major-minor system

Terms Related to Early Opera

opera
intermedio (pl., intermedi)
madrigal cycle
madrigal comedy
pastoral
monody
stile recitativo (recitative style)

air
solo madrigal
strophic variation
recitative
aria
bel canto

Terms Related to Vocal Music

strophic air
strophic variation
romanesca
ground bass
basso ostinato
chaconne
passacaglia
concerto (17th-century)
concertato medium

concertato madrigal
sacred concerto
stile concitato
cantata (17th century)
air de cour
cori spezzati
polychoral motet
grand concerto
oratorio

Terms Related to Instrumental Music

fuga	variation canzona
sonata da chiesa	sonata (17th-century)
partita (or partite)	affetti
passacaglia	trio sonata
chaconne	cantus firmus variation
chorale partita	style brisé
chorale prelude	agréments
suite	allemande, courante, sarabande,
fancy	gigue

NAMES TO KNOW

Names Related to Early Opera

Girolamo Mei	*Le nuove musiche*
Giovanni Bardi	*L'Orfeo*
Florentine Camerata	*Arianna*
Vincenzo Galilei	Francesca Caccini
Ottaviano Rinuccini	*La liberazione di Ruggiero*
Jacopo Peri	*Il ritorno d'Ulisse*
Dafne	*L'incoronazione di Poppea*
L'Euridice	Pier Francesco Cavalli
Giulio Caccini	Marc' Antonio Cesti
Emilio de' Cavalieri	*Orontea*
Rappresentatione di Anima e di Corpo	

Names Related to Vocal Music

Madrigali guerrieri et amorosi	Giacomo Carissimi
Il combattimento di Tancredi e Clorinda	*Historia di Jephte*
	Johann Hermann Schein
Barbara Strozzi	*Opella nova*
Johann Joseph Fux	Heinrich Schütz
Gradus ad Parnassum	*Psalmen Davids*
Giovanni Gabrieli	*Kleine geistliche Konzerte*
Lodovico Viadana	*Symphoniae sacrae*
Cento concerti ecclesiastici	*The Seven Last Words*
Alessandro Grandi	

Names Related to Instrumental Music

Girolamo Frescobaldi	Louis Couperin
Denis Gaultier	Johann Jakob Froberger
Jacques Champion de Chambonnières	

REVIEW QUESTIONS

1. Make a time-line for the pieces, composers, treatises, and theorists discussed in this chapter.

2. What are the principal characteristics that distinguish music of the Baroque period from music of the Renaissance?

3. What new concepts or procedures were developed in the period 1600–1650 as composers sought to find ways to capture human emotions in music?

4. Trace the development of opera in Italy from its origins to 1650. Include in your answer changes of aesthetic aims and ideas as well as changes of style and procedure.

5. What connections do you see between Monteverdi's madrigals and his operas? What effects did his experience as a madrigal composer have on his operas?

6. Write an expressive recitative in the style Monteverdi used in *L'Orfeo*. Use for your text the first two lines of his madrigal *Cruda Amarilli* (NAWM 41) in either the original Italian or in the English translation. Write it for male voice and continuo, as in Orfeo's recitative *Tu se' morta* from *L'Orfeo* (in NAWM 56c), and use the latter as a model for how to write a recitative, how to fit the music to the accentuation of the poetry, and how to use gestures and dissonances for expressivity. You may write only the voice and bass line or may fill in the harmony, and you may stop after a few measures or write an entire recitative using all eight lines of the poem, as you wish; the point is to see how recitative in this style works, from the inside.

   (If you use the Italian, please note that in Italian adjacent vowels elide into a single syllable. Thus the first line has eleven syllables, with the "-da" of "Cruda" elided into a single syllable with the "A-" of "Amarilli" and the "-me" of "nome" elided with the "an-" of "ancora.")

7. What new forms and styles of secular vocal music were introduced in the first half of the 17th century?

8. How was sacred music affected by the new developments in secular music in the first half of the 17th century? What new forms or styles of sacred music emerged during this time?

9. What was the concertato medium, and where was it used?

10. What types of instrumental music were practiced during the early 17th century? Which of these genres and styles were new, and which continued trends from the 16th century? Of the latter, how were the older genres or styles changed in the 17th century?

11. What are some elements that distinguish French from Italian instrumental style in the early Baroque?

OPERA AND VOCAL MUSIC IN THE LATE SEVENTEENTH CENTURY

10

CHAPTER OBJECTIVES

After you complete the reading, study of the music, and study questions for this chapter, you should be able to:

1. describe developments in Italian opera in the second half of the 17th century and the beginning of the 18th century;
2. trace the origins and development of musical theater in France, England, and Germany during the 17th and early 18th centuries and explain what makes each national tradition distinctive;
3. describe the cantata and other secular vocal genres in the late 17th century;
4. describe the varieties of sacred music being composed in the late 17th and early 18th centuries;
5. define and use the most important terms and identify some of the composers and works associated with opera and vocal music in the late 17th and early 18th centuries.

CHAPTER OUTLINE

I. Opera (HWM 323–37, NAWM 69–72)

A. Venice

In the late 17th century, opera spread throughout Italy and Europe. The main Italian center was Venice. Musical interest in operas lay primarily in the arias. Singers were the stars, and popular singers commanded much higher fees than composers (just as today film and popular music stars earn more than the screenwriters and songwriters whose works they perform). There were many types of aria, including strophic songs; arias over ostinato basses or a *running bass* (also called a *walking bass*), in which the bass moves in steady eighth notes; and arias which used march or dance rhythms, fanfare motives, or coloratura.   *Continuo arias* were accompanied only by continuo, with or without an orchestral ritornello.

B. Venetian Opera Exported

Many Italian composers made careers writing Italian operas in Germany. A common type of aria was a *motto aria,* in which the singer states the opening motive (the motto), the instruments interrupt, and then the singer begins again.

C. Naples

A new style of opera developed in Naples in the late 17th century and became dominant in the early 18th century.   Here the emphasis was on beautiful singing and elegant melodies, at the expense of drama.   There were two types of recitative, which became known as *recitativo secco* (dry recitative), for long dialogues or monologues, and *recitativo accompagnato* (accompanied recitative), for dramatic situations.   Composers also used *arioso,* a type of singing between aria and recitative.   The most common aria type was the *da capo aria,* in which the first section (with or without the opening ritornello) is repeated after a contrasting middle section.   *Alessandro Scarlatti* (1660–1725) was one of the leading composers of this kind of opera.   **Music: NAWM 69**

D. France

A distinctive style of opera developed in France in the second half of the 17th century under the patronage of Louis XIV.   *Jean-Baptiste Lully* (1632–1687) drew on two strong French traditions, court ballet and classical French tragedy, to create what he called a *tragédie lyrique* (tragedy in music).

E. Jean-Baptiste Lully

Lully was born in Italy, came to Paris, and was put in charge of theatrical music in France (where King Louis XIV controlled his realm in part through centralized control of the arts).   His librettos by *Jean-Phillippe Quinault* featured mythological plots often interrupted by *divertissements,* long interludes of choral singing and dancing.   Lully's recitative is in a new style, more dramatic and compelling than Italian recitativo secco and perfectly matched to the rhythms and inflections of French, especially as spoken on the dramatic stage.   There are two types: *récitatif simple,* in which the meter shifts freely between duple and triple, and *récitatif mesuré,* in a more songlike, measured style.   Lully's *airs* are simpler and much less florid than Italian arias.   **Music: NAWM 70b**

F. The Ouverture

The *ouverture* or *French overture* was used to introduce an opera, ballet, suite, or other large work.   A French overture usually has two parts, the first slow, stately, homophonic, and marked by dotted rhythms, and the second fast and imitative, often closing with a return to the slower first tempo.   *Georg Muffat* (1653–1740) introduced Lully's style into Germany, where it found many imitators.   French composers also mixed elements of opera and ballet in the *opera-ballet.*   **Music: NAWM 70a**

G. England

Musical theater in 17th-century England included the *masque,* akin to the French court ballet; plays with extensive incidental music, called *semi-operas*; and only two operas, in the sense of a drama that is sung throughout.

H. John Blow

John Blow (1649–1708) was organist and composer at Westminster Abbey and in the Chapel Royal. His masque *Venus and Adonis* (1684 or 1685) is sung throughout, like an opera. It combines French overture and dance styles, Italian recitative and bel canto, and English song and choral styles.

I. Henry Purcell

Henry Purcell (1659–1695) is considered the greatest English composer of the Baroque era. He wrote a large amount of music for chorus, voice, chamber ensembles, and keyboard, and incidental music for forty-nine plays, including five semi-operas such as *The Fairy Queen* (1692). His opera *Dido and Aeneas* (1689) combined French overture, dance, and choral styles with Italian and English vocal styles. **Music: NAWM 71–72**

J. Germany

While German courts supported Italian operas, some German cities, particularly Hamburg, supported opera in German, called *Singspiel* (play with music). These usually used spoken dialogue instead of recitative and featured a variety of aria types drawing on Italian, French, and German styles.

K. Reinhard Keiser

Reinhard Keiser (1674–1739) was the foremost composer of German opera in the early 18th century, unifying German and Italian traits.

II. Vocal Chamber Music (HWM 337–40)

A. The Cantata in Italy

In the second half of the 17th century, the Italian cantata was a dramatic narrative or soliloquy for voice and continuo laid out as a series of two or three recitative-aria pairs. It was like a scene from an opera, but performed in a chamber setting and without staging. The leading Italian composers of opera also wrote great numbers of cantatas.

B. Alessandro Scarlatti

Scarlatti wrote over 600 cantatas. His music is fully tonal and uses diminished-seventh chords, distant modulations, and unusual harmonies for expressive effect.

C. Other Vocal Chamber Music

Other types of Italian vocal chamber music included the vocal duet and the *serenata,* a semidramatic work for several singers and small orchestra.

D. Song in Other Countries

French and German composers also wrote cantatas, following Italian models. Solo songs continued to be written in the national styles of France, Germany, and England. English composers also wrote *catches,* unaccompanied canons to texts that were usually humorous, and *odes,* large works for soloists, chorus, and orchestra celebrating state occasions and holidays.

III. Church Music (HWM 340–55)

A. General
In the late 17th and early 18th centuries, Catholic church music was written in the old stile antico, in the modern styles, and in mixed styles.

B. Italy
The basilica of San Petronio in Bologna was a center of church music in both stile antico and the modern concerted style. The music of *Giovanni Battista Pergolesi* (1710–1736) of Naples exemplifies the plaintive chromaticism and sentimental tone of much Italian religious music of the early 18th century. German writers called this style *Empfindsamkeit* (sentimentality).

C. South Germany
South German composers of church music blended old and new styles and Italian and German traits. Masses were often on a grand scale, featuring chorus and soloists with full orchestral preludes and accompaniment.

D. Vienna
The Masses of *Antonio Caldara* (1670–1736) include a variety of styles and ensembles, with self-contained concerted arias and duets, choral movements, and movements that mix chorus and soloists.

E. Oratorio
Italian oratorios were performed in sacred concerts. Most of them were in Italian rather than in Latin, and were in two parts with a sermon or intermission between them. Oratorios were written in the same style as operas and substituted for opera during Lent and other seasons when theaters were closed.

F. French Church Music
Marc-Antoine Charpentier (1634–1704), a student of Carissimi's, introduced the Latin oratorio to France. He combined Italian traits with French ones, including a prominent role for the chorus. At Louis XIV's chapel, the leading genres were the motet for solo voice and continuo and the *grand motet* (large motet) for soloists, choruses, and orchestra.

G. Anglican Church Music
Services and anthems continued to be the leading genres of Anglican church music. Purcell and others wrote anthems and odes for special occasions and non-liturgical songs and ensembles for private devotional use.

H. Lutheran Church Music
Lutheran music reached its height in the period 1650–1750. Orthodoxy was challenged by *Pietism,* which emphasized individual freedom and simple, direct expression of feelings in music.

I. Chorales

Johann Crüger (1598–1662) wrote many new chorale tunes and edited the most influential Lutheran songbook of the second half of the 17th century. Many of these songs were intended for use in the home, but began to be used in church in the 18th century. Four-part settings of the chorales in cantional style, like those of J. S. Bach, were popular. Pietist songs were simple and sentimental, while Orthodox composers wrote sacred concertos that included concertato arias and choruses, concerted chorale settings, or a mixture of both.

J. Concerted Church Music

Among important composers of Lutheran concerted church music are *Matthias Weckmann* (1619–1674), *Franz Tunder* (1614–1667), *Johann Pachelbel* (1653–1706) and *Dietrich Buxtehude* (ca. 1637–1707). Buxtehude wrote *chorale variations,* in which each verse elaborates a chorale in a different way, as well as freer concerted pieces. Much of his church music was composed for the *Abendmusiken,* concerts after the afternoon church services. A standard format for concerted church music was an opening chorus, solo movements, and a choral setting of one verse of a chorale. Lutheran services included some Latin, and Lutheran composers set Latin texts as well as German ones.

K. The Lutheran Church Cantata

The *Lutheran church cantata* was devised around 1700 by *Erdmann Neumeister* (1671–1756) as a series of recitatives and arias meditating on a biblical text and closing with a chorale. Neumeister blended Orthodoxy with Pietism, and composers setting his cantata texts to music blended elements of chorale settings, solo song, the sacred concerto, and opera. Today J. S. Bach is considered the greatest exponent of the church cantata, but in his time *Georg Philipp Telemann* (1681–1767) was more highly regarded. Telemann wrote more than 1000 cantatas and published four complete cycles for the entire church year.

L. The Passion

The *historia* was a German genre setting a Bible story to music. The most important type was the *Passion,* telling the story of the suffering and death of Jesus. Plainchant Passions survive from the Middle Ages. Passions in the 16th and early 17th centuries were written in motet style throughout (the *motet Passion*) or alternating plainsong and motet style (the *dramatic* or *scenic Passion*). In the late 17th century a new type appeared that resembled an oratorio and is known as the *oratorio Passion*. Passions came to include not only the Bible story but also interpolated chorales sung by the choir or congregation and poetic texts set as solo arias.

STUDY QUESTIONS

Opera (HWM 323–37, NAWM 69–72)

1. What changes took place in Italian opera during the late 17th and early 18th centuries? What were the most important elements of opera in this time? How did drama and music relate in Italian opera of this period, and how did this compare with the ideals of the Florentine Camerata?

2. Describe each of the following types of aria.

   continuo aria

   motto aria

   da capo aria

3. Describe each of the following types of music. In what circumstances was each used?

   recitativo secco

   recitativo accompagnato

   arioso

Music to Study
> **NAWM 69**: Alessandro Scarlatti, *Griselda*, opera, excerpt: *Mi rivedi, o selva ombrosa* (1721)
> CD 4.36–38   Cassette 4.B

4. What type of aria is Scarlatti's *Mi rivedi, o selva ombrosa* (NAWM 69)? Chart the form of this aria as it would be performed.

5. Look at the words of this aria in translation. What emotions is Griselda experiencing?

   How does Scarlatti's music convey Griselda's feelings? How does the musical form help to capture the conflicting emotions Griselda feels?

---

6. From what two French traditions did French opera arise?

   _____   _____

7. Who was the leading opera composer in France in the late 17th century?

   _____

   Who was his librettist? _____

   How do their *tragédies lyriques* compare to Italian operas of the time?

Music to Study
> **NAWM 70**: Jean-Baptiste Lully, *Armide*, opera, excerpts (1686)
>> 70a: Ouverture
>>> CD 4.39–41   Cassette 4.B
>> 70b: Act II, Scene 5: *Enfin il est en ma puissance*
>>> CD 4.42–44   Cassette 4.B

8. What characteristics of the overture to *Armide* (NAWM 70a) mark it as a French overture?

9. How does the musical setting of Armide's recitative *Enfin il est en ma puissance* (NAWM 70b) reflect the form and accentuation of the text?

10. How does the musical setting reflect the dramatic situation and the emotional conflict Armide is feeling?

11. The scene ends with a minuet played by instruments and then sung by Armide. The minuet was associated at the time with surrender to love. In what ways is this appropriate to the dramatic situation?

12. How does this scene from Armide differ from the recitative and aria of Italian opera?

13. What are the characteristics of the following English genres of musical theater? Name and describe an example of each.

masque

semi-opera (also sometimes called "opera")

Music to Study
    NAWM 71: Henry Purcell, *Dido and Aeneas,* opera, excerpt from Act III
        (1689)
        Recitative: *Thy hand, Belinda*
            CD 5.1 (Concise 2.25)   Cassette 5.A (Concise 2.A)
        Aria: *When I am laid in earth*
            CD 5.2–3 (Concise 2.26–27)   Cassette 5.A (Concise 2.A)
        Chorus: *With drooping winds*
            CD 5.4
    NAWM 72: Henry Purcell, *The Fairy Queen,* semi-opera, excerpt: *Hark!*
        The ech'ing air (1692)
        CD 5.5   Cassette 5.A

---

14. Compare Purcell's recitative *Thy hand, Belinda* (in NAWM 71) to Lully's recitative from *Armide* (in NAWM 70b) and Peri's recitative in *L'Euridice* (in NAWM 55c). How does Purcell's music follow the accentuation of the English text? How does the music convey Dido's emotions?

15. Laments in Italian operas were often written over a descending ground bass, and Purcell's aria *When I am laid in earth* (in NAWM 71) follows this tradition. Part of the expressivity comes from dissonances or conflicts in phrasing between the ostinato bass and the vocal line. Where do these dissonances or conflicts in phrasing occur?

Besides these conventions, what other devices does Purcell use to give this music the feeling of a lament?

16. How does the air from Purcell's *The Fairy Queen* (NAWM 72) compare to the aria from Scarlatti's *Griselda* (NAWM 69) and the air from Lully's *Armide* (in NAWM 70b)? Would you say this Purcell air is more Italian or more French in style?

17. What is a *Singspiel,* and how does it differ from an Italian opera?

Vocal Chamber Music (HWM 337–40)

18. How did the secular cantata evolve in the late 17th and early 18th centuries? How does it compare to opera?

19. In addition to opera and cantata, what other vocal forms (other than church music) were popular in Italy, France, Germany, and England in the second half of the 17th century?

Church Music (HWM 340–55)

20. Describe the varieties of sacred music practiced in the late 17th and early 18th centuries in Catholic Europe, including Italy, southern Germany, and France.

21. Where and when were oratorios performed, and what were they like? What does André Maugars praise in oratorios in the passage on p. 345 of HWM?

22. What is *Pietism,* and what is its significance for music?

23. How did Lutheran composers in the second half of the 17th century use the concertato medium? Include in your discussion brief descriptions of at least three pieces excerpted or described in HWM, pp. 348–53.

24. How did Lutheran composers in the second half of the 17th century use chorales in their music? Include in your discussion brief descriptions of the works by Tunder and Buxtehude excerpted or described in HWM, pp. 350–52.

25. Who was *Erdmann Neumeister*? What sacred vocal genre did he devise, and when? What were the elements of this genre? Which parts did Neumeister write himself, which did he borrow from elsewhere, and which did he leave to other artists to create? What was the music like, and from which traditions did it draw?

26. What is an *historia*? What is a *Passion*? What kinds of Passion are there, and when was each important?

TERMS TO KNOW

Terms Related to Italian Opera

running bass (walking bass)
continuo aria
motto aria
recitativo secco

recitativo accompagnato
arioso
da capo aria

Terms Related to Opera in Other Regions

tragédie lyrique
divertissement
récitatif simple
récitatif mesuré
air

French overture (ouverture)
opera-ballet
masque
semi-opera
Singspiel

Terms Related to Other Vocal Music

cantata (in late-17th-century Italy)
serenata
catch
ode
Empfindsamkeit
grand motet
Pietism

chorale variations
cantata (in Lutheran Church)
historia
Passion
motet Passion
dramatic or scenic Passion
oratorio Passion

NAMES TO KNOW

Names Related to Opera

Alessandro Scarlatti
Jean-Baptiste Lully
Jean-Phillippe Quinault
Georg Muffat
John Blow

Venus and Adonis
Henry Purcell
Dido and Aeneas
The Fairy Queen
Reinhard Keiser

Names Related to Other Vocal Music

Antonio Caldara
Giovanni Battista Pergolesi
Marc-Antoine Charpentier
Johann Crüger
Matthias Weckmann
Franz Tunder

Dietrich Buxtehude
Abendmusiken
Johann Pachelbel
Erdmann Neumeister
Georg Philipp Telemann

Review Questions

1. Make a time-line for the pieces, composers, librettists, and theorists discussed in this chapter.

2. How did Italian opera develop and change during the 17th and early 18th centuries, from Monteverdi through Scarlatti?

3. Trace the origins and development of musical theater in France during the 17th century and explain what distinguishes it from Italian opera.

4. What factors influenced the development of English musical theater in the 17th century? What genres did the English use? What did the English borrow from the French and Italian traditions?

5. Write a new setting in the style of Lully's French recitative for Dido's four lines of recitative in NAWM 71 (from "Thy hand, Belinda" through "Death is now a welcome guest"). Use as a model the opening of Armide's recitative in NAWM 70b, which is also a setting of a rhymed quatrain (from "Enfin" to "son invincible coeur"). You may write only the voice and bass line or may fill in the harmony. Why is Purcell's recitative so different from Lully's, and what is he trying to achieve that Lully's style does not accomplish?

6. Trace the history of opera in Germany through the early 18th century.

7. Describe the secular cantata of the late 17th century. What other secular vocal genres were common, other than opera and cantata?

8. Describe the varieties of sacred music being composed in the late 17th and early 18th centuries. Take note of works in the Catholic, Anglican, and Lutheran traditions.

INSTRUMENTAL MUSIC IN THE LATE BAROQUE PERIOD

11

CHAPTER OBJECTIVES

After you complete the reading, study of the music, and study questions for this chapter, you should be able to:

1. name and describe the genres of instrumental music composed in the second half of the 17th century and the early 18th century;
2. trace the evolution of keyboard music in this period and describe the styles of various regions and individual composers;
3. trace the evolution of ensemble music and orchestral music in this period and describe the style of Corelli; and
4. distinguish between modal and tonal music in the 17th century.

CHAPTER OUTLINE

I. Introduction (HWM 359)

In the latter 17th and early 18th centuries, the medium for which music was composed helped to determine how it was composed. There are two main categories of instrumental music, keyboard and ensemble music.

A. Keyboard Music
The principal genres of keyboard music are these:
1. Toccata, prelude, or fantasia and fugue;
2. Settings of chorales or chants, such as a chorale prelude or verset;
3. Variations;
4. Passacaglia and chaconne;
5. Suite; and
6. Sonata (after 1700).

B. Ensemble Music
The principal genres of ensemble music are these:
1. Sonata (sonata da chiesa), sinfonia, and related forms;
2. Sonata da camera, dance suite, and related forms; and
3. Concerto.

II. Organ Music (HWM 359–66, NAWM 73–74)

A. The Baroque Organ

Baroque organs could achieve a variety of timbres, with several keyboards and many different ranks of pipes available for each keyboard. The organist selected the *registration* by pulling out a knob (called a stop) for each desired set of pipes. Among the prominent German organist-composers in the late 17th century were Buxtehude and Pachelbel. Much organ music was written for Protestant services, where it served as a prelude to part of the service.

B. The Toccata

The 17th-century German toccata or prelude includes not only sections in toccata style but also one or more sections in imitative counterpoint. The toccata sections have an improvisatory feel, with unpredictable harmony, surprising contrasts of texture, and virtuoso passagework. The imitative sections are like fugues embedded between toccata sections. From this contrast evolved the 18th-century form of toccata and fugue or prelude and fugue. **Music: NAWM 73**

C. The Fugue

The ricercare was gradually replaced by the *fugue,* which was composed as an independent piece or as part of a prelude. A fugue opens with an *exposition,* in which the *subject,* or *dux* (leader), in the tonic is imitated by the *answer,* or *comes* (companion), in the dominant and the other voices alternate tonic and dominant. Later appearances of the subject are also called expositions and are interspersed with *episodes* where the subject is absent and modulation may occur.

D. Equal Temperament

Preludes and fugues were also used as teaching pieces for performance and composition. Lute players could play in all 24 major and minor keys because their frets were equally spaced, giving *equal temperament.* Keyboard players in the Baroque era often preferred *meantone temperament,* an unequal tuning that gave better thirds in most keys but did not allow the use of all 24 keys.

E. Chorale Compositions

Chorales were used in several different types of organ compositions. Chorales could be accompanied with harmonizations or counterpoint; varied in *chorale variations* (also called a *chorale partita*); fragmented and developed in a *chorale fantasia*; or presented in embellished form. **Music: NAWM 74**

F. The Chorale Prelude

A *chorale prelude* presents a chorale once, varied or elaborated in a contrapuntal setting. Most chorale preludes use one of the following procedures: (1) each phrase of the melody is treated in imitation; (2) each phrase is presented cantus firmus style and is preceded by an imitative foreshadowing of the phrase in smaller note values; (3) the melody is ornamented over a contrapuntal accompaniment; (4) the melody is presented unadorned over an accompaniment marked by a repeating rhythmic figure.

G. Organ Music in the Catholic Countries

Organ composers in Italy, southern Germany, and Spain continued to use early-17th-century forms, writing ricercars, variation canzonas, settings of liturgical cantus firmi, and non-imitative toccatas. French composers wrote airs, antiphonal "dialogues" between parts of the organ, and versets and interludes for the Mass.

III. Harpsichord and Clavichord Music (HWM 366–71, NAWM 75)

The same sorts of works written for organ were also written for stringed keyboard instruments, but the most important genres for the latter were the *theme and variations* and the *suite*.

A. Theme and Variations

Variation sets continued to be popular. Composers often wrote variations on an original melody rather than an existing tune.

B. Suite

The suite was a popular form in the late 17th and early 18th centuries.

1. French *clavecinists* (harpsichordists) wrote many suites using a variety of dance movements. *Elisabeth-Claude Jacquet de la Guerre* (1665–1729) was hailed as a child prodigy and became renowned for her harpsichord, ensemble, and vocal music. The *ordres* of *François Couperin* (1668–1733) contain any number of short movements, most of them in dance rhythms and mostly with evocative titles. Couperin's treatise *L'Art de toucher le clavecin* (The Art of Playing the Clavecin, 1716) detailed how to play the harpsichord, including fingering and performing the *agréments* (French ornaments).   **Music: NAWM 75**

2. In Germany, the suite (also called *partita*) by 1700 always featured four dances of varying meter, tempo, and national origin in a set order:

   —an *allemande,* a German dance in continuous eighth or sixteenth notes in a moderately fast duple meter, with a short upbeat;

   —a *courante,* a French dance in moderate 6/4 or 3/2 time, often motivically related to the allemande;

   —a *sarabande,* a Mexican-Spanish dance in slow triple meter, often emphasizing the second beat, and usually more homophonic than the others; and

   —a *gigue,* an Anglo-Irish dance (the jig) usually in a fast 12/8 or 6/8 with a skipping melody and often in imitative counterpoint.

   A suite might also contain an introductory prelude or one or more dances added after one of the last three standard dances.

C. The Keyboard Sonata

The sonata, primarily a genre for ensembles, was transferred to the keyboard by Johann Kuhnau (1660–1722) at the end of the 17th century.

IV. Ensemble Music (HWM 372–85, NAWM 76–77)

A. Italy

Italian composers continued to dominate instrumental chamber music during the 17th and early 18th centuries, as they did in opera and cantata. This was also the the era of the great Cremona violin makers, Nicolò Amati (1596–1684), Antonio Stradivari (1644–1737), and Giuseppe Bartolomeo Guarneri (1698–1744).

B. The Ensemble Sonata

After 1630, "sonata" and "sinfonia" increasingly designated instrumental works independent of voices. The sonata was a work in several contrasting sections or movements for a small number of instruments with basso continuo. After about 1660, there were two main types, although in practice the two types were mixed:
1. *Sonata da chiesa* (church sonata), which was not based on dance styles;
2. *Sonata da camera* (chamber sonata), a suite of stylized dances.

A *trio sonata* is a sonata (of either type) for two treble instruments (usually violins) and basso continuo. This is the most common instrumentation for a sonata, followed by the *solo sonata* for one treble instrument and continuo. **Music: NAWM 76**

C. Italian Chamber Music

The Church of San Petronio in Bologna was an important center for chamber music.

D. Arcangelo Corelli

Arcangelo Corelli (1653–1713) was the greatest master of late-17th-century Italian instrumental music. After studies at Bologna, he lived in Rome. He published two sets each of trio sonatas da chiesa and trio sonatas da camera, a set of solo violin sonatas, and a set of concerti grossi, with twelve works in each set.

E. Corelli's Trio Sonatas

Corelli's trio sonatas feature lyrical violin lines within a limited range of technique. Suspensions and *sequences* drive the music forward and help to create the directed harmonic motion characteristic of common-practice *tonality* (which was new in Corelli's generation). His church sonatas most often include four movements in the pattern slow-fast-slow-fast. Most often the first movement is a majestic prelude, the second a fugue, the third like a slow aria or duet, and the finale a fast binary dance, such as a gigue. His chamber sonatas typically begin with a prelude and include two or three dance movements. Each movement presents and develops a single melodic idea. **Music: NAWM 77**

F. Corelli's Solo Sonatas

Corelli's violin sonatas also divide into equal numbers of church and chamber sonatas and use the same types of movement. Here the violin is given much more difficult passagework, including double and triple stops, rapid runs and arpeggios, and *moto perpetuo* movements. Corelli's playing and teaching were as influential on later violinists as his music was on later composers.

G. Improvisation in Musical Performance

Performers in the 17th and 18th centuries were expected to embellish written melodies, whether with small figures such as trills, turns, appoggiaturas, and mordents or with longer and freer ornamentation through scales, passagework, arpeggios, and the like. Ornamentation was not only decorative, but added interest and helped to convey the affections. A *cadenza* was an improvised extension of the six-four chord in a cadence near the end of a movement. Performers could also omit movements or sections and add instruments as desired. (In other words, pieces were regarded as opportunities for performance, not as hallowed works that were only to be performed as the composer intended.)

H. Ensemble Sonatas Outside Italy

Composers in England, Germany, and France wrote trio sonatas, following the Italian model. The most important trio sonatas in France are those by François Couperin, who sought a union of Corelli's style with the French style.

I. The Solo Sonata after Corelli

Composers in Germany, England, and France also wrote solo sonatas on the Italian model. An influential pupil of Corelli's was *Francesco Geminiani* (1687–1762), active in London as violinist and composer and author of the important treatise *The Art of Playing on the Violin* (1751).

J. Works for Larger Ensembles

Sonatas, dance suites, and other types of composition were also written for larger ensembles. In Germany, music was cultivated not only at courts by the nobility but also in the cities by the middle class. Many towns had a *collegium musicum,* a group that played and sang music for their own pleasure, and a town band, the *Stadtpfeifer.*

K. Orchestral Music

In the late 17th century, musicians began to distinguish between *chamber music* for one player on a part and *orchestral music* for more than one instrument playing a part. It is not clear from most scores which medium the composer preferred. Opera overtures and dances were always conceived as orchestral music. The Paris opera orchestra was the most famous in Europe, renowned for its discipline.

L. The Orchestral Suite

The *orchestral suite* was a German form based on the model of Lully's suites extracted from his operas and ballets. These suites were also called *ouvertures,* after the French overture which always opened each suite.

M. The Concerto

The instrumental *concerto* was a new genre that emerged in the late 17th century and became the most important orchestral genre in the 18th century. In the *orchestral concerto,* the first violin dominated and the texture was less contrapuntal than in the sonata and sinfonia. More important were the *concerto grosso,* which contrasted a small ensemble (called the *concertino,* or little ensemble) with the orchestra (called the *concerto grosso,* or large ensemble), and the *solo concerto,* which set a solo instrument with continuo against the orchestra. In both, the full orchestra was also called *tutti* (all) or *ripieno* (full). Concerto-like textures were frequent in 17th-century vocal and instrumental music before the concerto emerged as a separate form. Like sonatas and sinfonias, concertos were played in church before certain segments of the Mass or as a substitute for the Offertory. Corelli's concerti grossi were like sonatas punctuated by changes of texture.

N. Torelli

Giuseppe Torelli (1658–1709) helped to codify the concerto as a work in three movements in the pattern fast-slow-fast. The fast movements are in *ritornello form,* in which the large group states a *ritornello* in the tonic at the beginning; the soloist or soloists contribute an episode, which usually modulates; the large group states the ritornello (or a part of it) in the new key; this alternation of episode and ritornello continues for some time; and the movement draws to a close with the reappearance of the ritornello in the tonic.

STUDY QUESTIONS

Introduction (HWM 359)

1. What are the main types of keyboard music in the later Baroque period? How do these compare to the types of keyboard music practiced in the 16th century and in the early 17th century?

2. What are the main types of ensemble music in the later Baroque period? How do these compare to the main types of instrumental ensemble music practiced in the 16th century and in the early 17th century?

Organ Music (HWM 359–66, NAWM 73–74)

3. What were the components of a large Dutch or German organ of about 1700?

4. What function did toccatas and chorale preludes play in the Protestant church?

Music to Study
    NAWM 73: Dietrich Buxtehude, Praeludium in E, BuxWV 141, prelude for
        organ (late 17th century)
    CD 5.6–10   Cassette 5.A

5. How does Buxtehude's Praeludium in E (NAWM 73) fit the definition of a
    late-17th-century toccata or prelude given in HWM, pp. 360–62? What
    types of texture and figuration does it use? How does it fall into sections?

6. The first fugal section of Buxtehude's Praeludium begins in m. 13. Taking
    the subject to be eight beats long (from the second beat of m. 13 to the
    downbeat of m. 15), bracket all the entrances of the subject in your score.
    Then list here the measure and staff (right-hand [top], left-hand [middle],
    and pedal [bottom]) of each entrance of the subject. (Note: The last one is
    somewhat disguised, and then the fugue blends into the following toccata
    section.)

    measure   staff   measure   staff

    1._____   _____   8._____   _____

    2._____   _____   9._____   _____

    3._____   _____   10._____   _____

    4._____   _____   11._____   _____

    5._____   _____   12._____   _____

    6._____   _____   13._____   _____

    7._____   _____

7. The places between statements of the fugue subject, when the subject is not sounding, are called *episodes*. (Practically speaking, it is usually not considered an episode unless it is at least a measure long, which here would be four beats long.) Below, list where each episode of at least four beats begins (the beat after the subject concludes) and how many beats long each episode is.

begins in measure   number of beats   begins in measure number of beats

_____   _____   _____   _____

_____   _____

What does the longest episode take from the theme, and how does it treat this idea?

8. What are the advantages and disadvantages of Pythagorean tuning, meantone temperament, and equal temperament for keyboard music?

9. What types of organ composition in the late 17th and early 18th centuries were based on chorales? In each type, how was the chorale treated?

Music to Study
> **NAWM 74:** Dietrich Buxtehude, *Danket dem Herrn,* BuxWV 181, chorale
> variations (late 17th century)
> CD 5.11–13   Cassette 5.A

10. How does Buxtehude treat the chorale melody in his variations on *Danket dem Herrn* (NAWM 74)?

---

11. How does organ music in Italy, Spain, and France differ from that in northern Germany during the late 17th and early 18th centuries?

Harpsichord and Clavichord Music (HWM 366–71, NAWM 75)

12. What four dances are typically part of the German keyboard suite, and in what order? What is the meter, relative speed, nation of origin, and character of each?

dance	meter	speed	nation of origin	other characteristics
_____	____	_____	_____	_____
_____	____	_____	_____	_____
_____	____	_____	_____	_____
_____	____	_____	_____	_____

What other movements might be part of a German suite?

Music to Study

NAWM 75: François Couperin, *Vingt-cinquième ordre* (Twenty-fifth Order), keyboard suite (1730)

75a: *La Visionaire* (The Dreamer)
CD 5.14–15 (Concise 2.28–29)   Cassette 5.A (Concise 2.A)

75b: *La Misterieuse* (The Mysterious One)
CD 5.16 (Concise 2.30)   Cassette 5.A (Concise 2.A)

75c: *La Monflambert*
CD 5.17   Cassette 5.A

75d:*La Muse victorieuse* (The Victorious Muse)
CD 5.18   Cassette 5.A

75e: *Les Ombres errantes* (The Roving Shadows)
CD 5.19   Cassette 5.A

13. In what sense is *La Visionaire* (NAWM 75a) "a French overture," as it is described in HWM, p. 369?

14. What elements of *La Misterieuse* (NAWM 75b) suggest that it is an allemande?

15. What are the names of the following *agréments* in the upper melody of *La Misterieuse* (NAWM 75b), and how is each one played? (Hint: See HWM, pp. 370–71.)

first measure, second note (*E*) _____

first measure, fifth note (*A*) _____

first measure, notes 6–7 (*A–B*) _____

measure 25, fifth note (*A*) _____

16. Which movement of Couperin's *Vingt-cinquiéme ordre* (NAWM 75) is in rounded binary form, with a musical rhyme between the two repeated halves

of the form? _____

Ensemble Music (HWM 372–85, NAWM 76–77)

17. What two main types of sonata began to be distinguished after about 1660? Describe each type.

18. What was the most common instrumentation for sonatas in the late 17th century? What was a sonata in this instrumentation called?

Music to Study

NAWM 76: Giovanni Legrenzi, *La Raspona,* trio sonata (published 1655)
    CD 5.20–21   Cassette 5.B
NAWM 77: Arcangelo Corelli, Trio Sonata in D Major, Op. 3, No. 2
    (published 1689)
    1. Grave   CD 5.22   Cassette 5.B
    2. Allegro CD 5.23   Cassette 5.B
    3. Adagio CD 5.24 (Concise 2.31)   Cassette 5.B (Concise 2.B)
    4. Allegro CD 5.25–26 (Concise 2.32–33) Cassette 5.B (Concise 2.B)

19. How many sections are there in Legrenzi's *La Raspona* (NAWM 76)? (HWM calls them "movements," although they were probably played without a break.) How are they distinguished from each other?

20. In what ways are the violin melodies in *La Raspona* idiomatic for instruments and unlike the vocal style of the 17th century?

21. *La Raspona* is modal, not tonal. The absence of a key signature suggests that it is in the Mixolydian mode on *G*, not in G major, and three characteristics of the harmony make this especially clear. (1) The note *F* is quite common, as are the chords D minor and F major; these appear frequently in pieces in the Mixolydian mode but seldom in pieces in G major. (2) The music modulates more often and more prominently to *C* (IV) than to *D* (V); the reverse would be true for pieces in G major. (3) There are several passages that move harmonically up the circle of fifths in sequence; tonal pieces often feature sequences that move down the circle of fifths (as in the chord progression iii–vi–ii–V–I), but motion up the circle of fifths contradicts the strong sense of direction characteristic of tonal music.

For each of these three characteristics, find the evidence in the piece to support the statement that *La Raspona* is modal, not tonal. List below the evidence you find, including measure numbers as appropriate.

22. Using the modal *La Raspona* as a point of comparison, what characteristics of the first movement of Corelli's Trio Sonata in D major, Op. 3, No. 2 (NAWM 77), mark it as a tonal rather than as a modal work? (Hint: Look again at each characteristic listed in the previous question, and see if the reverse is true in the Corelli.) "Tonal" here means that the music follows the common practice of major-minor tonality.

23. Corelli's trio sonatas are marked by sequences and by suspensions, especially chains of suspensions in sequence. For each of these techniques, find two passages in which it is prominent.

	location of passage 1	location of passage 2
sequences	_____	_____
chain of suspensions	_____	_____

How do these techniques help to give these passages a sense of forward momentum toward the next cadence?

24. Is Corelli's Op. 3, No. 2, a church sonata or a chamber sonata? What traits mark it as this type of sonata?

It also has one or more traits of the other type of sonata. What are those traits?

25. In what ways are Corelli's solo violin sonatas like his trio sonatas, and in what ways are they different?

26. How did musicians in the late 17th century regard ornamentation of written melodies?

27. Describe the two main ways of ornamenting a melody in the Baroque period.

28. Why and how did Couperin seek to unite the French and Italian styles of instrumental music? Which composers did he particularly invoke to represent each style?

29. What is a *collegium musicum*? What are *Stadtpfeifer*? Where and when was each of these institutions active?

30. What is the difference between *chamber music* and *orchestral music*? In the 17th century, what kinds of pieces might have been played by either type of ensemble?

31. Describe the *orchestral suite* of about 1690–1740 and its components.

32. Name and describe the three types of *concertos* composed around 1700. How were Baroque principles of contrast embodied in each of them?

33. How many movements does a typical concerto by Giuseppe Torelli have, and what is the relative tempo of each movement?

34. Describe *ritornello form* as used by Torelli in the finale of his Concerto for Violin, Op. 8, No. 8. How does ritornello form embody the Baroque interest in contrast, and how does it draw contrasting parts into a unified whole?

TERMS TO KNOW

Terms Related to Keyboard Music

organ registration
fugue
fugal exposition
fugue subject, answer
dux, comes
fugal episode
equal temperament
meantone temperament
chorale variations
chorale partita
chorale fantasia

chorale prelude
theme and variations
suite
clavecinist
ordre
partita
allemande
courante
sarabande
gigue

Terms Related to Ensemble Music

sonata da chiesa
sonata da camera
trio sonata
solo sonata
sequences (in Baroque music)
tonality
moto perpetuo
cadenza
collegium musicum
Stadtpfeifer

chamber music, orchestral music
orchestral suite
ouverture (in Germany)
instrumental concerto
orchestral concerto
concerto grosso, solo concerto
concerto grosso, concertino
tutti, ripieno
ritornello
ritornello form

NAMES TO KNOW

Elisabeth-Claude Jacquet
    de la Guerre
François Couperin
L'Art de toucher le clavecin

Arcangelo Corelli
Francesco Geminiani
The Art of Playing on the Violin
Giuseppe Torelli

REVIEW QUESTIONS

1. Make a time-line for the pieces, composers, treatises, and theorists discussed in this chapter.

2. Name the varieties of keyboard music being composed in the late 17th and early 18th centuries. Name and briefly describe an example for as many of these genres as you can.

3. What functions did keyboard music serve in the late 17th and early 18th centuries? Name the functions for as many genres as you can.

4. Trace the evolution of keyboard music from ca. 1500 to the early 18th century.

5. Name the varieties of ensemble music composed in the late 17th and early 18th centuries. Name and briefly describe an example for as many of these varieties as you can.

6. What functions did ensemble music serve in the late 17th and early 18th centuries? Name the functions for as many genres as you can.

7. Trace the development of music for instrumental chamber ensemble from ca. 1500 to the early 18th century.

8. What characteristics distinguish tonal music from modal music in the 17th century? What makes Legrenzi's *La Raspona* (NAWM 76) modal, and what makes Corelli's Trio Sonata, Op. 3, No. 2 (NAWM 77), tonal? Couperin's *La Visionaire* (NAWM 75a) has a tonal center of E♭ and a key signature of two flats, suggesting it might be in a transposed Lydian mode; what elements in the music make clear that it is actually in E♭ major and is tonal, not modal?

9. What did Corelli and Torelli contribute to the development of instrumental ensemble music?

MUSIC IN THE
EARLY EIGHTEENTH
CENTURY

12

CHAPTER OBJECTIVES

After you complete the reading, study of the music, and study questions for this chapter, you should be able to:

1. summarize the careers, describe the musical styles, and name and describe some of the most significant works by each of four major composers of the early 18th century: Antonio Vivaldi, Jean-Philippe Rameau, Johann Sebastian Bach, and George Frideric Handel;
2. compare the music of each one to that of his predecessors and contemporaries; and
3. explain the historical significance of each of these composers.

CHAPTER OUTLINE

I. Background (HWM 389–91)

In the decades between 1720 and 1750, music of the high Baroque competed with a simpler, more songful style. Venice was still an important center for music printing, opera, church music, and instrumental composition.

II. Antonio Vivaldi (HWM 391–96, NAWM 78–79)

A. Vivaldi's Career

Antonio Vivaldi (1678–1741) was trained as a musican and priest. His main post was as music director, teacher, conductor, and composer at the *Pio Ospedale della Pietà* in Venice, a home and school for girls who were orphaned or abandoned. Music was an important part of the curriculum, and the concerts at the Pietà were well attended. At this time, there were no musical "classics," and audiences expected new music every season. Vivaldi composed very quickly and always for a specific occasion, writing concertos, oratorios, and church music for the Pietà and 49 operas for theaters in Venice and other cities. About 500 of his concertos survive, along with about 90 sonatas, and many operas and religious works.

B. The Vocal Works

Vivaldi is best known today as an instrumental composer, but in his time he was also successful as a composer of church music and of opera.

C. The Concertos

Vivaldi's concertos are marked by clear forms, memorable melodies, rhythmic energy, and masterful contrasts of sonority and texture. Two-thirds are for solo with orchestra, usually violin, but also cello, flute, or bassoon; others use two soloists or a concertino group of which one or two members are the main soloists. Most of his concertos are in three movements, with fast outer movements in ritornello form and a slow middle movement in a closely related key. In Vivaldi's hands ritornello form is infinitely variable, not at all a rigid scheme. The soloist in the fast movements is a real virtuoso, standing apart from the orchestra as a singer does in an opera. The slow movements are often aria-like. His *sinfonias* mark him as an early forerunner of the Classic-era symphony. Some of his works are programmatic, such as the four concertos in *The Four Seasons*. **Music: NAWM 78–79**

D. Vivaldi's Influence

Vivaldi had a strong influence on other composers of instrumental music, including J. S. Bach, who arranged several of Vivaldi's concertos for keyboard.

III. Jean-Philippe Rameau (HWM 396–403, NAWM 80)

A. Rameau's Career

Jean-Philippe Rameau (1683–1764) was the foremost French composer of the 18th century. He had a unique career, becoming known first as a theorist and only later as a composer and writing his major works late in life. His early training and positions were as an organist. In 1722 he published his *Traité de l'harmonie* (Treatise on Harmony), which made his reputation as a theorist, but he had difficulty establishing himself as a composer.

B. La Pouplinière

In 1731, Rameau became organist, conductor, and composer for Alexandre-Jean-Joseph Le Riche de la Pouplinière, a rich nobleman and tax collector and an avid patron of music. Rameau wrote numerous operas and opera-ballets which, with the aid of his patron, were produced in Paris. His operas secured his reputation as a composer, but they also inspired a debate between his devotees (the Ramistes) and those who attacked him as a subverter of the tradition of Lully (the Lullistes).

C. Rameau's Theoretical Works

Rameau sought to put music theory on a solid acoustical basis. He is the founder of the theory of tonal music (or functional harmony), as opposed to modal music, and all subsequent tonal theory is derived in some measure from his work. He posited the chord as the basic unit in music; derived it from the overtone series; and suggested that a chord maintained its identity and its original root even when inverted. He established the tonic, dominant, and subdominant chords as the pillars of harmony and related all other chords to them.

D. Musical Style

French interest in spectacle is exemplified in Rameau's *Les Indes galantes* (The Gallant Indies, 1735), an opera-ballet in four acts set in exotic locales in Asia and North and South America. Rameau's operas are like Lully's in using dramatic declamation, mixing recitatives with airs, choruses, and instrumental interludes, and including long divertissements. But his style is quite different. Rameau believed that melody was rooted in harmony; his melodies often are triadic, plainly revealing their underlying harmony, and much of Rameau's expressivity comes from his use of harmonic dissonance and modulation. His overtures expanded on the Lully model. His airs, like those of other French composers, are restrained in comparison to Italian arias, while his choruses are effective and his instrumental interludes remarkable in their ability to depict scenes.   **Music: NAWM 80**

E. Summary

Rameau was typical of French artists of his time in combining clarity and elegance with a talent for depiction and in being a thinker as well as a creator.

IV. Johann Sebastian Bach (HWM 403–4)

Johann Sebastian Bach (1685–1750) was not the most famous composer of his time but has become so in the last two centuries. He was born in Eisenach into a family of professional musicians and was trained by his father and elder brother. He served as a church organist at Arnstadt (1703–7) and Mühlhausen (1707–8), court organist and concertmaster for the duke of *Weimar* (1708–17), music director for a prince in *Cöthen* (1717–23), and cantor of *St. Thomas's Church and School* in *Leipzig* (1723–50), writing music for his immediate use in each position. He blended German, French, and Italian styles, which he learned by copying and arranging music by the leading composers of each region.

V. Bach's Instrumental Music (HWM 404–14, NAWM 81–82)

A. The Organ Works

Bach's first positions were as an organist, and his first major works were for the organ. His early works were influenced by Buxtehude. In his Weimar period, he arranged several of Vivaldi's concertos for keyboard, learned the Italian style, and adopted many aspects of Vivaldi's forms and styles in his own compositions. From Italian, French, and German elements he forged his own distinctive style.

B. The Preludes and Fugues

Some of Bach's organ toccatas intersperse fugue and toccata sections, but more common are works with separate fugues. Some fugues have more than one subject and more than one section. Most of Bach's important organ preludes and fugues date from his Weimar years, with some from Cöthen and Leipzig. **Music: NAWM 81**

C. Bach's Trio Sonatas

Bach adapted the Italian trio sonata to the organ in his six trio sonatas for organ composed in Leipzig.

D. The Chorale Preludes

Bach wrote about 170 chorale settings for organ, using all current types of setting. His *Orgelbüchlein* (Little Organ Book), compiled at Weimar and Cöthen, contains short chorale preludes in which the chorale is heard once, usually in the soprano. Ordinarily the chorale is unadorned, although some are embellished or treated in canon. In some chorale preludes, visual images in the chorale texts are suggested by appropriate figures in the accompaniment. In addition to their practical use for church services, Bach also intended these chorale preludes as teaching pieces for organists. Bach dedicated the *Orgelbüchlein* and many other works to the glory of God and made no distinction between sacred and secular music. He also made three later compilations of chorale settings for organ, which are longer and more varied in type than his earlier settings. **Music: NAWM 82**

E. The Harpsichord and Clavichord Music

Bach wrote for all genres of harpsichord and clavichord music of his time. Most of his clavier works were written at Cöthen and Leipzig. The intermingling of Italian, French, and German elements is prominent in these works.

F. The Toccatas

There are several notable toccatas for the clavier.

G. *The Well-Tempered Clavier*

Bach's best-known work for harpsichord or clavichord is *The Well-Tempered Clavier* (Book I, ca. 1722; Book II, ca. 1740), two cycles of 24 preludes and fugues in all 12 major and minor keys in rising chromatic order from C to B. Both sets demonstrate the usability of all keys with equal or near-equal temperament. Book I is a teaching manual in offering diverse technical challenges to the player, exemplifying numerous genres and forms in the preludes, and using a variety of approaches in the fugues. Book II includes pieces from many different periods in Bach's life.

H. The Clavier Suites

Bach wrote three sets of six suites each, the English Suites (Weimar, ca. 1715), the French Suites (in the *Clavierbüchlein,* Cöthen, 1722–25), and the six Partitas (1726–31, collected as Part I of the *Clavier-Übung*). All contain the standard four dances with additions; furthermore, the English Suites begin with preludes, and each of the partitas begins with a different kind of introductory movement.

I. *Goldberg* Variations

The *Goldberg Variations* (published 1741 or 1742 as part IV of the *Clavier-Übung*) is a set of 30 variations on a sarabande. The variations are in groups of three, with the last of each group a canon; the interval of imitation grows from a unison in variation 3 to a ninth in variation 27. The last variation is a quodlibet, followed by a reprise of the theme. The non-canonic variations are of many types.

J. Works for Solo Violin and Cello
Bach wrote six sonatas and partitas for unaccompanied violin, six suites for cello alone, and a partita for solo flute. These works suggest a polyphonic texture by using multiple stops or jumping back and forth between implied independent lines.

K. Ensemble Sonatas
Bach wrote sets of sonatas for violin and harpsichord, viola da gamba and harpsichord, and flute and harpsichord. Most have four movements, slow-fast-slow-fast, like a sonata da chiesa, and most are like trio sonatas, with the right hand of the harpsichord providing the other solo instrument while the left hand supplies the continuo.

L. Concertos
Bach composed a set of six concertos for the Margrave of Brandenburg in 1721. These follow Italian models, but expand the form. He also wrote violin concertos and was perhaps the first to write or arrange concertos for one or more harpsichords and orchestra.

M. The Orchestral Suites
Bach wrote four orchestral suites, or *ouvertures*.

N. Other Works
Two works are surveys of musical possibilities. *A Musical Offering* (1747) is based on a theme by King Frederick the Great of Prussia, on which Bach improvised while visiting the king; the finished work shows the possibilities of the theme by setting it in two ricercares, a trio sonata, and ten canons. *The Art of Fugue* (1749–50) sums up the fugue in a series of 18 canons and fugues of increasing complexity, all based on the same subject.

VI. Bach's Vocal Music (HWM 414–23, NAWM 83–84)

A. Bach at Leipzig
As cantor in Leipzig, Bach was responsible for the music at St. Thomas's and St. Nicholas's churches and for teaching Latin and music in the St. Thomas's school. Each Sunday, Bach directed a cantata, alternating between the two churches. The service also included a motet, a Lutheran Mass (Kyrie and Gloria), and chorales, using a choir of at least twelve singers (three for each part).

B. The Church Cantatas
For his orchestra, Bach drew on the school, town musicians, and the university's collegium musicum. The cantata followed the Gospel reading in the liturgy and often was related in subject. Bach composed four complete cycles of cantatas

for the church year (1723–29), plus cantatas for various occasions such as weddings. About 200 cantatas survive, representing a variety of forms and approaches.

C. Neumeister Cantatas

Bach set five cantata texts by Erdmann Neumeister and was deeply affected by his combination of chorale verses, Bible passages, and new poetry. In his cantatas, Bach frequently combined secular genres such as French overture, recitative, and da capo aria with chorale settings.

D. Chorale Cantatas

Bach's cantatas use chorales in various ways. The cantata *Christ lag in Todes Banden,* BWV 4, elaborates the chorale in a different way in each of its seven movements. More frequently, Bach based the opening chorus on a chorale and ended with the chorale in simple four-part harmony, with independent solos and duets and an occasional chorale setting in between. For example, *Wachet auf, ruft uns die Stimme,* BWV 140, sets the first verse of the chorale in an elaborate chorus, the second for tenor solo, and the third in simple harmonization; in between each chorale verse and the next are a recitative and duet whose words and music are not derived from the chorale.   **Music: NAWM 83**

E. The Secular Cantatas

Bach also wrote secular cantatas for various occasions. In some he experimented with the newer operatic style. Some were reworked as church cantatas.

F. Motets

A *motet* in Bach's time was a sacred choral work, usually in contrapuntal style, without obligatory instrumental accompaniment. Bach's six surviving motets were written for special occasions, and some use chorale texts or melodies. Bach also wrote a Magnificat and the *Christmas Oratorio,* a set of six cantatas for the Christmas and Epiphany season with the Bible story in recitative, and arias and chorales that comment on the story.

G. Passions

The high points of Bach's church music are his *St. John Passion* (1724) and *St. Matthew Passion* (1727), settings of the Passion story from the Gospels of John and Matthew respectively that were performed during Good Friday services. In both, the Bible story is narrated by the tenor soloist, with characters played by other soloists and the crowd by the chorus. Chorales, recitatives, and arias are interpolated as commentary on the story.

H. Mass in B Minor

Bach's *Mass in B Minor* was assembled in 1747–49 from some existing and some newly composed movements. It includes styles from stile antico and cantus firmus to the modern galant style. It is not a practical Mass, in view of its size, and Bach may have intended it as a universal statement of religious feeling. **Music: NAWM 84**

I. Summary

Even before his death, Bach's music was viewed as old-fashioned in comparison to the newer, more tuneful style of contemporary Italian opera. His music was known to relatively few in the latter 18th century, then gradually revived in the 19th century. His blending of different styles, genres, and forms and the balance in his music among harmony, melody, and counterpoint, and between expressivity and technique, have helped to make Bach seem in retrospect the greatest musician of his age.

VII. George Frideric Handel (HWM 423–35, NAWM 85–86)

George Frideric Handel (1685–1759) was a truly international composer. He was the first composer to be remembered by all later generations and to have his music performed in a continuous performing tradition down to the present.

A. Handel's Career

Handel was born in Halle and studied organ and composition. In 1703, he went to Hamburg, where he composed his first opera. In 1706, he went to Italy, where he associated with the leading composers and patrons of music, including Corelli, Steffani, Alessandro Scarlatti, and Domenico Scarlatti. He composed several cantatas, an oratorio, and an opera and solidified his command of the Italian style.

B. Handel in London

In 1710, Handel was named music director for the elector of Hanover, who was crowned King George I of England in 1714. Handel preceded his patron to London and quickly established himself as a composer of Italian opera. During the 1720s, Handel composed operas for a stock company called the *Royal Academy of Music*; after that company failed, he formed his own company to produce operas. When rising costs and falling interest made the opera no longer viable in 1739, Handel turned to oratorios in English, which could be performed in a concert hall without expensive Italian singers, sets, or costumes and which attracted a broader audience. The oratorios gave him a great and enduring popularity in England.

C. Suites and Sonatas

Although his reputation is founded on vocal music, Handel wrote a considerable amount of instrumental music, including three sets of concertos for harpsichord or organ, two collections of harpsichord suites, and numerous solo sonatas and trio sonatas in a style influenced by Corelli.

D. The Concertos

Handel's most significant instrumental works are those for orchestra, including the suites *Water Music* (1717) and *Music for the Royal Fireworks* (1749) and 18 concerti grossi. Corelli is the main influence on the concertos, which follow the sonata da chiesa format (slow-fast-slow-fast) and only rarely feature extensive or virtuosic solo playing.

E. The Operas

Handel's operas were among the most successful of his time and were produced in Germany and Italy as well as in London. His operas' plots were freely adapted from history and literature, and the music consists largely of recitatives to forward the action and arias that reflect on the characters' feelings. Handel's operas include a wide variety of aria types. His *Giulio Cesare* (1724) is judged one of his masterpieces, and *Serse* (1738) is a later work in a lighter, more modern style. **Music: NAWM 85**

F. The Oratorios

Handel's oratorios use recitatives and arias, as does opera, and these are similar in style to opera. But Handel and his librettists also incorporated elements from the English masque and choral anthem, the German historia, and French and ancient Greek drama. The oratorios were in English and often based on Old Testament stories, which appealed to a broader audience than the Italian language and the historical or mythological plots of opera. The prominence of the chorus in his oratorios is indebted to choral music in both Germany and England.

G. Choral Style

Handel's choruses often comment on the action, as in a Greek drama or German Passion. At other times, the chorus participates in the action. He often uses musical figures to depict images in the text or convey a feeling. His choral style was simpler and less contrapuntal than Bach's, but perhaps more dramatic in his use of contrasting textures. **Music: NAWM 86**

H. Handel's Borrowings

Handel frequently borrowed and reworked material from his own earlier music and from other composers. At this time, borrowing, transcribing, and reworking were universally accepted practices. When Handel borrowed, he "repaid with interest," using the borrowed material in new and more ingenious ways.

I. Summary

Handel was the first composer whose music endured after his death in an unbroken tradition of performance, particularly in his oratorios. His music's simpler texture, emphasis on melody, grandiose choruses, interest in contrast, and appeal to middle-class audiences suited the taste of the late 18th century and laid the foundation for his permanent place in the repertory.

STUDY QUESTIONS

Background (HWM 389–91)

1. Describe the cultural conditions in Venice in the early 18th century.

2. What does Charles Burney's report on Venetian opera indicate about the stature of opera singers in the early 18th century?

Antonio Vivaldi (HWM 391–96, NAWM 78–79)

3. In which city and for which institution did Vivaldi work for most of his career?

   What was the purpose of such institutions? What was the role of music in the curriculum?

4. What was the 18th-century attitude toward new music? How did this attitude affect Vivaldi?

5. In Vivaldi's concertos, what instruments does he favor as soloists?

6. What is the typical pattern of movements in Vivaldi's concertos, including the number of movements and their tempo, forms, and key relationships?

7. What innovations did Vivaldi contribute to the slow movement of the concerto?

Music to Study

NAWM 78: Antonio Vivaldi, Concerto Grosso in G minor, Op. 3, No. 2
(published 1712), excerpts
78a: First movement, Adagio e spiccato
CD 5.27   Cassette 5.B
78b: Second movement, Allegro
CD 5.28–34 (Concise 2.34–40)   Cassette 5.B (Concise 2.B)
NAWM 79: Antonio Vivaldi, Concerto for Violin, Op. 9, No. 2 (published
1728), second movement
CD 5.35   Cassette 5.B

8. How does Vivaldi treat texture and contrasts of texture in his concertos? How is this exemplified in the concerto movements in NAWM 78 and 79?

9. How are dissonances treated in the first movement of Vivaldi's Op. 3, No. 2 (NAWM 78a)? How does this compare to the treatment of dissonance in a work of the early 16th century such as Josquin's *Mille regretz* (NAWM 32a) and to a work of the early 17th century such as Monteverdi's *Cruda Amarilli* (NAWM 41)?

---

10. Chart the form of the second movement of Vivaldi's Op. 3, No. 2 (NAWM 78b) by completing the table below. Use the abbreviations "Rit" for ritornello, "Epi" for episode, and letters for the melodic material as it is introduced.

(Before you begin, what is the relationship between b and c in the table below?)

Beginning measure	Section	Tutti or soloists	Melodic material	Key
14	Rit	Tutti	a	g minor
17	↓	↓	b	↓
20	↓	↓	c	↓
23	Epi	Soloists	d	↓

11. What characteristics of the mid-to-late-18th-century Classic style are already present in Vivaldi's music? Which of these characteristics can you find in the slow movement from Op. 9, No. 2 (NAWM 79)?

Jean-Philippe Rameau (HWM 396–403, NAWM 80)

12. Briefly trace Rameau's career. What were his various occupations? How did he earn a living? What made it possible for him to write operas and opera-ballets?

13. What were Rameau's contributions to the theory of functional harmony?

> **Music to Study**
>
> **NAWM 80:** Jean-Philippe Rameau, *Hippolyte et Aricie,* opera (1733), excerpt: *Ah! faut-il* (Act IV, Scene 1)
>
> CD 5.36 (Concise 2.41)   Cassette 5.B (Concise 2.B)

14. At the opening of Act IV of Rameau's *Hippolyte et Aricie,* the noble young man Hippolyte is alone in the woods, banished from home, and despairing. How does Rameau use harmony, melody, rhythm, and choice of instrument in the instrumental prelude (NAWM 80, mm. 1-13) to convey his situation and mood? In particular, what suggests that he is in despair? in a rural setting? alone?

15. Diagram the form of this excerpt by completing the table below. Label sections in recitative "recit." and all other melodic material by letter; label modulatory sections "mod." and sections in stable keys by the key. (Note that the vocal line is in alto clef.)

Beginning measure	Singer or orchestra	Melodic material	Key
1	orchestra	A	a minor
4	↓	B	mod. to C
9	↓	C	mod.
11	↓	D	e minor

How would you describe this form? How does it reflect Hippolyte's emotions?

16. How does this excerpt compare with the scene from Lully's *Armide* in NAWM 75b? How are Rameau's approach and style similar to Lully's, and how are they different?

Johann Sebastian Bach (HWM 403–4)

17. How did Bach learn music?

18. Where did Bach work, and when? What were his duties in each position?

19. How did Bach's employment affect the music he composed?

Bach's Instrumental Music (HWM 499–511, NAWM 99–101)

20. What types of organ works did Bach write? For each type, what are its main characteristics, and when during his career did Bach write organ works of this kind?

21. What collections of his organ works did Bach compile, and what was the aim and focus of each collection?

Music to Study

 NAWM 81: Johann Sebastian Bach, Praeludium et Fuga in A minor for
  organ, BWV 543 (1710s?)
  81a: Praeludium (Prelude)
   CD 5.37 (Concise 2.42)   Cassette 5.B (Concise 2.B)
  81b: Fuga (Fugue)
   CD 5.38 (Concise 2.43)   Cassette 5.B (Concise 2.B)

22. How do the melodies in Bach's prelude and fugue (NAWM 81) show the influence of Italian violin style? Use the solo violin portions of Vivaldi's Concerto Grosso in G minor, Op. 3, No. 2, second movement (NAWM 78b) for comparison.

23. Diagram the form of Bach's fugue by completing the chart below. Indicate the expositions of the subject and the episodes; the staff on which each entrance of the subject appears by "top," "middle," or "pedal" (bottom); and the implied key of each entrance of the subject. The first four entrances of the subject comprise the exposition of the fugue, as each of the four voices enters in turn. Some of the entrances of the subject are disguised through embellishment of the opening few notes. Note that the piece ends with a free toccata section after the last entrance of the subject in the tonic.

Beginning measure	Subject or episode	Staff	Key	Relation of key to tonic (a minor)
1	subject	top	a minor	i
6	subject	top	e minor	v
11	episode			
15	subject	middle	a minor	i
20	episode			
26	subject	pedal	e minor	v

24. How does the form of Bach's fugue show the influence of Vivaldi's concertos? In what ways is it similar to ritornello form?

25. How does this Bach fugue compare to the first fugal section of Buxtehude's Praeludium in E (NAWM 73) in form and in other respects? (See chapter 11, study questions 6 and 7.)

26. Based on the comparisons you have made above, write a brief summary of how Bach's prelude and fugue blends north German and Italian influences.

Music to Study
NAWM 82: Johann Sebastian Bach, *Durch Adams Fall,* BWV 637, chorale
       prelude from the *Orgelbüchlein* (ca. 1716–23)
   82a: Chorale melody   not on recordings
   82b: Bach setting   CD 5.39   Cassette 5.B

27. How does Bach employ musical imagery in his chorale prelude on *Durch Adams Fall* (NAWM 82b) to convey the images in the chorale text?

28. What types of pieces did Bach write for clavier (harpsichord or clavichord)? What are the characteristics of each type?

29. When was *The Well-Tempered Clavier* written? What does it contain, and how is it ordered? What are the characteristics of this collection?

30. What is the *Goldberg Variations* and how is this work structured?

31. What types of chamber music and orchestral music did Bach write? Where were most of his works of this type written?

32. What are *A Musical Offering* and *The Art of Fugue*? When were they written? What does each one contain?

Bach's Vocal Music (HWM 414–23, NAWM 83–84)

33. What were Bach's duties as cantor of St. Thomas's and music director of Leipzig?

34. Where in the liturgy was the cantata performed? How did its subject matter relate to the rest of the liturgy?

35. What kinds of musicians (and how many of each) did Bach have available for performing cantatas in Leipzig?

Music to Study

NAWM 83: Johann Sebastian Bach, *Wachet auf, ruft uns die Stimme*
[Cantata No. 140], BWV 140 (1731)

1a: Philipp Nicolai, *Wachet auf, ruft uns die Stimme,* chorale (source
for first, fourth, and final movements)   not on recordings

1b: Chorus, *Wachet auf, ruft uns die Stimme*
CD 6.1–5 (Concise 2.44–48)   Cassette 6.A (Concise 2.B)

2: Tenor recitative, *Er kommt, er kommt*
CD 6.6   Cassette 6.A

3: Duet for soprano and bass, *Wann kömmst du, mein Heil?*
CD 6.7   Cassette 6.A

4: Tenor chorale verse, *Zion hört die Wächter singen*
CD 6.8   Cassette 6.A

5: Bass recitative, *So geh' herein zu mir*
CD 6.9   Cassette 6.A

6: Duet for soprano and bass, *Mein Freund ist mein!*
CD 6.10–11   Cassette 6.A

7: Chorale, *Gloria sei dir gesungen*
CD 6.12   Cassette 6.A

---

36. For which day of the church calendar did Bach write the cantata *Wachet auf, ruft uns die Stimme* (NAWM 83)? How do the words of the chorale Bach uses and of the added texts relate to the Gospel reading for the day?

37. How are the words and images of the text reflected in the music, particularly in the opening chorus (1b) and the two duets (3 and 6)?

38. The second recitative is accompanied by strings. What does that symbolize? And why are the third and sixth movements written as duets?

39. How is the chorale tune *Wachet auf, ruft uns die Stimme* used in the first movement (1b)?

    In the fourth movement (4)?

    In the final movement (7)?

40. What Italian forms and textures, adapted from opera, concerto, and sonata, are used in this cantata, and in which movements? What other Italian traits do you notice?

41. How do Bach's secular cantatas relate to his church cantatas?

42. What did the word *motet* mean in Bach's time? How was a motet different from a cantata?

43. What is the *Christmas Oratorio*? Why is it called an oratorio?

44. In the *St. Matthew Passion,* where do the words come from?

What are the functions of the tenor soloist? of the chorus?

In what respects do Bach's Passions resemble operas?

Music to Study

NAWM 84: Johann Sebastian Bach, Mass in B Minor, BWV 232 (assembled in 1747-49), excerpts from the Credo (*Symbolum Nicenum*)

84a: Bass Aria, *Et in Spiritum sanctum Dominum*
CD 6.13–14   Cassette 6.B
84b: Chorus, *Confiteor*
CD 6.15–17   Cassette 6.B
84c: Chorus, *Et expecto resurrectionem*
CD 6.18–19   Cassette 6.B

45. In what ways does the music of *Et in Spiritum sanctum Dominum* from Bach's B-minor Mass (NAWM 84a) show traces of an up-to-date style?

46. How many times does the cantus firmus appear in the chorus *Confiteor* (NAWM 84b)?

    Where does it appear, and in which voices?

    How is it treated?

47. In addition to cantus firmus technique, what other Renaissance traits appear in the music of the *Confiteor*?

    What Baroque traits make clear that this is a Baroque-era composition in stile antico, rather than a work from the Renaissance?

48. How does Bach use changes of musical style and texture to convey the sense of the words "and I await the resurrection of the dead"? (Note that these words are set twice, in two different styles, to bring out two different aspects of their meaning.)

49. On what grounds was Bach's music criticized during his lifetime?

50. What are some of the factors that have led later centuries to regard him as the greatest composer of his era?

George Frideric Handel (HWM 423–35, NAWM 85–86)

51. By the age of 25, where had Handel lived, studied, and worked? What genres had he tried? What influences had he absorbed? What made his music "international" in style?

52. In which genre was Handel first successful in England? Why and when did his success fade? Which new genre supplanted the first and allowed Handel to continue his career?

53. Which composer was the primary model for Handel's sonatas and concertos?

> **Music to Study**
>   **NAWM 85**: George Frideric Handel, *Giulio Cesare* (Julius Caesar), opera
>   (1724), excerpt from Act III, Scene 4
>   Accompanied recitative, *Dall'ondoso periglio*
>   CD 6.20–21 (Concise 2.49–50)   Cassette 6.B (Concise 2.B)
>   Aria, *Aure, deh, per pietà*
>   CD 6.22–25 (Concise 2.51–54)   Cassette 6.B (Concise 2.B)
>
> 54. In Act III, Scene 4, of *Giulio Cesare* (NAWM 85), Handel rearranges the
> ex-pected order of events for expressive reasons. We might expect to hear a
> recitative, then a da capo aria with an opening ritornello, first section, con-
> trasting middle section, and reprise of the first section. Instead of this, what
> is the order of events in this scene? How does this order of events in the
> music work to set the scene and convey Caesar's feelings? When the first
> section is finally repeated, how have Caesar's words gained in intensity by
> what has intervened?

55. What national styles and genres did Handel combine in his oratorios?

56. What language is used in his oratorios, and why? How did the language and the
subject matter influence the success of his oratorios? Where were they
performed, and for whom?

57. How did Handel use the chorus in his oratorios? How does this differ from the practice of Italian composers? What traditions influenced Handel in this regard?

Music to Study
　　　　NAWM 86: George Frideric Handel, *Jephtha*, oratorio (1752), excerpt:
　　　　　　　Chorus, *How dark, O Lord, are Thy decrees!*
　　　　　　Largo, *How dark, O Lord, are Thy decrees!*　　CD 6.7　　Cassette 6.B
　　　　　　Larghetto, *All our joys to sorrow turning*　　CD 6.8　　Cassette 6.B
　　　　　　A tempo ordinario, *No certain bliss*　　CD 6.9　　Cassette 6.B
　　　　　　Larghetto, *Yet on this maxim still obey*　　CD 6.10　　Cassette 6.B

58. In the chorus *How dark, O Lord, are Thy decrees!* from *Jephtha* (NAWM 86), how does Handel use contrasts between contrapuntal and homophonic writing to delineate the form and to convey the meaning of the text?

59. How does Handel's choral writing in this work differ from that of Bach in the choral movements from his cantata *Wachet auf* (NAWM 83) and Mass in B Minor (NAWM 84), and how is it similar?

60. What was the role of borrowing in Handel's music?

61. What characteristics of Handel's music helped to earn it a lasting place in the repertory of music?

NAMES TO KNOW

Antonio Vivaldi
Pio Ospedale della Pietà
The Four Seasons
Jean-Philippe Rameau
Traité de l'harmonie
Les Indes galantes
Hippolyte et Aricie
Johann Sebastian Bach
Weimar
Cöthen
Leipzig
St. Thomas's Church and School
Orgelbüchlein
The Well-Tempered Clavier
Goldberg Variations

A Musical Offering
The Art of Fugue
Wachet auf, ruft uns die Stimme,
  BWV 140
Christmas Oratorio
St. John Passion and *St. Matthew*
  Passion
Mass in B Minor
George Frideric Handel
Royal Academy of Music
Water Music
Music for the Royal Fireworks
Giulio Cesare
Serse

Review Questions

1. Add the composers, pieces, and *Traité de l'harmonie* to the time-line you made for the previous chapter.

2. Describe the career and music of Vivaldi. How did the circumstances of his employment relate to the music he wrote? How are his concertos similar to those of Corelli and Torelli, and how are they different?

3. How do the operas and opera-ballets of Rameau continue the tradition of Lully, and how do they differ? Describe the similarities and differences in objective terms. Then take a position as a Lullist (one who opposed Rameau's music as "difficult, forced, grotesque, thick, mechanical, and unnatural" in the words of HWM, p. 398) or a Ramist (a defender of Rameau, who said that, like Lully, he also took "nature herself—so beautiful and so simple—as a model") and write a paragraph in which you attack the other point of view.

4. Trace Bach's career and explain how the circumstances of his training and employment influenced the types of music he wrote and the styles he drew upon.

5. What did Bach's instrumental music draw from German sources? What did he draw from Italian models and from French models? Describe a piece by Bach that blends at least two of these national traditions, and explain how Bach combined elements from different nations into a coherent idiom.

6. Adopting the aesthetic position of Johann Adolph Scheibe (as quoted on p. 422 of HWM), describe what is wrong with Bach's Praeludium et Fuga in A minor (NAWM 81) and the opening chorus of his cantata *Wachet auf, ruft uns die Stimme* (NAWM 83).

7. Trace Handel's career and explain how his experiences as a composer influenced the types of music he wrote and the styles he drew upon.

8. Compare and contrast the musical ideals and styles of Bach and Handel, focusing particularly on their vocal music.

SONATA, SYMPHONY, AND OPERA IN THE EARLY CLASSIC PERIOD

13

CHAPTER OBJECTIVES

After you complete the reading, study of the music, and study questions for this chapter, you should be able to:

1. describe the intellectual, cultural, and aesthetic background to music in the Classic period;
2. name and describe the principal musical styles and genres current in the second half of the 18th century;
3. diagram and describe some of the principal forms used in this period, particularly aria forms, sonata form, and concerto first-movement form;
4. use and define terms appropriate to this period; and
5. name some of the composers of the period, describe their individual styles, and identify some of their works.

CHAPTER OUTLINE

I. The Enlightenment (HWM 439–51)

A. Enlightenment Thought

The *Enlightenment* was an intellectual movement that valued reason and asserted the equal rights of every person. Enlightenment ideas led to advances in science and were incorporated into the American Declaration of Independence and the Constitution.

B. Aspects of Eighteenth-Century Life

Eighteenth-century politics, culture, and the arts were cosmopolitan. The flutist and composer *Johann Joachim Quantz* held that the best music was that which combined features of many nations and thus was universally pleasing. Musicians from across western Europe were active in Vienna, facilitating a mixing of styles. Humanitarian ideals were strong. A growing middle-class public pursued learning and the arts and helped to support the new institutions of the public concert of music and the journal of musical news and criticism. As more people could afford instruments, had time to play them, and learned to read music, the market grew for published music that amateurs could play and enjoy.

C. Eighteenth-Century Musical Taste

The latter 18th century preferred music that was universal in appeal, both noble and entertaining, expressive yet tasteful, natural, simple, and immediately pleasing. Yet old and new styles, and national and cosmopolitan styles, coexisted and competed. (The entire 18th century can be viewed as a long argument about taste, as the attacks on Rameau and Bach discussed in chapter 12 might suggest.)

D. Terminology in the Classic Period

Several terms have been used for the styles current in the mid-to-late 18th century. *Classic* was applied retrospectively to the music of Haydn and Mozart and has been expanded to include the entire period of about 1720–1800. The term *galant* (elegant) was used in the 18th century to describe the new style that emphasized melody in clearly marked phrases over light accompaniment. *Empfindsamkeit* (sentimentality, from the German verb for "to feel") was a related style that added surprising harmonies, chromaticism, nervous rhythms, and speech-like melody.

E. New Concepts of Melody, Harmony, and Form

In contrast to the constant spinning-out of Baroque music, the new styles were *periodic,* divided into short phrases that combine into periods and larger sections, like the phrases, sentences, and paragraphs of a speech. Phrases were related through motivic similarities or through antecedent-consequent pairing. Harmonic change slowed down. In compensation, the texture was animated through devices such as the *Alberti bass.* Composers no longer sought to express one single affection in a movement, as in the Baroque, and instead explored contrasting styles and feelings within a single movement.

Sidebar: Musical Rhetoric in Depth

Several writers on music compared it to rhetoric, the art of giving an oration. The most thorough guide for beginning composers was that by *Heinrich Christoph Koch* (1749–1816), who showed how to put together short units into phrases, phrases into periods, and periods into larger forms.

II. Opera (HWM 451–60, NAWM 87–88)

Many elements of Classic-era style derive from Italian opera, and especially comic opera, of the early 18th century.

A. Early Italian Comic Opera

An *opera buffa* was a full-length Italian comic opera with several characters. Plots usually counterpoised comic and serious characters, and librettos often used dialect, especially for the comic characters. An *intermezzo* was a series of short comic scenes performed between acts of a serious opera or play. Plots revolved around a small number of characters drawn from ordinary life. The best-known intermezzo is *La serva padrona* (The Maid as Mistress, 1733), by *Giovanni Battista Pergolesi* (1710–1736). In opera buffa, as well as in the intermezzi, dialogue was set in rapid *recitative* with keyboard accompaniment,

and the *arias* used short tuneful phrases and periods over simple harmonies.
Music: NAWM 87

B. *Opera Seria*

An *opera seria* was a serious opera on a heroic classical theme without comic
interludes. The form was codified by the librettist *Pietro Metastasio* (1698–
1782), whose librettos were set hundreds of times throughout the 18th century.
His plots show a conflict of passions that is resolved through heroism or
renunciation, and his aim was to promote morality and to show examples of
enlightened rulers. The action proceeds in recitative, and characters comment on
the situation in arias.

C. The Aria

The standard aria form was the *da capo aria,* with a large A section in the tonic,
a shorter contrasting B section in a related key, and a reprise of the A section.
The A section normally includes an orchestral ritornello that introduces the main
melodic idea; a vocal statement that modulates to a related key, most often the
dominant; an abbreviated ritornello in the new key; a second vocal statement on
the same text that modulates back to the tonic; and a closing ritornello, full or
abbreviated, in the tonic. The B section sets a new text and usually lacks
orchestral interludes. This format could be abbreviated in various ways—for
instance, by omitting the opening ritornello on the repeat of A, or by expanding
the A section and omitting the rest altogether. Singers were expected to
ornament the written line as appropriate, especially on the repetition. There were
abuses: some composers treated the da capo format too rigidly, and some singers
added excessive embellishment or forced composers to alter or substitute arias to
suit their voices. But the form also continued to evolve, as composers introduced
a greater variety of moods and figuration and borrowed formal ideas from the
sonata and concerto.

D. Hasse

Johann Adolph Hasse (1699–1783), music director at the Saxon court in
Dresden, was the leading composer of opera seria around the middle of the 18th
century. He wrote in an Italianate style marked by careful accentuation of the
text and melodies grateful to the voice. His wife, *Faustina Bordoni* (1700-1781),
was one of the century's leading sopranos. She performed all over Europe,
including for Handel in London, and sang in most of Hasse's operas. **Music:
NAWM 88**

III. Comic Opera (HWM 461–63, NAWM 89–90)

A. General

Comic opera grew in importance after 1760. Each nation or region had its own
type, using the national language and musical styles. Comic opera exercised an
important influence on later music, in its style, its preference for naturalness, and
its use of national characteristics.

B. Italy

From the middle of the century, comic Italian operas—sometimes called *dramma giocoso* (cheerful drama) as well as opera buffa—incorporated serious and sentimental plots along with comic ones. The *ensemble finale* at the end of an act brought the characters on stage one by one until all were singing together.

C. France

French *opéra comique* began as a show with *vaudevilles* or other simple tunes. The 1752 visit of an Italian comic opera troupe inspired French composers to write comic operas in a mixed style with original airs called *ariettes*. One of the first is *Le Devin du village* (The Village Soothsayer, 1752) by *Jean-Jacques Rousseau*. Although the Italians set dialogue as recitative, the French and other national comic opera traditions used spoken dialogue. Later in the century, the opéra comique was also used for serious subjects, as in *André Ernest Modeste Grétry*'s *Richard Coeur-de-Lion* (Richard the Lion-Hearted, 1784), the first *rescue opera*. **Music: NAWM 89**

D. England

Ballad opera became popular in England after John Gay's success with *The Beggar's Opera* (1728), a mostly spoken play which set new words to popular tunes and parodied operatic conventions. **Music: NAWM 90**

E. Germany

The success of ballad opera inspired a revival of *Singspiel* in Germany, beginning with translations or adaptations of English ballad operas and French comic operas. Some Singspiel tunes were so popular that they have virtually become folksongs. In the north, Singspiel merged with native opera in the early 19th century; in the south, it was influenced by Italian comic opera.

IV. Beginnings of Opera Reform (HWM 463–66, NAWM 91)

A. Italian Reformers

Some mid-century Italian composers, such as *Nicolò Jommelli* (1714–1774) and *Tommaso Traetta* (1727–1779), sought to make opera more expressive, flexible, and varied, and thus better able to reflect real human drama and sentiment.

B. Gluck

Christoph Willibald Gluck (1714–1787), working with his librettist *Raniero de Calzabigi* (1714–1795), reformed opera by making music once again subservient to the poetry and the plot. As exemplified in *Orfeo ed Euridice* (1762) and *Alceste* (1767), Gluck's reform opera blends Italian, German, and French traits; emphasizes the chorus, dance, and orchestra and links them closely with the dramatic action; restrains the freedom of singers to indulge in vocal display; lessens the gulf between aria and recitative; and unifies a variety of elements in extended scenes. Gluck brought his new style to Paris and French opera with *Iphigénie en Aulide* in 1774, scoring a great triumph. Serious French opera had been in decline since the *Querelle des bouffons* (Quarrel of the comic actors), a debate in 1752 about the relative merits of traditional French opera and the new comic Italian opera. Gluck's new style was praised and imitated, establishing a new tradition of serious opera in French.   **Music: NAWM 91**

V. Song and Church Music (HWM 466–69)

A. The Lied

Many collections of *Lieder* (German songs) were published in the 18th century, intended primarily for amateur performance at home. Composition of lieder was centered in Berlin. Most lieder were syllabic settings in folksong style with simple accompaniment.

B. Church Music

Masses, motets, and especially oratorios increasingly adopted operatic style in the late 18th century, although some composers continued to use the *stile antico*. English composers often wrote in Baroque styles, partly due to the continuing influence of Handel.

VI. Instrumental Music: Sonata, Symphony, and Concerto (HWM 469–79, NAWM 92–96)

A. Domenico Scarlatti

Domenico Scarlatti (1685–1757), son of Alessandro Scarlatti, worked mainly in Portugal and Spain. His music was little known outside those countries, although he is now well known for his 555 harpsichord sonatas. Typically his sonatas are one movement (or two paired movements) in rounded binary form: two sections, both repeated, the first moving from tonic to dominant or relative major, the second modulating back to the tonic and ending with a tonic-key restatement of the material that closed the first section. Rather than themes *per se*, Scarlatti often presents a series of strongly etched ideas that plainly project the key through pedal points, arpeggiation, and other figuration.   **Music: NAWM 92**

B. The Sonata

Sonatas, symphonies, and chamber works typically had three or four movements in related keys and contrasting moods and tempos. What we now call *sonata form* or *first-movement form* was described by Koch in the 1770s as an expanded binary form in two sections, both normally repeated. The first has one large period comprising a series of four or five extended phrases, the first two presenting the movement's main idea in the tonic, the third phrase modulating to the dominant or relative major, and the others in the new key. The second section has two large periods, the first modulating back to the tonic, and the second shaped like the first section but transposing the latter part into the tonic. Theorists writing in the 1830s and later divided the form not into two parts but into three, corresponding to Koch's three periods: (1) an *exposition* with a first theme in the tonic, a modulatory transition, and second and closing themes in the dominant or relative major; (2) a *development* section which fragments and varies the themes and modulates to new keys; and (3) a *recapitulation*, restating all three themes in the tonic, sometimes followed by a *coda*. Koch's description emphasizes the tonal plan, the later (and now more familiar) description the thematic content.

C. Early Symphonies and Chamber Music

In the early 18th century, the Italian opera overture, called *sinfonia*, had three movements in the order fast-slow-fast, ending with a dance. These were also performed independently, and composers such as *Giovanni Battista Sammartini* (1701–1775) began to write *symphonies* for concert performance, works in the same form that were not attached to operas. Sammartini's first movements often follow Koch's description of the form and present a number of ideas. **Music: NAWM 93**

D. The *Empfindsam* Style

The *empfindsam* style, originated by Italians, is especially identified with *Carl Philipp Emanuel Bach* (1714–1788), the most famous of Johann Sebastian Bach's sons and a very influential composer in his own right. He wrote in a variety of genres but is best known for his keyboard music, especially several sets of sonatas, marked by constantly changing rhythms, sudden surprising changes of harmony, texture, or dynamic level, and instrumental evocations of recitative and aria. His *Essay on the True Art of Playing Keyboard Instruments* is an important source for ornamentation and performance practice. **Music: NAWM 94**

E. German Symphonic Composers

Composers at *Mannheim,* Vienna, and Berlin were the leading German composers of symphonies at mid-century. The Mannheim orchestra, led by *Johann Stamitz* (1717–1757), was renowned for its virtuosity, dynamic range, and controlled crescendo. **Music: NAWM 95**

F. J. C. Bach's Concertos

Johann Christian Bach (1735–1782), J. S. Bach's youngest son, studied and worked in Italy before going to London. There he had a successful career and met the young Mozart, on whom he had a profound influence. His *concertos* for piano or harpsichord and orchestra follow in their first movements a form that alternates tutti ritornellos with solo episodes, as in the Baroque concerto, but also features the contrasting themes and keys of sonata form. **Music: NAWM 96**

G. Orchestral Music in France

Many publishers and composers were active in Paris. An important genre was the *symphonie concertante* for two or more soloists and orchestra.

H. The Symphony Orchestra

The orchestra of the Classic era had about twenty to thirty-five players, including strings, winds in pairs, horns, and harpsichord. The practice of basso continuo was gradually abandoned, and conducting duties passed from the harpsichordist to the leader of the violins. The winds, often used to double the strings and fill in harmonies, gained more independent roles late in the century. The *serenade* was a hybrid Viennese form combining aspects of the symphony and the concerto.

I. Chamber Music

Instrumental roles were unequal in chamber music, with the piano dominating any group with which it played and the first violin dominating in string quartets.

VII. Summary (HWM 479)

The early Classic period saw many innovations, especially in comic opera. The desire to reach a wide and varied audience led to music, both vocal and instrumental, that was simple, natural, and easy to grasp on first hearing. This intelligibility made possible the increasing independence—and with it the growing significance—of instrumental music in the Classic period.

STUDY QUESTIONS

The Enlightenment (HWM 439–51)

1. What was the Enlightenment? How did the wider cultural climate of the 18th century affect music?

2. How did musical life change, in response to a growing public interest in music?

3. According to Johann Joachim Quantz (quoted in HWM, p. 443) and other critics, what were the characteristics of the best music?

4. What factors distinguish the stylistic tendencies known as the *galant* style and *Empfindsamkeit* from Baroque style, and from each other?

5. According to Johann Nikolaus Forkel (as quoted in HWM, p. 448), how is a piece of music like a speech?

6. According to Heinrich Christoph Koch, how is a melodic period put together from smaller units? How does this process resemble that of an orator making an argument?

Opera (HWM 451–60, NAWM 87–88)

7. What are the characteristics of an *opera buffa*? How does the aria by Leonardo Vinci excerpted in HWM, pp. 452–53, exemplify some of these characteristics?

8. How is an *intermezzo* different from an opera buffa, and how is it similar?

Music to Study
> **NAWM 87:** Giovanni Battista Pergolesi, *La serva padrona* (The Maid as Mistress), intermezzo, excerpt: Recitativo and Recitativo obbligato, *Ah quanto mi sta male*, and Aria, *Son imbrogliato io* (1733)
> CD 7.1–6 (Concise 3.1–6)   Cassette 7.A (Concise 3.A)

9. What is funny in Uberto's recitative soliloquy in this scene from Pergolesi's *La serva padrona* (NAWM 87)? How do his vocal line, the changes of harmony, and the interjections of the string orchestra convey yet parody his emotions?

---

10. How are repeated notes and phrases and sudden changes of texture and mood used in Uberto's aria *Son imbrogliato io* to create a comic flavor? What other humorous touches do you notice?

11. What are the characteristics of the *opera seria* libretto as established by Pietro Metastasio? What moral lessons did his operas aim to teach?

12. What are the musical characteristics of opera seria?

13. Describe and chart the typical form of an aria in an opera seria. What alterations in this form were made by some composers?

14. What does "da capo" mean, and what does it ask the performer to do?

What does "dal segno" mean, and what does it signify?

Music to Study
> **NAWM 88:** Johann Adolf Hasse, *Cleofide,* opera seria, excerpt: Act II,
> Scene 9, *Digli ch'io son fedele* (1731)
> CD 7.7–11   Cassette 7.A

15. Compare Cleofide's aria *Digli ch'io son fedele* (NAWM 88) to the standard da capo form you charted in question 13. In what respects does it follow this form? Where does it deviate?

16. Where does material from the opening ritornello (mm. 1-10) return later in the aria, either in the vocal statements or in later ritornellos, and how is it changed?

17. In what ways does the B section contrast with the A section?

18. What characteristics of the new Classic-era styles (as described in the first section of this chapter) are apparent in the music of both sections of this aria?

19. How does the embellished melody in the upper staff of Example 13.5 in HWM (p. 459) relate to the written melody in the staff below? It was transcribed (by King Frederick the Great of Prussia, no less) from a live performance. What can you deduce from this example about how singers embellished arias in opera seria? (You may also consider the embellishments added by Emma Kirkby in the performance that accompanies NAWM.)

Comic Opera (HWM 461–63, NAWM 89–90)

20. How did Italian comic opera change after the middle of the 18th century?

21. What are the distinctive features of comic opera in France, England, and Germany in the 18th century?

Music to Study
> **NAWM 89:** Jean-Jacques Rousseau, *Le Devin du village* (The Village
> Soothsayer), opéra comique, excerpt: Scene 1, Air, *J'ai perdu tout
> mon bonheur* (1752)
> CD 7.12–15   Cassette 7.A
> **NAWM 90:** John Gay (librettist and arranger), *The Beggar's Opera,* ballad
> opera, excerpt: Scenes 11–13 (1728)
> CD 7.16–20   Cassette 7.A

22. How does the scene from Rousseau's *Le Devin du village* (NAWM 89) com-pare to Pergolesi's *La serva padrona* (NAWM 87)? What musical charac-teristics do the two works share, and how do they differ? What elements in the music mark the Rousseau as distinctively French?

23. In what ways does the Rousseau reflect the new musical tastes of the later 18th century (as described earlier in this chapter)?

24. In what ways does *The Beggar's Opera* differ from the other forms of musical theater we have considered? What is this type of musical theater called? What did John Gay do to "compose" this work?

Beginnings of Opera Reform (HWM 463–66, NAWM 91)

25. How did Jommelli and Traetta seek to reform Italian opera in the 1750s?

Music to Study
NAWM 91: Christoph Willibald Gluck, *Orfeo ed Euridice,* opera, excerpt
from Act II, Scene 1 (1762)
CD 7.21–25   Cassette 7.A

26. What operatic reforms did Gluck introduce in *Orfeo ed Euridice* and *Alceste*? How are those reforms apparent in the scene from *Orfeo ed Euridice* in NAWM 91? How does this differ from the other operas we have seen so far in this chapter?

27. What dramatic musical devices does Gluck use to set the scene and portray the characters (the Furies in the underworld, and Orpheus, who has come down to bring back his beloved Euridice)?

Song and Church Music (HWM 466–69)

28. In what ways is J. F. Reichardt's *Erlkönig* (excerpted in HWM, pp. 467–68) typical of 18th-century lieder?

Instrumental Music: Sonata, Symphony, and Concerto (HWM 469–79, NAWM 92–96)

Music to Study
   NAWM 92: Domenico Scarlatti, Sonata in D Major, K. 119 (ca. 1749)
      CD 7.26–27 (Concise 3.7–8)   Cassette 7.A (Concise 3.A)

29. In the first half of his Sonata in D Major, K. 119 (NAWM 92), Scarlatti
     introduces a string of ideas with contrasting figuration and function. For
     each of the following ideas or groups of ideas (shown by measure numbers),
     indicate the implied key when it is tonally stable or "mod." if it changes
     key, and briefly describe the figuration (e.g., arpeggios, scales, octaves,
     repeated notes or chords, trills, stepwise melody, or a combination of these).

	Mm.	Implied key	Figuration	Where in 2nd half?
a.	1–5	_____	_____	_____
b.	6–13	_____	_____	_____
c.	14–17	_____	_____	_____
d.	18–35	_____	_____	_____
e.	36–55	_____	_____	_____
f.	56–64	_____	_____	_____
g.	65–72	_____	_____	_____
d'.	73–95	_____	_____	_____

     Of these ideas, some return in the second half, and some do not. For those
     that do, indicate above where they begin, and in what key they are presented.

30. Based on your answers above, write a brief description of the form and the
     kinds of figuration Scarlatti uses in his sonata.

31. In this sonata, how does Scarlatti imitate the sound or style of Spanish guitar music?

32. Diagram a sonata first movement as described by Koch. Then diagram it as described by theorists of the 1830s and later, and show the correspondences between these two descriptions by indicating which elements of the later description parallel particular elements of the Koch model.

33. What role did opera play in the birth of the independent symphony?

Music to Study

NAWM 93: Giovanni Battista Sammartini, Symphony No. 32 in F Major, first movement (ca. 1744)
CD 7.28–30   Cassette 7.A

NAWM 94: Carl Philipp Emanuel Bach, Sonata in A Major, H. 186, Wq. 55/4, second movement (1765)
CD 7.31–32 (Concise 3.9–10)   Cassette 7.B (Concise 3.A)

NAWM 95: Johann Stamitz, Sinfonia a 8 in E♭ Major, first movement (published 1758)
CD 7.33–37   Cassette 7.B

NAWM 96: Johann Christian Bach, Concerto for Harpsichord or Piano and Strings in E♭ Major, Op. 7, No. 5, first movement (ca. 1770)
CD 7.38–50   Cassette 7.B

34. How does the first movement of Sammartini's Symphony No. 32 in F Major (NAWM 93) compare in style to the aria from Pergolesi's *La serva padrona* in NAWM 87) or the Scarlatti sonata in NAWM 92? What elements does it have in common with each?

35. Which description of sonata form or first-movement form applies better to this movement, that of Koch or that of theorists of the 1830s and later? Why?

36. In the second movement of C. P. E. Bach's Sonata in A Major (NAWM 94), where does the opening material repeat, and in what key? What else is repeated, and in what key does it appear each time? Diagram the form of the piece. How does it relate to sonata form, and how is it different?

37. What elements of this movement are typical of Bach's expressive style?

38. Compare the melodic writing in this sonata movement to the vocal embellishments added to Hasse's aria from *Cleofide* (NAWM 88), as shown in the upper staff of Example 13.5 in HWM (p. 459; see also question 19, above). Although the melodic range is too wide for a singer, how does Bach create the sense in this instrumental work of a vocal melody, like a slow aria?

39. What are some of the techniques that made the Mannheim orchestra famous, and how are they used in the Stamitz symphony movement in NAWM 95?

40. Compare this movement to the Sammartini symphony movement in NAWM 93. How are they similar, and how are they different, in instrumentation, style, and form?

41. What traits mark Johann Christian Bach's keyboard concerto movement (NAWM 96) as *galant* in style? How does it differ from the *Empfindsamkeit* of C. P. E. Bach's sonata movement (NAWM 94)?

42. In the J. C. Bach concerto movement, what elements of the opening orchestral ritornello return later, and where does each return?

43. When the keyboard solo enters, what new material does it introduce? Which of these new ideas are later recapitulated, and where?

44. How does the form of this first movement resemble a Baroque concerto movement in ritornello form (in which the orchestra interjects transposed and often abbreviated statements of the ritornello between solo episodes), and how does it differ? How does it resemble a Classic-era sonata-form movement, and how does it differ?

45. How large was the orchestra in the Classic period? In addition to the strings, what other instruments were members, about how many of each were there, and what was their function?

Who conducted? _____

Summary (HWM 479)

46. How did the new Classic-era styles make possible the rise of instrumental music to a position of unprecedented prominence and prestige?

TERMS TO KNOW

Terms Reviewed from Earlier Chapters

recitative
aria
da capo aria
castrati

vaudeville
Singspiel
stile antico

Terms Related to the Classic Style

the Enlightenment
galant style
Empfindsamkeit (empfindsam style)

periodicity
Alberti bass

Terms Related to Opera and Vocal Music

opera buffa
intermezzo
opera seria
dramma giocoso
ensemble finale

opéra comique
ariette
rescue opera
ballad opera
lied (18th-century)

Terms Related to Instrumental Music

sonata form
exposition, development,
    recapitulation, coda
sinfonia

symphony
concerto (late-18th-century)
symphonie concertante
serenade

NAMES TO KNOW

Names Related to the Classic Style and to Opera

Joseph Joachim Quantz
Heinrich Christoph Koch
Giovanni Battista Pergolesi
La serva padrona
Pietro Metastasio
Johann Adolph Hasse
Cleofide
Faustina Bordoni
Jean-Jacques Rousseau
Le Devin du village

André Ernest Modeste Grétry
Richard Coeur-de-Lion
The Beggar's Opera
Nicolò Jommelli
Tommaso Traetta
Christoph Willibald Gluck
Raniero de Calzabigi
Orfeo ed Euridice
Alceste
Querelle des bouffons

Names Related to Instrumental Music

Domenico Scarlatti   Mannheim
Giovanni Battista Sammartini   Johann Stamitz
Carl Philipp Emanuel Bach   Johann Christian Bach
Essay on the True Art of Playing
   Keyboard Instruments

REVIEW QUESTIONS

1. Make a time-line for the pieces, composers, librettists, and theorists discussed in this chapter.

2. How did the Enlightenment ideals of reason and individual equality help to create a climate in which the older Baroque styles were replaced by simpler, immediately pleasing styles with wide appeal?

3. What parallels did 18th-century writers observe between music and rhetoric? How does Cleofide's aria (NAWM 88) or C. P. E. Bach's sonata movement (NAWM 94) resemble a speech?

4. Trace the development of comic opera in the 18th century in Italy, France, England, and Germany.

5. What did comic opera styles contribute to instrumental music in the second half of the 18th century?

6. Trace the development of serious opera from the 1730s to the 1770s, including both opera seria and reform opera.

7. If you are familiar with jazz improvisation on a standard tune, what comparisons can you draw between jazz performance and the improvised embellishments in opera seria, as exemplified in Example 13.5 in HWM (p. 459)?

8. What social functions were served by the various instrumental works discussed in this chapter? Which were concert pieces, and which were for amateur or private performance?

9. What elements of form do all or most of the instrumental works in NAWM 92–96 have in common? (For instance, do they all have similar harmonic plans? Do they repeat musical material in similar ways? What elements does each share with the standard model of sonata form?) Can you distill from these five movements a short list of formal strategies that are shared by all or most of these pieces?

THE LATE EIGHTEENTH CENTURY: HAYDN AND MOZART

14

CHAPTER OBJECTIVES

After you complete the reading, study of the music, and study questions for this chapter, you should be able to:

1. trace the careers of Haydn and Mozart and the evolution of their musical idioms;
2. describe the major genres practiced by Haydn, Mozart, and their contemporaries; and
3. name several important works by each of these composers and describe some works by each in their mature styles.

CHAPTER OUTLINE

I. Introduction (HWM 484)

The leading composers of the late 18th century were *Franz Joseph Haydn* (1732–1809) and *Wolfgang Amadeus Mozart* (1756–1791). They were friends and wrote in many of the same genres, yet their careers were strikingly different.

II. Franz Joseph Haydn (HWM 484–87)

A. Haydn's Career

Haydn learned music through lessons, experience as a choirboy, and his own studies in counterpoint. He entered the service of Prince Paul Anton Esterházy in 1761. On the latter's death in 1762, *Prince Nicholas Esterházy* succeeded to the title and became Haydn's patron. Haydn's duties were to compose music at the prince's request, as well as to conduct performances, train singers, supervise the musicians, and keep the instruments in repair. Haydn led the 25-person orchestra in weekly concerts and operas at the prince's country estate, *Eszterháza.* He composed numerous chamber pieces with *baryton,* a string instrument the prince played. Writing so much music for immediate performance allowed Haydn to experiment and develop a fresh and effective style that made him the most popular composer in Europe. He also wrote music for publication and on commission. When Prince Nicholas died in 1790, his son Anton disbanded the orchestra and gave Haydn a pension. In 1791–92 and 1794–95 Haydn went to London, where he gave concerts for the impresario *Johann Peter Salomon* and wrote symphonies Nos. 93–104 (the *London* Symphonies). From 1795 he was again in Vienna, where the court resided, as music director for Anton's son Prince Nicholas II, with much lighter duties. His major late works are Masses and two oratorios, *The Creation* (1798) and *The Seasons* (1801).

III. Haydn's Instrumental Music (HWM 487–505, NAWM 97–101)

A. Symphonic Form

Many of Haydn's early symphonies use the three-movement format of the Italian opera sinfonia; others have four movements in the order Andante–Allegro–Minuet–Presto. Soon he adopted the standard four movements in the order Allegro–Andante–Minuet-and-Trio–Allegro. First movements are in sonata form, alternating harmonically stable and symmetrically phrased periods (the themes) with unstable transitions and developments. Haydn often repeats and alters the opening theme to lead into the transition, an orchestral tutti which modulates to the dominant or relative major. The second thematic section is lightly scored and may introduce a new theme or rework the opening idea, and the exposition closes with a cadential tutti. The development, which grew longer in his later symphonies, varies and recombines material from the exposition, changing keys and often taking sudden digressions. The recapitulation repeats all the themes in the tonic, sometimes altered, and often amplifies the transition and closing section. The slow movement provides a respite from the speed and strong contrasts of the first. The Minuet-and-Trio pairs two minuets, graceful triple-meter dances in rounded binary form, the second of which (the Trio) is more lightly scored and is followed by a return of the first, for an overall ABA form. The fourth movement, in sonata or rondo form, is full of high spirits and surprises.

B. Early Symphonies

Haydn used themes that were readily broken up and recombined. Symphonies Nos. 6-8, titled *Le Matin, Le Midi,* and *Le Soir* (Morning, Noon, and Evening, 1761) are the best-known early symphonies and have several unusual features.

C. The Symphonies of 1768–74

The symphonies of 1768–74 are longer and more serious works than earlier symphonies and require the listener's close attention. The emotional, agitated, minor-key character of some has been linked to the slightly later literary movement *Sturm und Drang* (storm and stress, from the title of a 1776 play). Haydn introduces more startling dramatic contrasts, richer harmonies, more distant modulations, and more counterpoint. Increasingly, each symphony has unique features that mark it as an individual.

D. The Symphonies of 1774–88

The symphonies after 1774 are less experimental, more cheerful, and infused with the appealing style of comic opera. The six *Paris* Symphonies (Nos. 82–87) were commissioned for a concert series in Paris. In Symphonies Nos. 88–92, Haydn often begins with a slow introduction; uses contrasting second themes less often; features the winds more; and infuses the finale with counterpoint, increasing its weight without sacrificing popular appeal. **Music: NAWM 97–98**

E. The *London* Symphonies

Haydn wrote music to suit particular occasions, performers, and halls and to please both the expert and the untutored music lover. His *London* Symphonies were aimed at the London audience, with greater tunefulness (including Slovenian and Croatian peasant tunes), more varied orchestration, and striking changes of key. First movements tend to focus on the first theme rather than introducing a contrasting second theme, the slow movements use theme and variations or a variant of sonata form, and the minuet-and-trio movements are faster and often humorous. The finales use sonata form, *rondo form* (ABACA or ABACABA), or a blend of the two. **Music: NAWM 99**

F. The Quartets up to 1781

Haydn wrote 36 string quartets between 1757 and 1781 and published them in sets of six. His Opp. 17 (1771) and 20 (1772) collections established his reputation as the first great master of the string quartet. The same movement types are used as in the symphony, although the minuet-and-trio sometimes precedes the slow movement. Three finales in Op. 20 are fugal. The Op. 33 quartets (1781) are lighter, with the minuet transformed into a *scherzo* (joke) through a faster tempo and witty hemiolas, syncopations, and rhythmic surprises. Quartets were intended primarily for amateurs to play for their own amusement, and Haydn's witty touches must have added to their pleasure.

G. The Quartets of 1785–90

The 19 quartets of 1785–90 show a trend toward monothematic first movements and slow movements in theme-and-variation form. **NAWM 100**

H. The Last Quartets

Haydn wrote 15 more string quartets between 1793 and 1803. These are marked by widely ranging harmonies, stark juxtapositions of contrasting styles, and many witty touches. **Music: NAWM 101**

I. Keyboard Sonatas

Haydn's early keyboard sonatas are suitable for harpsichord, clavichord, or piano, but his later ones are intended for the piano. His piano sonatas generally develop in parallel with his symphonies and quartets.

IV. Haydn's Vocal Works (HWM 505–8)

A. Operas

Haydn wrote many operas, most of them Italian comic operas. They met with success but soon passed from the repertory and are now rarely heard.

B. Church Music

Haydn's most important works for church were six festive Masses he composed between 1796 and 1802 for Princess Esterházy's nameday. These were in symphonic style, with full orchestra, soloists, and chorus.

C. Oratorios

While in England, Haydn heard some of Handel's oratorios, and his own late oratorios *Die Schöpfung* (The Creation, 1798) and *Die Jahreszeiten* (The Seasons, 1801), to librettos by *Baron Gottfried van Swieten,* show that influence.

V. Wolfgang Amadeus Mozart (HWM 508–14)

A. Early Life

Mozart was born in Salzburg, where his father Leopold Mozart served the archbishop as performer and composer. Wolfgang and his older sister Marianne ("Nannerl") were both child prodigies as performers—as was Wolfgang a prodigy as improviser and composer—and their father took them on a series of tours around Europe. Through these tours, Mozart learned every style of music then current in western Europe and imitated each one in his own compositions. His mature works synthesize these various styles and types in music of unprecedented variety. His more than 600 works are identified by their number in the catalogue of his works by Ludwig von Köchel.

B. Early Works

Mozart's first teacher was his father Leopold. On tour in London, he met Johann Christian Bach, whose strong thematic contrasts and infusion of Italian opera style into instrumental works became hallmarks of Mozart's style. Stays in Italy and Vienna resulted in strong influences from Italian opera and symphony and from Haydn and other Viennese composers.

C. The Salzburg Years

Mozart was in Salzburg for most of 1774–81 but actively sought a position elsewhere. His reputation as a composer was growing, and he was commissioned to write an opera seria, *Idomeneo,* for Munich.

D. Piano and Violin Sonatas

Mozart wrote numerous piano variations for his pupils and piano sonatas for his own concert performances. The sonatas are varied in form, style, and content. Reflecting the influences of opera and of J. C. Bach, Mozart's themes are usually graceful, singing melodies that grow without apparent effort from the initial ideas. In his early violin sonatas, the violin is an optional reinforcement of the melody in the piano, but by the late 1770s it was a virtually equal partner.

E. Serenades and Divertimentos

Mozart wrote many serenades and *divertimentos,* pieces for background music or entertainment. They are scored for strings, strings and winds, or winds in pairs (if meant for outdoor performance). The most famous is *Eine kleine Nachtmusik* (A Little Night Music, 1787) for string quintet.

F. Solo Concertos

Also dating from the Salzburg years are the Violin Concertos, the first original Piano Concertos, and the Symphonie concertante.

VI. Mozart's Vienna Years (HWM 514–28)

A. Mozart in Vienna

Mozart moved to Vienna in 1781, hoping to earn a living as a freelance composer. He met with great initial success, but he failed to find a permanent position and his popularity and earnings later declined. His music struck a perfect balance between immediate universal appeal and the depth of feeling and technique that earned the respect of the learned. He was strongly influenced by Haydn and by Johann Sebastian Bach, whose music he discovered through Baron Gottfried van Swieten.

B. Piano Works

Among Mozart's most important piano works in these years are the Fantasia and Sonata in C Minor, K. 475 and 457.

C. The *Haydn* Quartets

In 1785, Mozart published six quartets dedicated to Haydn. The fruit of long effort and much revision (unusual for Mozart, who normally wrote quickly and easily), they show his ability to absorb Haydn's techniques yet remain original.

D. The Vienna Symphonies

Mozart wrote only six symphonies after 1781, but they were longer and more substantial than their predecessors, with more difficult wind parts, more harmonic and contrapuntal complexity, and weightier finales. The last two characteristics are exemplified in the finale of Symphony No. 41 in C Major (the *Jupiter*), which combines its fugal first theme in counterpoint with five other motives.

E. Concertos for Piano and Orchestra

Mozart wrote 17 piano concertos in Vienna for his own performances as a soloist, primarily during his first five years there. In them, as in all his music, he sought to please both the connoisseur and the less learned listener, although they challenge the best players. The first movements are like those of Johann Christian Bach's concertos in blending ritornello and sonata procedures. Before the final tutti, the orchestra pauses on a tonic six-four chord and the soloist plays a *cadenza*. Mozart's second movements are like slow arias, and the finales are rondos or sonata-rondos. **Music: NAWM 102**

F. Operas

In Vienna, Mozart composed a Singspiel, *Die Entführung aus dem Serail* (The Abduction from the Harem, 1786); three Italian comic operas on librettos by *Lorenzo da Ponte* (1749–1838), that is, *Le nozze di Figaro* (The Marriage of Figaro, 1786), *Don Giovanni* (premiered at Prague in 1787), and *Così fan tutte* (Thus Do They All, 1790); an opera seria, *La clemenza di Tito* (The Mercy of

Titus, 1791); and a German opera, *Die Zauberflöte* (The Magic Flute, 1791). Mozart's music captured each character, and the ensembles showed them interacting in dramatic ways. *Don Giovanni* was the first opera on the Don Juan theme to take the Don seriously, resulting in characters and a drama of unprecedented depth. *Die Zauberflöte* mixes comedy with the humanistic imagery and symbolism of the Freemasons, and Mozart's music blends elements of opera seria, Singspiel, opera buffa, accompanied recitative, sacred choral style, and Baroque counterpoint.   **Music: NAWM 103**

G. Church Music

Mozart's Masses are written in the modern symphonic-operatic style, alternating chorus and soloists. His Requiem was left unfinished at his death and completed by Mozart's student and collaborator Franz Xaver Süssmayr.

VII. Epilogue (HWM 528–29)

Haydn and Mozart wrote in all major genres and represent the best music the Classic era produced. Yet there are many other composers who made significant contributions.

STUDY QUESTIONS

Introduction (HWM 484)

1. What are the significant differences between the careers of Haydn and Mozart?

Franz Joseph Haydn (HWM 484–87)

2. Who was Haydn's main patron? What was Haydn required to do as part of his employment?

3. What other sources of income did Haydn have during his service with this patron?

4. Trace Haydn's career after 1790, including his sources of income and his major compositions.

Haydn's Instrumental Music (HWM 487–505, NAWM 97–101)

5. What are the standard four movements of a Haydn symphony, and what are the main characteristics of each?

6. What is *Sturm und Drang* style, and what are its typical features?

Music to Study

    NAWM 97: Franz Joseph Haydn, Symphony No. 56 in C Major, first movement (1774)

    CD 7.51–57 (Concise 3.11–17)   Cassette 7.B (Concise 3.A)

    NAWM 98: Franz Joseph Haydn, Symphony No. 92 in G Major (*Oxford*), second movement (1789)

    CD 7.58–61   Cassette 7.B

    NAWM 99: Franz Joseph Haydn, Symphony No. 104 in D Major (*London*), finale (1795)

    CD 7.62–72   Cassette 7.B

(Note on reading scores: Instruments like the horn and clarinet are written as they are fingered to allow players to move easily between different members of the same family of instruments. Clarinets in *A*, in *B♭* and in *E♭*, for instance, will all use the same fingering when they see a *C*, but the instrument will produce an *A*, a *B♭*, or an *E♭* respectively. In 18th- and 19th-century scores, these "transposing instruments" are given in the score as they are notated for the player, which means the conductor or score-reader must transpose in the same way the instrument does to determine the pitch that will sound. In the latter two movements, Haydn uses horns in D, which sound a minor seventh lower than written—*D* when *C* is notated; in Symphony No.104, he also uses trumpets in D, sounding a whole step higher, and clarinets in A, sounding a minor third lower—*A* when *C* is notated.)

7. In the exposition of Haydn's Symphony No. 56, first movement (NAWM 97), how are the following sections distinguished from each other? Mention these and any other features you find significant: harmonic stability or instability; key (when stable); chromaticism or largely diatonic music; orchestration; dynamics; phrasing (clearly articulated phrasing or continuous, overlapping phrasing); and melodic content.

first theme area (mm. 1–28)

transition (mm. 29–52)

second theme area (mm. 53–67, with a contrasting extension in mm. 68–78)

closing group (mm. 79–99)

Notice how many different ways there are to follow the form. A listener may attend to any of these distinguishing features and will still be able to follow the course of the music clearly. This is one of the ways in which Classic-era music is notable for its intelligibility to a wide range of listeners.

8.   In what measure does the recapitulation begin? _____

     The recapitulation repeats material from the exposition, but with some changes. What is different in the recapitulation, in comparison to the exposition?

9.   What happens in the development, in terms of harmony and key?

     How are orchestration and dynamics used in the development?

     What kind of phrasing appears in the development: articulated phrases, in which each phrase comes to a cadence before the next one begins (as in mm. 1-28 of this movement), or continuous phrasing, in which ideas overlap without pause?

10. What ideas from the exposition are used in the development, where do they appear, and how are they changed from the exposition?

11. Chart the form of the slow movement of Haydn's Symphony No. 92 (NAWM 98), and give the key of each main section.

   How do the opening motives of the first two sections relate?

   What elements of both sections appear in the coda (mm. 94–111)?

12. Compare the melodic writing in this movement first to the vocal embellishments added to Hasse's aria from *Cleofide* (NAWM 88 and Example 13.5 in HWM, p. 459) and second to the melodic style in the slow movement from C. P. E. Bach's piano sonata (NAWM 94; see also chapter 13, questions 19 and 38). How does Haydn embellish his melodies?

13. How are the wind instruments used in this movement? How does this compare to the earlier Haydn symphony movement in NAWM 97?

14. What elements give the finale of Symphony No. 104 (NAWM 99) its popular character?

15. In what ways does the exposition of this sonata-form movement differ in form from the first movement of Haydn's Symphony No. 56 (NAWM 97)?

16. What occurs in the development section of the Symphony No. 104 finale, in terms of harmonic plan; orchestration and dynamics; phrasing; and use of material from the exposition? How does this compare to the development of Haydn's Symphony No. 56, first movement (compare question 9, above)?

17. In the Symphony No. 104 finale, at the end of the recapitulation there is a long coda (mm. 265–334) instead of the expected closing material. What happens during this coda, in terms of harmonic plan; orchestration and dynamics; phrasing; and use of material from the exposition?

18. What characteristics of these three movements (NAWM 97–98) are typical of Haydn symphonies from the mid-1770s, late 1780s, and London period respectively?

No. 56, first movement (1774):

No. 92, second movement (1789):

No. 104, finale (1795):

19. String quartets were written primarily for amateurs to play for their own enjoyment. What aspects of Haydn's quartets were particularly well suited to give pleasure to the players themselves?

Music to Study
> **NAWM 100:** Franz Joseph Haydn, String Quartet in D Major, Op. 64, No. 5, finale (1790)
> CD 8.1–8 (Concise 3.18–25)   Cassette 8.A (Concise 3.A)
> **NAWM 101:** Franz Joseph Haydn, String Quartet in C Major, Op. 76, No. 3, second movement (1797)
> CD 8.9–13   Cassette 8.A

20. The finale of Haydn's String Quartet in D Major, Op. 64, No. 5, blends features of rondo and sonata form. In a rondo, the theme itself is normally a little binary form with two repeated sections, often a rounded binary form (in which both halves end with the same music): ‖: a :‖: b a :‖ This is indeed what appears at the start of this movement. What follows, however, is a contrapuntal, almost fugal development section that begins in the parallel minor and modulates freely. This eventually leads back to the rondo theme, now without repetitions and with a varied close, and the movement ends with a coda. The overall form is this:

‖: a :‖: b a :‖ development a b a' coda

The binary-form rondo theme is the "wrong" shape for the exposition of a sonata (despite the chart in NAWM that shows the parallels); if it were the same shape as an exposition, of course, this movement would be in sonata form, not an amalgam. On the other hand, the large development is out of proportion for a rondo, and in a normal rondo one would expect more than one episode. It is as if Haydn substituted the binary-form theme of a rondo for the exposition of a sonata, or replaced the episodes of a rondo with a sonata-form development.

We may conclude from this example that the "forms" of the Classic period are best thought of as procedures to be used—and, in this and many other cases, mixed with each other—rather than molds to be filled. The flexibility with which Haydn and other composers applied these procedures is amazing.

You expected a question? Here is one: which of the following aspects of mm. 1-28 make it *unlike* a sonata exposition? Explain your answer.

1. The repeat mark in m. 8, marking the repetition of mm. 1–8 and 8–28.
2. The modulation to the dominant.
3. The lack of a thematic statement on the dominant.
4. The return to the tonic and the opening material before the double bar.

21. In the second movement of his String Quartet in C Major, Op. 76, No. 3
    (NAWM 101), Haydn presents a series of variations on a tune that later
    became the Austrian and German national anthems. In each variation, how
    is the tune varied? How is the accompaniment changed?

    variation I:

    variation II:

    variation III:

    variation IV:

Haydn's Vocal Works (HWM 505–8)

22. Briefly describe Haydn's late Masses and oratorios.

Wolfgang Amadeus Mozart (HWM 508–14)

23. Describe Mozart's career and the influences on his music to 1781.

Mozart's Vienna Years (HWM 514–28)

24. How did Mozart make a living in Vienna?

25. How did Mozart become acquainted with the music of Johann Sebastian Bach? How was he influenced by Bach's music?

26. What are the characteristics of the quartets and symphonies Mozart wrote in Vienna? How do they compare to Haydn's works in the same forms?

Music to Study
    NAWM 102: Wolfgang Amadeus Mozart, Piano Concerto in A Major, K.
        488, first movement (1786)
    CD 8.14–29   Cassette 8.A

27. In this Mozart concerto movement, what segments of the opening orchestral ritornello return later in the work, and where does each return? How is it varied on its return? How does this compare with J. C. Bach's concerto in NAWM 96 (see chapter 13, question 42)?

---

28. How does the form of this first movement resemble a Baroque concerto movement in ritornello form, how does it resemble a sonata-form first movement, and how does it differ from each? How does it compare with the first movement of J. C. Bach's concerto in NAWM 96 (see chapter 13, question 44)?

29. Describe Mozart's melodic style. How do his melodies compare with those in Haydn's symphonies (NAWM 97–99)?

30. Compare mm. 114–37 in the piano to mm. 46–62 in the first violins, and mm. 149–56 in the piano to mm. 143–49 in the first violins. Describe what Mozart is doing in the piano part. What procedure treated in this or the previous chapter does this recall?

31. In a Classic-period concerto, what is a *cadenza*?

Where does it fall in the form, and how is it prepared?

The cadenza printed in NAWM 102 is Mozart's own. How would you describe it, in terms of melodic figuration, harmony, and treatment of the instrument?

32. What are Mozart's five best-known operas of his Vienna period, and when was each premiered?

_____   _____

_____   _____

_____

33. In Mozart's view, what was the proper relationship between the words and the music in opera?

Music to Study
  NAWM 103: Wolfgang Amadeus Mozart, *Don Giovanni*, K. 527, opera, Act
     I, Scene 5 (1787)
     103a: No. 3, Aria: *Ah chi mi dice mai*
        CD 8.30–31 (Concise 3.26–27)   Cassette 8.A (Concise 3.A)
        Recitative: *Chi è là?*
        CD 8.32 (Concise 3.28)   Cassette 8.A (Concise 3.A)
     103b: No. 4, Aria: *Madamina! Il catalogo è questo*
        CD 8.33–34 Concise 3.29–30)   Cassette 8.A (Concise 3.A)

34. How does Mozart's music help to delineate the three characters and portray their feelings in *Ah chi mi dice mai* from *Don Giovanni* (NAWM 103a)?

35. In what ways does the form of this aria resemble sonata form? What element of sonata form does it omit?

36. In Leporello's *Catalogue* aria (103b), how are the different characteristics of Don Giovanni's victims depicted in the music? That is, what musical means does Mozart use to depict the images in the text?

TERMS TO KNOW

baryton
Minuet and Trio
Sturm und Drang
rondo form

scherzo
divertimento
cadenza

NAMES TO KNOW

Franz Joseph Haydn
Wolfgang Amadeus Mozart
Prince Nicholas Esterházy
Eszterháza
Johann Peter Salomon
the *London* Symphonies
Die Schöpfung (The Creation)
Die Jahreszeiten (The Seasons)
Baron Gottfried van Swieten

Mozart's *Haydn* Quartets
Die Entführung aus dem Serail (The
   Abduction from the Harem)
Lorenzo da Ponte
Le nozze di Figaro (The Marriage of
   Figaro)
Don Giovanni
Così fan tutte (Thus Do They All)
Die Zauberflöte (The Magic Flute)

REVIEW QUESTIONS

1. Add Haydn, Mozart, and the major events and works discussed in this chapter to the time-line you made for chapter 13.

2. Compare the careers of Haydn and Mozart, including the circumstances of their lives and the genres and styles they cultivated. What are the main similarities between their careers, and what are the major differences?

3. Briefly describe each of the following genres as practiced by Mozart and Haydn in terms of form, style, content, and social function: symphony, string quartet, piano sonata, concerto, and comic opera.

4. Describe the principal characteristics of Haydn's mature style in his instrumental works. Use NAWM 97–101 as examples for your discussion, referring to and describing passages as appropriate.

5. Building on the previous question, what aspects of Haydn's style did Mozart absorb into his own? And in what ways does Mozart's mature music differ from that of Haydn? Use NAWM 102–3 and other works described in HWM as examples for your discussion, referring to and describing passages as appropriate.

LUDWIG VAN BEETHOVEN

15

CHAPTER OBJECTIVES

After you complete the reading, study of the music, and study questions for this chapter, you should be able to:

1. briefly recount Beethoven's career and the circumstances of his life;
2. list the main characteristics of the music of each of his three periods;
3. name several works and describe at least one complete movement for each period.

CHAPTER OUTLINE

I. The Composer and His Music (HWM 533–36)

A. Background

Ludwig van Beethoven (1770–1827) was born in Bonn in northwestern Germany and was taught music by his father and a local organist. From 1792, when he went to Vienna, he studied first with Haydn and then with other composers. Building on the genres, styles, and conventions of the Classic period, he created highly individual works that brought him unprecedented success and that became models for later composers. These included 9 symphonies, 5 piano concertos, 16 string quartets, 32 piano sonatas, and many other orchestral, chamber, and vocal works. He was neither as prolific nor as speedy a composer as Haydn or Mozart, but took each piece through many drafts and revisions, as we can see in his surviving *sketchbooks*. Starting in his twenties, Beethoven gradually went deaf, writing movingly of his suffering in an 1802 letter called the *Heiligenstadt Testament*. His deafness tended to isolate him from society.

B. Beethoven's "Three Periods"

Beethoven's career is traditionally divided into three periods. In the first, to about 1802, he assimilated the musical language, genres, and styles of his time. In the second, ca. 1803–16, his works are more individual, longer, and grander than before. In the last period, ca. 1816–27, his music becomes more introspective (and often more difficult to play and understand).

II. First Period (HWM 536–41, NAWM 104–5)

A. Patrons

Beethoven was supported by aristocratic patrons both in Bonn and in Vienna. In Bonn he worked only for the elector of Cologne, but in Vienna he had several noble benefactors, including three who gave him an annuity to keep him in Austria. He also sold his works to publishers, performed as a pianist, and taught piano. Thus he was able to make a living without being dependent for employment on a single patron, as Haydn had been.

B. The Piano Sonatas

Beethoven's piano sonatas continue the tradition of Haydn but show individual features. Several traits of his piano style may be indebted to the sonatas of *Muzio Clementi* (1752–1832) and *Jan Ladislav Dussek* (1760-1812): economy of material, symphonic breadth, sudden changes of harmony, dynamics, texture, and mood, and certain kinds of pianistic figuration. **Music: NAWM 104–5**

C. Chamber Music

Beethoven's first six String Quartets, Op. 18 (1798–1800), follow the model of Haydn in motivic development and use of counterpoint but show his individuality in their themes, surprising modulations and turns of phrase, and formal structure. Other chamber works of the first period include piano trios, violin sonatas, cello sonatas, and a septet for strings and winds.

D. First Symphony

Beethoven's First Symphony in C Major (1800) also follows Haydn's example, but has a scherzo as the third movement and features long codas in the other movements.

E. Second Symphony

Beethoven's Second Symphony in D Major (1802) is longer than previous symphonies, with more thematic material and long codas that develop the main ideas.

III. Second Period (HWM 541–54, NAWM 106)

A. Beethoven's Reputation

By his early thirties, Beethoven was renowned as a pianist and composer, had many aristocratic patrons, and was sought after by publishers.

B. The *Eroica* Symphony

The Third Symphony in E♭ Major, the *Eroica* (1803), was of unprecedented length and complexity, with many unusual features. The first movement has a great number of melodic ideas, including a "new theme" in the development, but almost all derive from the material presented near the beginning. Most novel is that the main theme is treated as a person in a drama, struggling and finally triumphing. The sketches show that many of the unusual features, such as the horn's "too early" entrance at the recapitulation, were planned from early on. Beethoven originally titled the work *Bonaparte,* after Napoleon, but changed the title to *Sinfonia Eroica* (Heroic Symphony). The second movement is a funeral march that evokes the style of French Revolutionary marches and hymns. The third movement is a scherzo, and the finale a mixture of variations (on a theme from Beethoven's ballet *The Creatures of Prometheus*) with elements of fugue and march style. **Music: NAWM 106**

C. *Fidelio*

In Beethoven's one opera, *Fidelio* (1804-5, rev. 1806 and 1814), Leonore assumes the disguise of a man in order to free her husband from wrongful imprisonment. Beethoven revised the work repeatedly before it was a success.

D. The *Rasumovsky* Quartets

Beethoven's second group of string quartets consisted of the three in Op. 59 (1806), dedicated to Count Rasumovsky, Russian ambassador to Vienna and lover of music. They share the heroic, individual style of the *Eroica* Symphony, and two movements include Russian themes.

E. The Fourth to Eighth Symphonies

Beethoven's Fourth and Fifth Symphonies project opposite moods; the Fourth in B♭ Major (1806) is jovial, while the Fifth in C Minor (1807–8) portrays struggle and final triumph. The Sixth Symphony in F Major, named the *Pastoral* (1808), evokes country scenes. The Seventh Symphony in A Major (1811–12) is large in scale, while the Eighth in F Major (1812) is quite condensed. Beethoven also wrote several overtures, which resemble in form the first movement of a symphony.

F. Piano Sonatas and Concertos

Many of Beethoven's piano sonatas show individual features. For example, the *Moonlight* Sonata, Op. 27, No. 2 (1801), begins with a fantasia movement; the Sonata in D Minor, Op. 31, No. 2 (1802), uses a melody that resembles a recitative; and the *Waldstein* Sonata in C Major, Op. 53 (1804), uses traditional forms with intense themes and strongly contrasting textures. His first three piano concertos belong to his first period, and the Fourth in G Major (1805–6) and Fifth (*Emperor*) in E♭ Major (1809) to his middle period, along with his one Violin Concerto (1806).

IV. Third Period (HWM 554–60, NAWM 107)

A. The Late Style

Although Beethoven was famous across Europe and well supported by patrons and publishers, his deafness led to greater social isolation. His music became more abstract and introspective, with extremes from the meditative to the grotesque conjoined in works that referred to Classical conventions without being constrained by them.

B. Characteristics of Beethoven's Late Style

Beethoven's late compositions work out the full potential of themes and motives. The *Diabelli Variations* (1819–23) do not simply embellish the theme as do earlier variation sets but rework material from it to create a new design, mood, and character in each variation. Several individual movements, especially slow movements, also use this kind of variation technique. Beethoven's late style is also marked by changes in other aspects:

1. He creates a new sense of *continuity* by blurring phrase and section divisions and de-emphasizing cadences.
2. He includes passages that have an *improvisatory character* or use *instrumental recitative.*
3. He often uses *fugal textures* in developments, and several movements or large sections are fugues.
4. He uses new *sonorities,* including wide spacings and exceptionally dense textures.
5. He often uses an unusual number of movements and unusual kinds of movements.

The *String Quartet in C♯ Minor,* Op. 131 (1826), exemplifies all of these characteristics. **Music: NAWM 107**

C. The *Missa solemnis*

The *Missa solemnis* (1822), or Mass in D, is a massive work that recalls the choral style of Handel while resembling the symphonic conception and mix of chorus and soloists typical of Haydn's late Masses.

D. The Ninth Symphony

Beethoven's Ninth Symphony (1824) is longer than his others. Its finale is innovative in recalling the themes of the earlier movements and introducing soloists and chorus to sing stanzas from Friedrich von Schiller's *Ode to Joy.*

E. Beethoven and the Romantics

Beethoven's middle-period works were the most influential on later composers, particularly for their conception of music as a vehicle to express the composer's own feelings and experiences. (This was perhaps the most innovative aspect of Beethoven's music; composers since Josquin had sought to express the feelings in a text, composers of opera to depict a character's emotions, and instrumental composers to represent the generalized affections, but apparently no composer before Beethoven's middle period had sought to represent his own feelings and experiences. This idea became so influential that modern listeners often assume that this is what all composers have had in mind, even before Beethoven.) Through this and through his innovations in form and procedure, he became a revolutionary force in the history of music.

STUDY QUESTIONS

The Composer and His Music (HWM 533–36)

1. Who were Beethoven's teachers, and when and where did each teach him?

Teacher	Dates	Place
_____	_____	_____
_____	_____	_____
_____	_____	_____
_____	_____	_____
_____	_____	_____
_____	_____	_____

2. What are two reasons Beethoven wrote fewer symphonies than Haydn or Mozart?

   a.

   b.

3. What is the *Heiligenstadt Testament*? What does it discuss, and what attitudes does Beethoven express? What does Beethoven say in it about his relations with other people and about the role of his art in his life?

4. Beethoven's career is often divided into three periods. Provide the dates for each period and a brief characterization of each.

First period:

Second period:

Third period:

First Period (HWM 536–41, NAWM 104–5)

5. How did Beethoven make a living in Vienna? How was his situation different from that of Haydn?

Music to Study
>   **NAWM 104:** Ludwig van Beethoven, *Sonate pathétique* for piano, Op. 13
>   (1797–98), Rondo: Allegro (finale)
>   CD 8.35–44 (Concise 3.31–40)   Cassette 8.A (Concise 3.A)
>   **NAWM 105:** Muzio Clementi, Sonata in G Minor, Op. 34, No. 2 (1795),
>   Largo e sostenuto—Allegro con fuoco (first movement)
>   CD 8.45–53   Cassette 8.B

6. In what ways is the finale of Beethoven's *Pathétique* Sonata (NAWM 104) like traditional rondos?

In what ways is it different?

7. What are some of the effects Beethoven uses to make this movement dramatic?

8. Compare the later repetitions of the rondo refrain to its initial presentation. What changes are made, if any?

Compare the rondo's first episode (mm. 25–61) to its reprise near the movement's end (mm. 134–69). In the reprise, how is it changed from its initial presentation?

How do these changes in the rondo refrain and first episode contribute to the dramatic quality of the music?

9. In the first movement of Clementi's Sonata in G Minor, Op. 34, No. 2 (NAWM 105), the exposition may be diagrammed as follows:

Measure:	1	10	23	41	48	63
	Intro	P	T	S	Extension	K
Key:	g	g	mod	B♭		b♭

Diagram the rest of the movement. Where does the recapitulation begin? How are the elements of the exposition changed in the recapitulation?

10. What is the motivic relationship between the slow introduction and the first and second themes (P and S)?

11. Both the Clementi and the Beethoven sonata movements use sudden changes in harmony, texture, or dynamic level for dramatic effect or to demarcate the form. Find and describe two such moments of sudden change in each movement.

12. When did Beethoven compose his first set of string quartets? _____

When did he compose his First Symphony? _____

What composer served as Beethoven's main model for these works? _____

13. What else was played on the concert in 1800 in which Beethoven's First Symphony was premiered? How does this program differ from a modern concert program?

Second Period (HWM 541–54, NAWM 106)

14. What was Beethoven's reputation as a pianist and composer by the early 1800s? How did he relate to his patrons and publishers?

Music to Study
> **NAWM 106:** Ludwig van Beethoven, Symphony No. 3 in E♭ Major (*Eroica*)
> (1803), Allegro con brio (first movement)
> CD 8.54–68   Cassette 8.B

15. What are some of the unusual features of the first movement of Beethoven's *Eroica* Symphony (NAWM 106)?

16. What in the sketches (shown in NAWM, pp. 277–280) suggests that the second theme of the first movement is to be heard as arriving in m. 83 rather than at m. 57, when the key of the dominant is first reached?

---

17. What in the sketches (shown in HWM, p. 544, and NAWM, p. 283) suggests that the "new theme" in the oboe at m. 284 is only a counterpoint to a variant of the main theme?

18. According to HWM and NAWM, the principal theme is treated as a person in a drama, struggling against other players and triumphing in the end. How does Beethoven use changes in the principal motive (mm. 3–8) to convey struggle and triumph? (Hint: Look at the versions of this idea in the development, at mm. 408 and 424 in the recapitulation, and at mm. 639ff. in the coda.)

19. What other devices does Beethoven use in this movement to suggest a dramatic struggle ending in triumph? How do the very long development and coda contribute to this effect?

20. Based on the descriptions in HWM, briefly describe the second and fourth movements of the *Eroica* Symphony.

21. What do Beethoven's *Eroica* Symphony and his opera *Fidelio* owe to the arts and politics of France in the Revolutionary period?

22. When were the *Rasumovsky* Quartets composed? _____

What elements distinguish them from earlier quartets?

23. How does Beethoven's Fifth Symphony portray the progress from struggle to triumph?

24. How does the music of Beethoven's Sixth Symphony (the *Pastoral*) suggest scenes from life in the country?

25. For each of Beethoven's first eight symphonies, what key is it in and when was it completed?

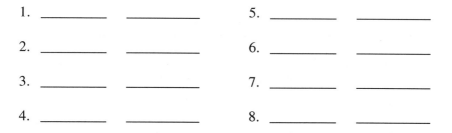

    1. _____ _____   5. _____ _____

    2. _____ _____   6. _____ _____

    3. _____ _____   7. _____ _____

    4. _____ _____   8. _____ _____

26. What vocal genre is evoked in the first movement of Beethoven's Sonata in D Minor, Op. 31, No. 2?

27. In the excerpts from the *Waldstein* Sonata shown in HWM, p. 553, how does Beethoven use contrasts of texture for dramatic effect?

Third Period (HWM 554–60, NAWM 107)

28. According to HWM, how did Beethoven's growing deafness affect his personality and his music?

29. For each of the following aspects of music, how does Beethoven's late style differ from Haydn, Mozart, and his own earlier style?

a. juxtaposition of disparate elements

b. variation technique

c. delineation of phrases and sections

d. evocation of improvisation and recitative

e. use of fugue

f. sonority

g. number of movements

Music to Study
    NAWM 107: Ludwig van Beethoven, String Quartet in C♯Minor, Op. 131
        (1826), excerpts
      107a. First movement: Adagio ma non troppo e molto espressivo
        CD 8.69–71 (Concise 3.41–43)   Cassette 8.B (Concise 3.A)
      107b. Second movement: Allegro molto vivace
        CD 8.72   Cassette 8.B

30. Beethoven's String Quartet in C♯ Minor, Op. 131, is in seven movements. Give the tempo marking, meter, key, and form for each movement.

	Tempo	Meter	Key	Form
1.	_____	_____	_____	_____
2.	_____	_____	_____	_____
3.	_____	_____	_____	_____
4.	_____	_____	_____	_____
5.	_____	_____	_____	_____
6.	_____	_____	_____	_____
7.	_____	_____	_____	_____

How can this sequence of movements be reconciled with the traditional four-movement plan of a string quartet?

31. It has been observed that the key scheme of the string quartet is unusual, and that there is a correspondence between the keys used for each movement and the important pitches of the opening fugue subject. Write out the following notes for the fugue subject as presented in violin I and the answer as stated in violin II:

	subject in violin I	answer in violin II
first note (same as last note):	_____	_____
highest note:	_____	_____
lowest note:	_____	_____
most emphasized note (longest, and marked with a sforzando):	_____	_____

Of these notes, circle the ones that are used as the key of one of the movements in the quartet, as you listed them in question 30.

32. From the evidence in the previous question, can you suggest a reason why Beethoven might have chosen to have the answer in the subdominant, rather than in the dominant as expected?

33. What traditional fugal techniques does Beethoven use in the first movement, and where is each one used?

34. What aspects of the music give the second movement its particularly light and folklike character?

35. Where in the second movement is there a recollection of the key of the first movement, to match the hint in the first movement of the key of the second?

36. In what ways does this quartet exemplify the characteristics of Beethoven's late style as you described them in question 29 above? (Hint: Answers for part d. of question 29 will be found in HWM and for parts e. and g. in the questions above. For parts a., b., c., and f., look both in HWM and at the two movements in NAWM.)

    a. juxtaposition of disparate elements

    b. variation technique

(continued)

c. delineation of phrases and sections

d. evocation of improvisation and recitative

e. use of fugue

f. sonority

g. number of movements

37. What does Beethoven's *Missa solemnis* owe to Handel, and what does it owe to Haydn?

38. Describe the sequence of events in the finale of Beethoven's Ninth Symphony.

39. What was Beethoven's impact on later composers?

TERMS TO KNOW

Beethoven sketchbooks   instrumental recitative
Beethoven's three periods

NAMES TO KNOW

Ludwig van Beethoven   *Fidelio*
Heiligenstadt Testament   the *Rasumovsky* Quartets, Op. 59
Muzio Clementi   *Diabelli* Variations, Op. 120
Jan Ladislav Dussek   String Quartet in C♯ Minor, Op. 131
Sonate pathétique, Op. 13   *Missa solemnis*
Six String Quartets, Op. 18   Beethoven's Ninth Symphony
Eroica Symphony   *Ode to Joy*

REVIEW QUESTIONS

1. Write an essay in which you recount Beethoven's career, including the changing circumstances of his life, his three major style periods, and major compositions of each period.

2. You have examples in NAWM 104, 106, and 107 of movements from each of Beethoven's three periods. For each of these works, describe the form and other significant features of the movements in NAWM and explain what makes this work characteristic of its period.

3. What other composers particularly influenced Beethoven's music, and what did he absorb from each?

4. Take the first eight measures of either of the Haydn String Quartet movements you have studied (NAWM 100 and 101) and recompose it to feature one or more of the characteristics of Beethoven's late style. You can change as many notes and rhythms as you wish, as well as dynamics, articulations, registration, and any other aspect. You may recast it for piano or for another ensemble if you prefer. Try to make it sound as much like Beethoven as possible. Then write a short statement explaining what aspects of Beethoven's late style you have tried to imitate and how you have done so.

ROMANTICISM AND NINETEENTH-CENTURY ORCHESTRAL MUSIC

16

CHAPTER OBJECTIVES

After you complete the reading, study of the music, and study questions for this chapter, you should be able to:

1. describe some of the differences between music of the Classic and Romantic periods, particularly in their aesthetic orientation;
2. explain how 19th-century symphonic composers responded to the influence of Beethoven;
3. identify some of the most important symphonic composers in the 19th century and suggest what makes each composer individual; and
4. briefly describe one or more characteristic works for each one.

CHAPTER OUTLINE

I. Romanticism (HWM 563–65)

There is more historical continuity than contrast between the Classic and Romantic periods. Most music between 1770 and 1900 uses a common set of conventions. The main differences are of degree: Romantic music is more individual in expressing feelings and transcending conventions. Music was seen as the most Romantic art. But music was also closely identified with literature, particularly in the *art song* and in *program music*.

II. Orchestral Music (HWM 565–87, NAWM 108–9)

A. The Beethoven Legacy

Beethoven cast a long shadow, and later composers sought to differentiate their music from his, typically by extending some elements of his music while rejecting others. Schubert introduced songlike themes into the symphony; Berlioz found precedents in Beethoven's symphonies for both the programmatic basis and the thematic drama of his *Symphonie fantastique*; Schumann,

Mendelssohn, Brahms, and Bruckner continued the symphony in individual ways; and Wagner saw the choral finale of Beethoven's Ninth Symphony as pointing to the future—a more intense union of music with words and drama.

B. Schubert

Franz Schubert (1797–1828) composed almost 1,000 works in his short life, including more than 600 lieder. His *Unfinished* Symphony has been called the first Romantic symphony because of its lyrical themes, harmonic excursions, and striking orchestration, traits also true of his "Great" C-major Symphony.

C. Mendelssohn

Felix Mendelssohn (1809–1847) combined adherence to Classic forms with themes reminiscent of foreign lands in his Symphonies Nos. 4 (*Italian*) and 3 (*Scottish*). Among his other important orchestral works are his Violin Concerto, his concert *overtures* (independent one-movement works), and his incidental music to Shakespeare's *A Midsummer Night's Dream*.   **Music: NAWM 109**

D. Berlioz

The *Symphonie fantastique* (1830) by *Hector Berlioz* (1803–1869) is a musical drama whose words are not spoken or sung but are written in a program handed out to the audience. The central theme, or *idée fixe* (fixed idea or fixation), stands for the woman with whom the artist is infatuated and appears in every movement, sometimes transformed; this procedure helped to initiate the cyclic symphony. *Harold en Italie* (Harold in Italy, 1834) is also a program symphony, with a solo violist playing the protagonist, and *Roméo et Juliette* (1839) is a "dramatic symphony" for orchestra, soloists, and chorus, extending Beethoven's example in the Ninth Symphony into what is almost an unstaged opera. These innovative works influenced all later program music and began a new era of colorful orchestration.   **Music: NAWM 108**

E. Schumann

Robert Schumann (1810–1856) composed his first symphonies (published as No. 1 and No. 4) in 1841. The four movements of Symphony No. 4 are played without a break and linked by thematical recall.

F. Liszt

Franz Liszt (1811–1886) wrote 12 *symphonic poems* between 1848 and 1858 and another in 1881–82. He was the first to use the term, which designates a programmatic work, usually in one movement, that evokes ideas and feelings associated with its subject and may follow the course of a poem or narrative with a similar sequence of moods and events. His symphonies are also programmatic. Some works introduce numerous transformations of a single motive or theme, an approach that had a strong impact on later composers. Several later composers wrote symphonic poems, and Liszt's harmonies influenced Wagner and others.

G. Brahms

Johannes Brahms (1833–1897) wrote four symphonies, four concertos, two overtures, two serenades, and a set of orchestral variations. He combined Classic structure with Romantic melodic gesture and emotional intensity. Middle movements are often in keys a third away from the main key of the symphony, instead of in the dominant or subdominant. His textures are often contrapuntal, with active melodic basses or countermelodies in the inner parts. The superimposition of duple and triple divisions of the beat or measure is frequent, as are other metric clashes and melodic cross-relations between parts.

H. Bruckner

Anton Bruckner (1824–1896) was an organist, and his symphonies show that background in his orchestration and in their serious, religious spirit. Their length, massive orchestra, and harmony show the influence of Wagner. They often begin like Beethoven's Ninth, with the gradual emergence of a theme, and end with chorale-like themes. While outwardly conforming to Classic structures, his symphonies depend upon the continuous development of musical ideas.

I. Tchaikovsky

Piotr Il'yich Tchaikovsky (1840–1893) wrote six symphonies, of which the last three are the best known. The Fourth has a private program about relentless fate, depicted in the opening horn theme that returns in the first and fourth movements. The key structure of the first movement is unusual, moving around the circle of minor thirds. The opening theme of the Fifth recurs in all movements. The Sixth (the *Pathétique*) has as its second movement a waltz in 5/4, and is exceptional in ending with a slow movement. Tchaikovsky's ballets are very well known.

J. Dvořák

Antonín Dvořák (1841–1904) is best known for his Symphony No. 9 (*From the New World,* 1893), written during his sojourn in the United States.

STUDY QUESTIONS

Romanticism (HWM 563–65)

1. What are some of the differences between music in the Classic era and music in the Romantic period? What are some of the similarities?

2. According to Liszt and Schopenhauer, what is special about music as an art?

3. What are some of the links between music and literature in the 19th century?

Orchestral Music (HWM 565–87, NAWM 108–9)

4. HWM sums up more than a century of music history in two succinct sentences (p. 565): "Composers who followed Beethoven had to come to terms somehow with this towering figure of the immediate past. They followed Beethoven or rejected his legacy in different ways, according to their personalities and talents."

   Although we have seen important figures since medieval times who exercised a strong influence on the next generation—such as Léonin, Machaut, Dufay, Josquin, Gabrieli, and Vivaldi—their music soon faded from the repertory, replaced by more recent styles that performers, listeners, and patrons of music preferred to the older styles. For the first time in the history of music, the last decades of the 18th century and first half of the 19th saw the development of a permanent repertory of immortal classics: the oratorios of Handel and Haydn, the late symphonies of Haydn and Mozart, and the Beethoven symphonies, concertos, string quartets, and sonatas. This body of works has been added to, but the original core has never been replaced.

This imposed a fundamentally new dilemma on composers. Whereas writers of music from the troubadours to Beethoven had to compete for performances and attention with other living composers, those born after 1800 had to compete with classical works of uncontested quality and universal acceptance. They have endured what the literary critic Harold Bloom has called "the anxiety of influence," the need to absorb yet transcend the influence of their very prominent predecessors. This anxiety of influence begins to appear as early as Beethoven, who had to make his way in the genres so fully explored by Haydn and Mozart and therefore composed much more slowly; it was unavoidable for symphonic composers in the 19th century, who had to write works that would stand up to being programmed next to a Beethoven symphony; and it has intensified with each generation, as space has filled up in what Lydia Goehr has called "the imaginary museum of musical works." In response, composers have sought to continue some aspects of the past tradition while also creating something new and distinctively their own.

According to HWM, how did each of the following composers confront the influence of Beethoven's symphonies and find an individual path?

Schubert

Berlioz

Brahms

Wagner

5. What does Schumann praise in Schubert's "Great" C-major Symphony (quoted in HWM, p. 570)?

6. How do Schubert's symphonies differ in approach from those of Beethoven?

7. What is "Italian" in Mendelssohn's *Italian* Symphony (No. 4)? What is "Scottish" in his *Scottish* Symphony (No. 3)?

Music to Study
NAWM 109: Felix Mendelssohn, Incidental Music to *A Midsummer Night's Dream,* Op. 61 (1843), excerpt: Scherzo
CD 9.7–9   Cassette 9.A
NAWM 108: Hector Berlioz, *Symphonie fantastique* (1830), excerpts
III. *Scène aux champs* (Scene in the Country)   not on recordings
IV. *Marche au supplice* (March to the Scaffold)
CD 9.1–6 (Concise 3.44–49)   Cassette 9.A (Concise 3.B)

8. What musical techniques does Mendelssohn use in the scherzo from the incidental music to *A Midsummer Night's Dream* (NAWM 109) to suggest the fairies in flight? How does he suggest the braying of Bottom, a character whose head has been changed by a spell into the head of a jackass?

9. How does the form of this scherzo differ from the traditional form of a scherzo? How does it resemble a sonata form without the repetition of the exposition?

10. What devices of orchestration, melody, and rhythm does Berlioz use to suggest that the third movement of his *Symphonie fantastique* (NAWM 108) is set in the country? (One device not mentioned in the commentary is the dotted siciliano rhythm, long associated with pastoral settings, first introduced in mm. 28–30.)

11. Where does the *idée fixe* appear in this movement? How is it transformed, and how is it introduced and developed, to suit the program (given in NAWM, p. 336)?

12. Chart the form of the fourth movement, *Marche au supplice*.

13. How does Berlioz develop and vary the theme introduced by the cellos and basses in mm. 17–25 over the course of the movement?

14. Where does the *idée fixe* appear? How is it treated, and how do its treatment and the surrounding music fit the program of the movement?

15. What special instrumental effects does Berlioz use, and how do they suit the program? What other aspects of the music help to support the program?

16. What was Berlioz's significance for later generations?

17. What is a *symphonic poem*? Who invented it, and when?

18. How did Liszt use thematic transformation in his *Les Préludes*? What did this procedure allow him to accomplish?

19. In what ways do the Brahms symphonies continue the Classic tradition, and in what ways are they Romantic?

20. What are the distinctive features of Bruckner's symphonies?

21. How does Tchaikovsky link the movements together thematically in his Fourth and Fifth Symphonies?

TERMS TO KNOW

art song
program music

concert overture (19th-century)
symphonic poem

NAMES TO KNOW

Franz Schubert
Unfinished Symphony
Felix Mendelssohn
Hector Berlioz
Symphonie fantastique
Harold en Italie
Roméo et Juliette

Robert Schumann
Franz Liszt
Les Préludes
Johannes Brahms
Anton Bruckner
Piotr Il'yich Tchaikovsky
Antonín Dvořák

REVIEW QUESTIONS

1. Make a time-line for the 19th century, and place on it the composers and most significant pieces discussed in this chapter. Add to it the three periods of Beethoven's career and his most important works, as discussed in chapter 15. Make your time-line large enough to allow further additions, as you will be adding to it in chapters 17–19.

2. How are Classic and Romantic music similar, and how are they different? Use examples from the orchestral works you know to illustrate these similarities and differences.

3. Describe the symphonic works of Schubert, Mendelssohn, Berlioz, Schumann, Liszt, Brahms, Bruckner, and Tchaikovsky. What traits distinguish each composer's works from those of Beethoven, and from the other composers discussed here?

SOLO, CHAMBER, AND VOCAL MUSIC IN THE NINETEENTH CENTURY

17

CHAPTER OBJECTIVES

After you complete the reading, study of the music, and study questions for this chapter, you should be able to:

1. name some of the most prominent 19th-century composers of piano music and chamber music, characterize their styles, trace influences upon them, and describe representative works by Schumann, Chopin, and Brahms;
2. trace the history of the 19th-century German lied from Schubert to Brahms; and
3. describe the social roles for and varieties of choral music in the 19th century and name some important composers of choral music.

CHAPTER OUTLINE

I. The Piano (HWM 592–93)

The 19th-century piano had a larger range, more varied dynamics, and faster response than the 18th-century piano. (It was also now mass-produced and thus widely available and affordable, so that it became the most common household instrument.) There were two schools of playing in the early 19th century, one emphasizing clarity and fluency, the other large sound and dramatic orchestral effects. The 19th century saw the rise of the traveling virtuoso. Some pianists emphasized technical display; others linked technique to interpretative substance.

II. Music for Piano (HWM 593–607, NAWM 110–13)

A. Romantic Piano Music

In order to sustain lyrical melodies with an active accompaniment, pianists often created a three-layer texture of melody, bass, and inner figuration shared between the hands. The new, more resonant piano also invited chordal textures. The most frequent forms were short dances or lyrical pieces.

B. The Early Romantic Composers

There were many composers of piano music, including *Carl Maria von Weber* (1786–1826) and a number of Bohemian composers.

C. Schubert

Schubert wrote marches, dances, and lyrical works that create a distinctive mood. His longer works include 11 sonatas and the *Wanderer Fantasy,* which uses a theme from his song *The Wanderer.* His sonatas often present three keys in the exposition rather than two and, while following Classic form, use lyrical themes that resist development.

D. Mendelssohn

Mendelssohn wrote a variety of piano works, including preludes and fugues that show his interest in J. S. Bach. His most popular piano works are his *Lieder ohne Worte* (Songs without Words), which capture the lyrical quality of the lied in works for piano alone. He also wrote important music for organ.

E. Robert Schumann

Schumann planned to be a concert pianist, but after he injured his right hand he turned to composition and to writing about music in the journal he founded, the *Neue Zeitschrift für Musik.* All his published music before 1840 was for piano. In addition to several longer works, he specialized in short character pieces, often grouped into collections such as *Papillons* (Butterflies), *Carnaval,* and *Phantasiestücke* (Fantasy Pieces). His pieces carry titles that suggest extramusical associations. In his criticism and his music, he used the imaginary characters Florestan, Eusebius, and Raro to reflect different sides of his own personality. He also wrote fugues and fugal passages that pay homage to Bach. **Music: NAWM 110**

F. Chopin

Fryderyk Chopin (1810–1849) wrote almost exclusively for piano. He was born in Poland and lived in Paris from 1831. His *mazurkas* and *polonaises* are stylized Polish dances and are among the first nationalist works of the 19th century. His playing style was more personal than theatrical, and his music is accordingly introspective. He used *tempo rubato,* in which the right hand pushes forward or holds back the tempo while the left hand accompanies in strict time. He followed *John Field* (1782–1837) in composing *nocturnes,* slow works with embellished melodies over wide-ranging accompaniments. Chopin also wrote preludes, under the influence of Bach; *ballades* (a term he apparently coined); scherzos; fantasias; sonatas; and concertos. His *études* are studies in piano technique, but are unusual for études in that they are also for concert performance. **Music: NAWM 111–12**

G. Liszt

Liszt was born in Hungary and trained in Vienna. He was a touring virtuoso from a young age, seeking to match on the piano the dazzling virtuosity of the violinist *Nicolò Paganini* (1782–1840). Liszt made many transcriptions for piano of other music. His original compositions for piano include *Hungarian Rhapsodies,* études, and many short descriptive pieces, and his works for piano and orchestra include two concertos; he also wrote for organ, using Baroque forms and styles. His Piano Concerto No. 1 in E♭ Major and his one-movement

Piano Sonata in B Minor exemplify his use of *thematic transformation,* a device also used in his symphonic poems. Liszt experimented with chromatic harmony, especially in his late works. **Music: NAWM 113**

H. Brahms

Brahms avoided pianistic display but achieved a great variety of textures by combining simple ideas. He often used broken-chord accompaniments, cross-rhythms, and melodies doubled in octaves, thirds, or sixths. He wrote three early sonatas, variation sets, and two concertos in mid-career, and numerous small, lyrical piano pieces in later life, when he also composed a set of chorale preludes for organ in emulation of J. S. Bach.

I. Other Composers

Other significant works for keyboard were Modest Musorgsky's *Pictures at an Exhibition* (1874) and pieces for piano and organ by *César Franck* (1822–1890).

III. Chamber Music (HWM 607–14, NAWM 114)

The best chamber music of the Romantic period came from composers who felt closest to the Classic tradition.

A. Schubert

Schubert wrote several significant chamber works, notably the *Trout* Quintet, three late string quartets, an octet for strings and winds, and the String Quintet in C Major, widely regarded as his best chamber work.

B. Mendelssohn

Mendelssohn wrote an octet, six string quartets, two piano trios, and other chamber works.

C. Schumann

Schumann wrote all his major chamber works (three string quartets, piano quartet, and piano quintet) in 1842, the year after his first two symphonies; he later added three piano trios. His quartets particularly show the influence of Beethoven.

D. Brahms

Brahms is Beethoven's true successor in the realm of chamber music, with a large body of works of high quality spanning his entire career. Perhaps anxious about competing with Beethoven, he delayed writing string quartets until mid-career. Like most of Brahms's works, the well-known Piano Quintet in F Minor, Op. 34 (1864), uses *developing variation,* in which a musical idea is varied to create a string of interrelated but different ideas, producing both unity and variety. His chamber works with clarinet or natural horn are peaks of the literature for those instruments. **Music: NAWM 114**

E. Franck

Franck wrote several chamber works united by the *cyclical use of themes,* recalling themes in two or more movements.

IV. The Lied (HWM 614–19, NAWM 115–18)

A. The Ballad

Ballads were long narrative poems written in imitation of folk ballads. They called for more variety and emotional expressivity from composers than did the lyrical strophic poem. In response to these demands, the piano became more of an equal partner with the voice in conveying the meaning of the poetry.

B. Schubert

Schubert had a gift for creating song melodies that were both lovely in themselves and perfectly suited to the text. He often used chromaticism and harmonic contrast to create drama or highlight the meaning of the words. Many songs are strophic; those that are through-composed are based on recurring themes and a clear tonal structure. The accompaniments often include figures that convey an image or feeling in the text. He set dozens of poems by Goethe and composed two *song cycles* (groups of songs intended to be performed in sequence and often implying a story) to poems by Wilhelm Müller, *Die schöne Müllerin* (The Lovely Miller's Daughter, 1823) and *Winterreise* (Winter's Journey, 1827). **Music: NAWM 115–16**

C. Robert Schumann

In Schumann's lieder, the piano is equal to the voice in interest and expressivity. He wrote more than 100 songs in 1840, the year of his marriage, including the song cycle *Dichterliebe* (A Poet's Love) on poems by Heinrich Heine. **Music: NAWM 117**

D. Clara Schumann

Clara Wieck Schumann (1819–1896) was a child prodigy on the piano who became an important soloist and composer. Her marriage to Robert Schumann and raising a family limited her touring, but she continued to perform, compose, and teach. **Music: NAWM 118**

E. Brahms

Among Brahms's over 250 songs, many are in a folklike style over simple accompaniment, such as the famous "Brahms lullaby." He also arranged German folksongs. His principal model in song composition is Schubert, and his usual tone is serious and reflective. His piano parts seldom depict an image in the poem, and they are quite varied in texture (unlike Robert and Clara Schumann, who often use the same figuration throughout a song).

V. Choral Music (HWM 620–24, NAWM 119)

A. Types of Choral Music

The 19th century saw a revival of choral works from earlier centuries, such as Palestrina, Lasso, Handel, and Bach. (Partly as a result, new choral music tended to be relatively conservative or even to hearken back to earlier eras; it was not the trailblazer of new styles it had been in the Renaissance.) There were three main types of choral music composed in the 19th century:

1. *Part-songs* on secular texts, usually short and mostly homophonic;
2. Music on liturgical texts, for church or home performance; and
3. Concert works for chorus and orchestra, often with soloists.

B. Part-Songs and Cantatas

Singing societies, amateur choruses who sang together for their own pleasure, were very popular in the 19th century, and composers produced hundreds of part-songs, cantatas, and other works for these amateur men's, women's, or mixed choirs. Brahms especially was a master of choral music of all types.

C. Church Music

The Cecilian movement, named after St. Cecilia, the patron saint of music, was a movement within the Catholic Church to revive the a cappella style of Palestrina and restore Gregorian chant to purer form. Other composers continued to write church music with orchestra or organ, including Catholic Masses and English anthems. In St. Petersburg, *Dmitri Bortnyansky* (1751–1825) helped to found a new choral style of Russian church music based in part on traditional Orthodox chant.

D. Other Music on Liturgical Texts

A number of composers wrote large works for chorus, soloists, and orchestra on texts from the liturgy. These were written for special occasions or intended to be performed in concert rather than in church. Berlioz's *Requiem* (1837) and *Te Deum* (1855) are dramatic symphonies with voices, scored for large orchestras with interesting instrumental effects. Several of Liszt's works are on a similarly large scale. Gioachino Rossini's *Stabat Mater* (1832, rev. 1841) and Giuseppe Verdi's *Requiem* (1874) are in operatic style, dramatizing their subjects. Bruckner was a church organist; his Masses share qualities and some themes with his symphonies, and his motets show the influence of the Cecilian movement. **Music: NAWM 119**

E. The Romantic Oratorio

Several German, French, and English composers composed oratorios, most notably Mendelssohn's *St. Paul* (1836) and *Elijah* (1846). Brahms's *Ein deutsches Requiem* (A German Requiem, 1868) uses biblical passages rather than the liturgical texts, and blends old and new styles.

STUDY QUESTIONS

The Piano (HWM 592–93)

1. How did the 19th-century piano differ from earlier keyboard instruments, including 18th-century pianos?

2. Describe the variety of approaches to piano playing in the 19th century.

Music for Piano (HWM 593–607, NAWM 110–13)

3. What were some ways composers for piano imitated textures from vocal and orchestral music?

4. How do Schubert's sonatas differ from Beethoven's?

5. What are Mendelssohn's most popular piano pieces, and what are they like?

Music to Study
    NAWM 110: Robert Schumann, *Phantasiestücke,* Op. 12 (1837), excerpts
        4: *Grillen* (Whims)
            CD 9.10–12 (Concise 3.50–52)   Cassette 9.A (Concise 3.B)
        5: *In der Nacht* (In the Night)
            CD 9.13–15   Cassette 9.A

6. What is the form of Schumann's *Grillen* (NAWM 110)?

How does it compare to a traditional ABA form?

How does this piece, titled "Whims," convey a sense of whims or whimsy?

7. What is the form of Schumann's *In der Nacht*?

How does this piece convey passionate emotions? How does its form resemble a narrative—that is, how does it suggest that it is relating a story?

8. What textures does Schumann use in these piano pieces that are different from textures used by Classic-era composers such as C. P. E. Bach (NAWM 94), Mozart (NAWM 102), or Beethoven (NAWM 104)?

9. What was Chopin's national heritage, and how is this reflected in his music?

10. What genres of piano music did Chopin use?

Music to Study
NAWM 111: John Field, Nocturne in A Major, No. 8 (1815)
    CD 9.16   Cassette 9.A
NAWM 112: Frédéric Chopin, Nocturne in E♭ Major, Op. 9, No. 2 (1830–31)
    CD 9.17 (Concise 3.53)   Cassette 9.A (Concise 3.B)

11. In what ways does Field embellish the melodic line in his Nocturne in A Major (NAWM 111)? How do his melodies resemble the style of opera?

12. How does Chopin embellish the melodic line of his Nocturne in E♭ Major (NAWM 112)? How is it like operatic singing? How is it like Field's nocturne?

13. How is chromaticism used in the Field? How is it used in the Chopin?

14. What elements of style, sound, and texture distinguish Chopin's Nocturne from Schumann's *Phantasiestücke* (NAWM 110) and from earlier keyboard styles? Can you describe Chopin's style, based on this example?

15. Who was Nicolò Paganini? What was his significance for Liszt's career?

16. What genres of keyboard music did Liszt cultivate?

17. What is *thematic transformation*? How does Liszt use it in his Piano Concerto No. 1 in E♭ Major (excerpted in HWM, p. 604)?

Music to Study
    NAWM 113: Franz Liszt, *Nuages gris* (Gray Clouds), for piano (1881)
        CD 9.18 (Concise 3.54)   Cassette 9.A (Concise 3.B)

18. What is unusual about the harmony of *Nuages gris* (NAWM 113)?

19. What is unusual about the piano texture of this work? How is it unlike the earlier, virtuosic Liszt?

---

20. What is Brahms's approach to texture on the piano, and how does it differ from that of Chopin or Liszt?

Chamber Music (HWM 607–14, NAWM 114)

21. Which Schubert chamber works borrow material from his songs or theatrical music, and how is that material used?

22. Who coined the phrase *developing variation*? _____

    Define and describe this procedure, using as an example the first movement of Brahms's Piano Quintet in F Minor, Op. 34 (excerpted in HWM, p. 611).

23. How does Brahms's developing variation compare to Liszt's thematic transformation? (For Liszt, see question 17, above.)

Music to Study
NAWM 114: Johannes Brahms, Piano Quintet in F Minor, Op. 34 (1864),
     excerpt: Scherzo
CD 9.19–25 (Concise 3.55–61)   Cassette 9.B (Concise 3.B)

24. How does the scherzo movement of Brahms's Piano Quintet in F Minor (NAWM 114) recall the style of Beethoven?

25. Chart the form of the scherzo, indicating changes of meter, thematic ideas, and keys.

26. How do the piano and strings interact with each other in this movement?

27. What elements of this movement strike you as characteristic of Romantic music?

The Lied (HWM 614–19, NAWM 115–18)

28. What is a *ballad*? Why did ballads call for greater variety and expressivity from composers? What effect did this have on the piano accompaniments to art songs?

Music to Study

NAWM 115: Franz Schubert, *Gretchen am Spinnrade* (Gretchen at the Spinning Wheel), Lied (1814)
   CD 9.26–30 (Concise 3.62–66)   Cassette 9.B (Concise 3.B)

NAWM 116: Franz Schubert, *Der Lindenbaum* (The Linden Tree), Lied, from the song cycle *Winterreise* (1827)
   CD 9.31–34   Cassette 9.B

NAWM 117: Robert Schumann, two songs from *Dichterliebe* (A Poet's Love), song cycle (1840)
   117a: *Im wunderschönen Monat Mai* (In the marvelous month of May)
   CD 9.35   Cassette 9.B
   117b: *Ich grolle nicht* (I bear no grudge)
   CD 9.36   Cassette 9.B

29. Schubert's *Gretchen am Spinnrade* (NAWM 115) sets a famous scene from Goethe's *Faust* in which Gretchen sits spinning thread while thinking of Faust. How is the spinning wheel depicted in this song? Why is this an effective device for depicting the spinning wheel?

How does this device also capture Gretchen's mood?

Where does the wheel suddenly stop, and then gradually start again? What does this suggest about Gretchen's feelings at this point?

---

30. Diagram the form of this song. How does Schubert use changes in melody, harmony, and key to portray Gretchen's changing emotions?

31. How does Schubert alter or repeat Goethe's words as given in NAWM? How does this help convey Gretchen's feelings?

32. In *Der Lindenbaum,* how does Schubert use figuration in the piano and contrasts between major and minor to suggest the images and meaning of the poem?

33. The text of *Im wunderschönen Monat Mai* (NAWM 117a) speaks of new love. How does Schumann's music imply, through melody and harmony, that this love is unrequited—as yet all "longing and desire" and no fulfillment? How are the opening piano prelude and closing postlude crucial in conveying this meaning?

34. What is the key of this song? Where does the tonic chord appear? What is unusual about the beginning and ending harmonies?

35. How does Schumann alter the poetry in his setting of *Ich grolle nicht* (NAWM 117b)?

36. In what way is the setting ironic, with the emotional tone of the music contradicting what the words claim?

37. Briefly trace the career of Clara Wieck Schumann.

Music to Study
   NAWM 118: Clara Wieck Schumann, *Geheimes Flüstern hier und dort*
      (Secret Whispers Here and There), Lied (1853)
   CD 9.37   Cassette 9.B

38. In Clara Schumann's song *Geheimes Flüstern hier und dort* (NAWM 118),
   how does the figuration in the piano capture the imagery in the poem? In
   what other ways does the music suit the poetry?

---

39. What are some characteristics of Brahms's songs?

Choral Music (HWM 620–24, NAWM 119)

40. What types of choral music were written in the 19th century?

41. What are *singing societies*? What effect did they have on the composition of choral music in the 19th century?

42. What was the *Cecilian movement,* and what were its goals?

43. Who was Dmitri Bortnyansky, when was he active, and what did he accomplish?

44. How do Berlioz's *Requiem* and *Te Deum* differ from traditional church music of the previous hundred years?

Music to Study
NAWM 119: Anton Bruckner, *Virga Jesse,* motet (ca. first century A.D.)
CD 9.38   Cassette 9.B

45. How does Bruckner evoke or suggest 16th-century polyphony in his motet *Virga Jesse* (NAWM 119)?

46. What elements in the music make clear that this could not have been written earlier than the 19th century?

Terms to Know

mazurka

polonaise

tempo rubato

nocturne

ballade

étude

thematic transformation

developing variation

cyclical use of themes

ballad

song cycle

part-song

singing societies

Names to Know

Carl Maria von Weber

Lieder ohne Worte (Songs
without Words)

Neue Zeitschrift für Musik

Phantasiestücke

Fryderyk Chopin

John Field

Nicolò Paganini

César Franck

Die schöne Müllerin

Winterreise

Dichterliebe

Clara Wieck Schumann

the Cecilian movement

Dmitri Bortnyansky

Review Questions

1. Add the composers and major works discussed in this chapter to the time-line you made for chapter 16.

2. Trace the history of piano music in the 19th century. Include in your discussion the changed character of the piano and the genres composers used, as well as describing the styles and works of the most prominent composers for the instrument.

3. What are the distinctive features of chamber music in the 19th century?

4. Trace the development of the German lied from the turn of the 19th century through Brahms.

5. Name the varieties of choral music in the 19th century and describe one or more examples of each type. What were the social roles and contexts for choral music in the 19th century, and how did this affect the types and styles used by choral composers? What roles did amateurs play in choral performance, and how might this have affected the relative prestige of choral music in comparison to orchestral music?

OPERA AND MUSIC DRAMA IN THE NINETEENTH CENTURY

18

CHAPTER OBJECTIVES

After you complete the reading, study of the music, and study questions for this chap-ter, you should be able to:

1. trace the history of opera in France, Italy, and Germany in the 19th century and distinguish between the characteristics of the various national traditions;
2. define and use the terminology associated with 19th-century opera;
3. name the most significant composers in each nation and describe the style and approach of each of them; and
4. describe characteristic excerpts from operas by Rossini, Bellini, Verdi, Weber, and Wagner.

CHAPTER OUTLINE

I. France (HWM 625–30)

A. Background

Paris was a center for opera in the early 19th century, with governmental support that varied through changes of regime.

B. Grand Opera

Grand opera was a new kind of opera on historical subjects, as much spectacle as music, that appealed to a broad audience. The genre was established by the librettist *Eugène Scribe* (1791–1861) and the composer *Giacomo Meyerbeer* (1791–1864), whose opera *Les Huguenots* (1836) is an early example.

C. Opéra Comique

Opéra comique used spoken dialogue rather than recitative, used a smaller cast, and used simpler music than grand opera. Its plots were comic or romantic rather than historical. After the 1851 declaration of the Second Empire under Napoleon III, the satiric genre of *opéra bouffe* emerged with *Jacques Offenbach* (1819–1880). His comic style influenced the later operettas of Gilbert and Sullivan in England and of Johann Strauss and others in Vienna.

D. Lyric Opera

Lyric opera developed from romantic comic operas, with similar romantic plots and a focus on melody, but on a somewhat larger scale. A famous example is *Faust* (1859) by *Charles Gounod* (1818–1893). *Carmen* (1875) by *Georges Bizet* (1838–1875) is classed as an opéra comique because it has spoken dialogue, but is a drama that reflects *exoticism* and a late-19th-century taste for *realism*.

E. Berlioz
Berlioz's *La Damnation de Faust* (1846) is not an opera, but a series of scenes from *Faust* set for concert performance by soloists, chorus, and orchestra. *Les Troyens* (1856–58) is his operatic masterpiece and has as much in common with the operas of Lully, Rameau, and Gluck as with 19th-century grand opera.

II. Italy (HWM 630–33, NAWM 120–21)

A. General
Italian opera was less influenced by Romanticism than were other operatic traditions. Opera was the only internationally significant music from Italy during this period. The 18th-century reforms of Jommelli and Traetta affected Italy in the 19th century, including more use of winds and horns and more important roles for the chorus and the orchestra.

B. Rossini
Gioachino Rossini (1792–1868) was the most successful opera composer of the early 19th century. His 32 operas include both serious and comic works, all with a strong emphasis on shapely, ornamented melody over a spare accompaniment. His most popular works today are his comic operas, such as *Il barbiere di Siviglia* (The Barber of Seville, 1816). Many arias move from a slow, highly embellished *cavatina* to a faster, brilliant *cabaletta*. Both sections often use vocal *coloratura*. Rossini often used repetition of an idea combined with a crescendo to build excitement. After composing many operas for Italian opera houses, Rossini moved to Paris in 1824, wrote some operas in French, and then wrote smaller vocal and piano works. **Music: NAWM 120**

C. Donizetti
Gaetano Donizetti (1797–1848) composed about 70 serious and comic operas as well as many songs, oratorios, cantatas, religious works, symphonies, and chamber works.

D. Bellini
Vincenzo Bellini (1801–1835) wrote 10 serious operas in a refined style marked less by Rossini's coloratura than by a flexible, elegant style of embellishment that influenced Chopin. French opera influenced the plots of Italian opera; *opera semiseria* featured a serious plot with Romantic sentimentality, as in French lyric opera. **Music: NAWM 121**

III. Giuseppe Verdi (HWM 633–38, NAWM 122)

A. General
Giuseppe Verdi (1813–1901) was the major figure in Italian opera after Donizetti. He continued the Italian operatic tradition and was a strong

nationalist. His career divides into three periods: to 1853 (the year of *Il trovatore* and *La traviata*); to 1871 (the year of *Aida*); and his last two operas, *Otello* (1887) and *Falstaff* (1893). His operas focused on human drama, and his librettos, drawn mostly from Romantic authors, provided high emotions, strong contrasts, and quickly moving plots. Most of his operas are in four main segments, with ensemble finales in the middle two, a big duet in the third, and a prayer or meditation for the heroine to begin the fourth.

B. Early Works

Verdi's early operas are especially notable for their choruses. Instead of a strict sequence of discrete musical numbers (such as arias, duets, and choruses), he mixed a variety of musical forces in a single scene to create a more compelling drama. In his second period operas appeared less frequently, as Verdi experimented with Parisian grand opera, daring harmonies, comic roles, *reminiscence motives,* and other new elements.   **Music: NAWM 122**

C. Late Works

After a long hiatus, Verdi returned to opera with *Otello* (1884–87), responding to intervening developments in German and French opera by making the music more continuous and by using several unifying motives. *Falstaff* (1893) takes to a new level the elements of comic opera, particularly the ensemble.

IV. Germany (HWM 638–41, NAWM 123)

A. Background

German opera derived from Singspiel, absorbed French Romantic features, and was closely linked to German Romantic literature.

B. Weber

Carl Maria von Weber (1786–1826) was director of the opera at Prague and later at Dresden. His *Der Freischütz* (1821) established the tradition of German Romantic opera. Plots draw from medieval history, legend, or fairy tale, and involve supernatural beings and events in a natural setting. Characters stand for good or evil principles, and good triumphs in a kind of spiritual deliverance. These traits and some musical elements such as use of folklike style, chromatic harmony, and emphasis on the inner voices as well as the main melody distinguish German from French or Italian opera, despite similarities in genre and musical style. The famous Wolf's Glen Scene uses *melodrama* (spoken dialogue over music), startling chromatic harmony, and unusual orchestral effects to create an eerie atmosphere. Weber often used recurring themes for dramatic effect and to unify the drama. **Music: NAWM 123**

C. Other German Opera Composers

German composers after Weber wrote comic, lyric, and dramatic operas.

V. Richard Wagner and the Music Drama (HWM 641–48, NAWM 124)

A. Career

Richard Wagner (1813–1883) was the most important composer of German opera and has been a pivotal figure for music since the middle of the 19th century, for he (1) brought German Romantic opera to its peak, (2) invented the *music drama,* and (3) developed a harmonic idiom whose greater chromaticism and freer modulation influenced most later composers. His opera *Der fliegende Holländer* (The Flying Dutchman, 1843) set the pattern for his later works with a libretto by the composer himself, a plot based on a legend, the use of recurring themes, and the hero's redemption through the loving sacrifice of the heroine. *Tannhäuser* (1845) combines German Romantic opera with grand opera; *Lohengrin* (1850) is still more continuous, with less division into numbers, more use of recurring themes, and the association of keys with characters. The 1848 Revolutions forced Wagner into exile in Switzerland, where he wrote a series of essays on his musical and social theories (including both *Opera and Drama* and the notorious *Jewishness in Music*) and the librettos to his cycle of music dramas, *Der Ring des Nibelungen* (The Ring of the Nibelungs), whose music he completed over two decades: *Das Rheingold* (The Rhine Gold, 1853–54), *Die Walküre* (The Valkyrie, 1854–56), *Siegfried* (1856–71), and *Götterdämmerung* (The Twilight of the Gods, 1869–74). They are linked by a continuous story, common characters, and shared motives. His other music dramas are *Tristan und Isolde* (1857–59), *Die Meistersinger von Nürnberg* (The Mastersingers of Nuremberg, 1862–67), and *Parsifal* (1882). Wagner's notion of music drama links drama and music in the service of a single dramatic idea. Together with scenery, staging, and action, they comprise a "total artwork" (*Gesamtkunstwerk*). Vocal lines are part of the entire texture, and music is continuous throughout an act rather than being broken into separate numbers, despite echoes of earlier types such as recitative, arioso, aria, and scene.

B. The Leitmotif

In Wagner's music dramas, a person, thing, or idea may be associated with a motive called a *Leitmotif.* By recalling and developing these motives, Wagner creates unity and makes the music itself the locus of dramatic action. These differ from the reminiscence motives of Verdi and Weber by being briefer, more numerous, and more pervasive in the music. **Music: NAWM 124**

C. Wagner's Influence

The complex chromatic chords, constant modulation, and evasion of resolutions that characterize Wagner's harmony in *Tristan und Isolde* created ambiguities that depart from common-practice tonality and led in the music of later composers to new systems of harmony. His concept of opera as a combination of many arts and his notion of continuous music ("endless melody") strongly influenced later composers.

STUDY QUESTIONS

France (HWM 625–30)

1. What is *grand opera*? In what ways does *Les Huguenots* exemplify grand opera?

    Who were the librettist and composer for *Les Huguenots*?

    librettist: _____ composer: _____

    What theater was associated with grand opera, and who was its director?

    theater: _____ director: _____

2. What is *opéra bouffe,* and when and why did it come into existence?

    Who was a major composer of *opéras bouffes*? _____

    Who were major composers of comic opera in England and Vienna?

    England: _____ Vienna: _____

3. What is *lyric opera*? How does it differ from grand opera and opéra bouffe?

4. Who wrote the following operas, and when?

Carmen _____   *Les Troyens* _____

What are the special qualities of each of these operas?

Italy (HWM 630–33, NAWM 120–21)

5. Briefly trace Rossini's career.

6. Who were the most important composers of Italian opera in the 1830s? What types of opera did each compose?

Music to Study
> **NAWM 120:** Gioachino Rossini, *Il barbiere di Siviglia* (The Barber of Seville), opera (1816), Act I, Scene 5: Cavatina, *Una voce poco fa*
> CD 9.39–42   Cassette 9.B
> **NAWM 121:** Vincenzo Bellini, *Norma,* opera (1831), Act I, Scene 4: Scena e Cavatina, *Casta diva*
> CD 10.1–5   Cassette 10.A

7. What is a *cavatina*?　What is a *cabaletta*?　Where are these types represented in Rosina's aria *Una voce poco fa* from Rossini's *Il barbiere di Siviglia* (NAWM 120)?　How do they correspond to and help to convey what Rosina is saying and feeling?

8. What is the relationship in the first section (Andante) between the instrumental introduction and the vocal melody that follows?

   In the second section (Moderato)?

   Diagram the form of the whole aria, including indications of instrumental and vocal sections and the change of tempo.

9. What in this aria is characteristic of Rossini's style?　How does it compare to the operatic styles of Pergolesi (NAWM 87), Hasse (NAWM 88), Gluck (NAWM 91), and Mozart (NAWM 103)?

10. In this scene from *Norma* (NAWM 121), how does Bellini use the contrast of cavatina and cabaletta to convey Norma's inner conflict?

   What does he add to the scene, beyond these two sections of an aria, and how do these added elements heighten the conflict?

11. Chart the form of this scene, including indications for changes of tempo and performing forces.

12. Compare the melodic writing of Bellini's Andante section to that in the Andante section of Rossini's *Una voce poco fa* (NAWM 120). What differences and similarities do you see? What characteristics mark the styles of Rossini and Bellini in their slow arias?

13. Now compare both to the melodic writing in Chopin's Nocturne in E♭ Major (NAWM 112). What does Chopin's melodic style have in common with Rossini's? With Bellini's?

Giuseppe Verdi (HWM 633–38, NAWM 122)

14. In what ways was Verdi a nationalist composer? How was his name used as a nationalist emblem?

15. How did Verdi's basic approach to opera contrast with that of German and French composers?

16. Describe the three periods of Verdi's career and the main features of each.

Music to Study
> **NAWM 122:** Giuseppe Verdi, *Il trovatore* (The Troubadour), opera (1853),
> Part 4, Scene 1, No. 12: Scene, Aria, and *Miserere* (1853)
> CD 10.6–9 (Concise 3.67–68)   Cassette 10.A (Concise 3.B)

17. How does Verdi use various musical forces, textures, and types to further the drama in this scene from *Il trovatore* (NAWM 122)? How does this compare with the textures and types used in the excerpts from Rossini's *Il barbiere di Siviglia* (NAWM 120) and Bellini's *Norma* (NAWM 121)?

18. In the slow aria section of the scene, *D'amor sull'ali rosee*, how does Verdi's melodic style compare to that of the slow arias in the excerpts from Rossini and Bellini (NAWM 120–21, and see question 12 above)?

Germany (HWM 638–41, NAWM 123)

Music to Study
> **NAWM 123:** Carl Maria von Weber, *Der Freischütz* (The Free Shot), opera
> (1821), Act II, Finale (Wolf's Glen Scene)
> CD 10.10–20   Cassette 10.A

19. What are the distinguishing characteristics of German Romantic opera plots in the early 19th century? How are they exemplified in Weber's *Der Freischütz* as a whole and in the Wolf's Glen Scene (NAWM 123)?

20. What supernatural events occur in the Wolf's Glen Scene? For each one, how does Weber depict it in the music? How does he use tritones, diminished or augmented harmonies, orchestration, sudden dynamic change, or other effects to create a feeling of the supernatural or spooky? (Note: In examining the harmony, remember that the clarinets in A sound a minor third lower than written; the horns in D a minor seventh lower than written; and the trumpets in D a whole step higher than written.)

21. What is *melodrama*? How is it used in this scene? Why do you think it
    might be more effective here than recitative?

Richard Wagner and the Music Drama (HWM 641–48, NAWM 124)

22. Give the name (in English or German) and the date for Wagner's last three
    Romantic operas:

    _____   _____

    _____

    Give the name (in English or German) and the date for his seven music dramas
    and indicate by (R) which are part of his cycle *The Ring of the Nibelungs*:

    _____   _____

    _____   _____

    _____   _____

    _____

23. What is a *music drama*? How does a music drama such as *Tristan und Isolde*
    differ from a Romantic opera?

24. What does *Gesamtkunstwerk* mean? What is its importance for Wagner?

25. Who wrote the librettos for Wagner's operas and music dramas? _____

Music to Study
>**NAWM 124:** Richard Wagner, *Tristan und Isolde,* (1857–59), excerpt from
>>Act I, Scene 5
>>CD 10.21–29 (Concise 4.1–9) Cassette 10.B (Concise 4.A)

26. How do text, action, scenery, and music reinforce each other in this scene from *Tristan und Isolde* (NAWM 124)? How is this like, and how is it different from, the scene from Verdi's *Il trovatore* in NAWM 122?

27. In the section from m. 132 to 188, how do the singers' melodies relate to the melodies in the orchestra? Where does the musical continuity lie, with the singers or with the orchestra? How does this compare to the excerpts from operas by Rossini, Bellini, and Verdi in NAWM 120–22?

28. How do Wagner's vocal melodies here and throughout the scene compare to those of Rossini, Bellini, and Verdi in NAWM 120–22? Include observations on phrasing and overall shape as well as on vocal embellishment. What are the main characteristics of Wagner's vocal style?

29. What is a *Leitmotif*? Where do leitmotifs appear in this scene from *Tristan und Isolde,* and how are they used? (Note: Several appeared earlier, in the overture, and will recur in Acts II and III.)

30. How does the harmonic language used for the sailors (e.g., at mm. 196–203, *Hail! King Mark, hail!*) differ from that used for Tristan and Isolde after they have drunk the love potion? Why is this contrast appropriate, and how does it heighten the drama?

31. What aspects of Wagner's music were especially influential on later composers?

TERMS TO KNOW

grand opera
opéra comique
opéra bouffe
lyric opera
exoticism
realism
cavatina
cabaletta

coloratura
opera semiseria
Viva Verdi!
reminiscence motive
melodrama
music drama
Gesamtkunstwerk
leitmotif

NAMES TO KNOW

Names Related to French Opera

Eugène Scribe
Giacomo Meyerbeer
Les Huguenots
Charles Gounod
Faust

Georges Bizet
Carmen
Hector Berlioz
La Damnation de Faust
Les Troyens

Names Related to Italian Opera

Gioachino Rossini
The Barber of Seville
Gaetano Donizetti
Vincenzo Bellini
Norma

Giuseppe Verdi
Il trovatore
Aida
Otello
Falstaff

Names Related to German Opera

Carl Maria von Weber
Der Freischütz
Richard Wagner
The Flying Dutchman
Tannhäuser
Lohengrin
The Ring of the Nibelungs

Das Rheingold
Die Walküre
Siegfried
Götterdämmerung
Tristan und Isolde
Die Meistersinger von Nürnberg
Parsifal

REVIEW QUESTIONS

1. Add the composers and major works discussed in this chapter to the time-line you made for chapter 16.

2. What types of opera were written for production in Paris during the 19th century? Trace the emergence of the new types of opera, name a significant composer and opera for each type, and briefly describe what makes each type distinctive.

3. Describe the operas and operatic styles of Rossini, Bellini, and Verdi, noting the similarities and differences among them. Use examples from NAWM 120–22 to illustrate your points.

4. Trace the development of Verdi's operas through his three periods. What changed, and what remained constant, from *Nabucco* to *Falstaff*?

5. How does the German Romantic opera of Weber and early Wagner differ from Italian and French opera in the first half of the 19th century? Use examples from the works excerpted in NAWM or described in HWM to support your answer.

6. Describe the mature style of Wagner in his music dramas, using the scene from *Tristan und Isolde* in NAWM 124 as an example. At the end of your essay, explain the elements of this style that were particularly influential on later composers.

EUROPEAN MUSIC FROM THE 1870S TO WORLD WAR I

19

CHAPTER OBJECTIVES

After you complete the reading, study of the music, and study questions for this chapter, you should be able to:

1. name some of the most prominent European composers from the late 19th and early 20th centuries, characterize their styles, and describe some of their music;
2. describe the varieties of musical nationalism that were prominent at this time;
3. define and describe impressionism and related trends in music of this period.

CHAPTER OUTLINE

I. The German Tradition (HWM 654–65, NAWM 125–27)

A. Overview

The late 19th and early 20th centuries saw an increasing tendency for composers to develop a style so individual that it departed from the shared conventions of common-practice tonality. These new styles were sometimes hard for listeners to understand or accept. Wagner was a strong influence on many composers.

B. Hugo Wolf

Hugo Wolf (1860–1903) is best known for his 250 lieder, which brought to the art song Wagner's harmony and fusion of voice and instrument. Wolf sought an equality between words and music, choosing only excellent poets and writing collections of lieder on poems by a single poet or group as if to keep poet and composer on an equal basis. The musical continuity is often in the piano, while the voice has a speechlike arioso. **Music: NAWM 125**

C. Mahler

Gustav Mahler (1860–1911) made a career as a conductor, including serving as director of the Vienna Opera (1897–1907) and the New York Philharmonic (1907–11). He completed nine symphonies and five song cycles with orchestra.

D. Mahler's Symphonies

Mahler's symphonies are long and often programmatic. He uses a large orchestra but creates delicate effects with solo instruments and unusual combinations. Several symphonies are based in part on his songs, and four include voices, most notably the Second (*Resurrection*) and the Eighth, which is in two large choral movements. Mahler included a greater diversity of elements and styles than did earlier symphonists, seeking to suggest a world in all its variety. His music often suggests irony or parody. Several symphonies begin and end in different keys.

E. Mahler's Lieder with Orchestra

The orchestral song cycle *Kindertotenlieder* (Songs on the Death of Children, 1901–4) uses the large orchestra and chromatic harmony of Wagner in a spare, haunting style. *Das Lied von der Erde* (The Song of the Earth, 1908), on poems translated from Chinese, captures both ecstasy and dread in a very symphonic song cycle. Heir to the 19th-century symphony and the Viennese tradition, Mahler was a primary influence on Schoenberg, Berg, and Webern in the next generation. **Music: NAWM 126**

F. Richard Strauss

Richard Strauss (1864–1949) is renowned for his symphonic poems, most of them written before 1900, and operas, most from after 1900. Like Mahler, he also wrote lieder and was well known as a conductor.

G. Strauss's Symphonic Poems

Symphonic poems may have a philosophical program, like Strauss's *Death and Transfiguration* (1889) and *Also sprach Zarathustra* (So Spoke Zoroaster, 1896, after a poem by Nietzsche), or a descriptive tale, like his *Till Eulenspiegels lustige Streiche* (Till Eulenspiegel's Merry Pranks, 1895) and *Don Quixote* (1897). In each, the transformation of motives with extramusical connections helps to convey the plot, as in Wagner's music dramas. **Music: NAWM 127**

H. Operas

Strauss achieved new fame as an opera composer with *Salome* (1903–5), whose decadent subject he captured with heightened dissonance and contrast. *Elektra* (1908) uses even sharper, apparently unresolved dissonance contrasted with diatonic passages to tell the tragic story, along with leitmotifs and the association of certain keys with characters. *Der Rosenkavalier* (The Cavalier of the Rose, 1910) has a lighter setting and plot and is thus much less dissonant, while using the same Straussian techniques of leitmotifs, key association, and colorful orchestration. *Ariadne auf Naxos* (Ariadne at Naxos, 1912, rev. 1916) hearkens back to the sounds and conventions of the Classic era.

I. Humperdinck, Reger, and Pfitzner

Engelbert Humperdinck's opera *Hänsel und Gretel* (1893) combined Wagnerian leitmotifs with folklike melodies, while Hans Pfitzner's *Palestrina* (1917) used Wagner's approach to relate the legend of the *Pope Marcellus Mass*. *Max Reger* (1873–1916) combined Brahms's interest in form and counterpoint with Wagner's chromatic and modulatory harmony.

II. Nationalism (HWM 665–77, NAWM 128–29)

A. General

Nationalism in the 19th and early 20th centuries was an attempt to capture in music the character of one's own people, through the choice of patriotic subjects or topics drawn from national literature; the use of national, folk, or folklike melodies or rhythms; or setting texts in one's national language. It lay behind Wagner and Verdi's choice of subject matter and Brahms and Mahler's use of folk styles and poetry. Composers in Russia, eastern Europe, England, France, and the United States especially sought a national style.

B. Russia

Mikhail Glinka (1804–1857) was the first Russian composer to be recognized for a distinctively Russian style, notably in his operas *A Life for the Tsar* (1836) and *Ruslan and Lyudmila* (1842). Tchaikovsky was more a cosmopolitan than a nationalist, but chose Russian subjects for his operas. *The Mighty Handful* (or Mighty Five) was a group of five composers who sought a fresh Russian style. César Cui is the least well known today. *Mily Balakirev* (1837–1910) collected folksongs and used folk melodies in a romantic style. *Alexander Borodin* (1833–1887) was a chemist best known for symphonic works, quartets, and his opera *Prince Igor*; he seldom used folk tunes, but his lovely melodies have some of their flavor.

C. Musorgsky

Modest Musorgsky (1839–1881) was the most original of the Five, best known for the piano suite *Pictures at an Exhibition* (1874) and the opera *Boris Godunov* (premiered 1874). His vocal melodies follow Russian speech accents closely and imitate Russian folksongs, which move in a narrow range, repeat rhythmic motives, and are modal rather than tonal. Musorgsky's harmony is innovative and his music depicts physical gestures realistically. **Music: NAWM 128**

D. Rimsky-Korsakov

Nikolay Rimsky-Korsakov (1844–1908) was one of the Five but later developed a smoother, more correct idiom. He was less interested in nationalism than in exotic and fairy-tale subjects. His main works were symphonic poems and operas, which often rendered human characters in a diatonic, modal style and supernatural characters and events in a chromatic, fanciful style marked by *whole-tone* and *octatonic scales* (respectively, scales made up of all whole tones or whole and half steps in strict alternation). Rimsky-Korsakov taught Alexander Glazunov and Igor Stravinsky. *Sergei Rakhmaninov* (1873–1943), a virtuoso pianist, wrote passionate, melodious piano concertos and other works in a style that was Romantic and sometimes Russian but not deliberately nationalist.

E. Skryabin

Alexander Skryabin (1872–1915) wrote mostly for the piano, beginning in a style derived from Chopin and evolving to an individual style that was no longer tonal but used a complex chord or collection of notes as a reference point akin to a tonic chord. He sought a synthesis of the arts and intended his orchestral work *Prometheus* (1910) to be performed with changing colored lights. **Music: NAWM 129**

F. Central Europe
Bedrich Smetana (1824–1884) and Antonín Dvorák, the leading 19th-century Czech composers, are nationalist in choosing national subjects for program music and operas and in incorporating national dance rhythms and folklike tunes. *Leoš Janáček* (1854–1928) collected folk music and cultivated a style based on Czech speech and song; he is best known for operas, in addition to choral works, chamber music, and symphonic works.

G. Norway
Edvard Grieg (1843–1907) was a nationalist who incorporated Norwegian national traits particularly in his short piano pieces and vocal works.

H. Other Countries
Nationalist composers were also active in Poland, Denmark, and the Netherlands.

I. Finland
Finnish composer *Jean Sibelius* (1865–1957) drew programs and song texts from the literature of Finland, especially the national epic the *Kalevala*. He does not use or imitate folksongs. He is best known for orchestral program music, seven symphonies, and the Violin Concerto. Sibelius is most original in his themes, his treatment of form, and the way his themes grow, develop, and interact.

J. England
Edward Elgar (1857–1934) wrote in a style derived from Brahms and Wagner rather than from English folksong.

K. Spain
Spanish nationalism was sparked by the operas of *Felipe Pedrell* (1841–1922) and the piano music of *Isaac Albéniz* (1860–1909). The major Spanish composer of the early 20th century was *Manuel de Falla* (1876–1946), whose earlier works use rhythms and melodic turns of Spanish popular music and whose later works are more neo-Classic.

III. New Currents in France (HWM 677–86, NAWM 130–32)

A. General
The National Society for French Music, founded in 1871, gave performances of living French composers and revived French music of the 16th through 18th centuries, helping to strengthen an independent French musical tradition. Three traditions coexisted in French music after 1871: a cosmopolitan tradition around Franck and d'Indy, a French tradition around Saint-Saëns and Fauré, and a new style developed by Debussy.

B. The Cosmopolitan Tradition
César Franck and his student *Vincent d'Indy* (1851–1931) represent a cosmopolitan tradition in France influenced by Wagner and German counterpoint.

C. The French Tradition

French music from Couperin to Gounod is typified by emotional reserve, lyricism, economy, refinement, and interest in well-ordered form rather than self-expression. The works of *Camille Saint-Saëns* (1835–1921) and the operas of *Jules Massenet* (1842–1912) combine this tradition with Romantic touches. *Gabriel Fauré* (1845–1924) studied with Saint-Saëns, worked as an organist, helped to found the National Society for French Music, taught composition at the Paris Conservatoire, and became its director. He is esteemed in France for his refined songs, piano pieces, and chamber works marked by lyrical melodies, lack of virtuosic display, and harmony that does not drive toward a tonic resolution, but instead suggests repose. His students included Ravel and *Nadia Boulanger* (1887–1979), a famous teacher of composition. **Music: NAWM 130**

D. Debussy

Claude Debussy (1862–1918) exercised a major influence on 20th-century music. His style, called *impressionism* (a term he disliked) by analogy with the impressionist painters, suggested a mood or atmosphere rather than expressing the deep emotions of Romanticism. He absorbed influences from many composers, including Wagner, Musorgsky, and Liszt. Although his music usually has a tonal center, the harmony is often coloristic and the strong pull to resolution is missing, creating a sense of movement without direction and of pleasure without urgency. His most important music includes orchestral pieces, many songs and piano works, and the opera *Pelléas et Mélisande*. He was one of the most influential composers of the 20th century. **Music: NAWM 131**

E. Satie

Erik Satie (1865–1925) was an avant-garde iconoclast who changed his style but consistently opposed sentimentality. His early piano pieces challenged Romantic pretension through deliberate simplicity and a modal, nonfunctional harmony that paved the way for impressionism. His later piano works mocked impressionism with parodistic music, surreal titles, and satirical commentary printed in the score. *Socrate* (1920) for singers and chamber orchestra is strangely moving in its austere simplicity, stylistic monotony, and avoidance of emotion.

F. Ravel

Maurice Ravel (1875–1937) looked back to the 18th-century French tradition in *Le Tombeau de Couperin* (for piano 1917, orchestrated 1919) and other works. He preferred clear forms and more pungent harmonies than Debussy but also wrote several impressionist works, such as the ballet *Daphnis et Chloé* (1909–11). Some of his music, such as the famous *Boléro* (1928), uses Spanish idioms. **Music: NAWM 132**

G. Other French Composers

Other French composers of the early 20th century include Paul Dukas, Florent Schmitt, and Albert Roussel.

IV. Italian Opera (HWM 678–87)

One trend in Italian opera in the late 19th century is *verismo* (realism or naturalism), which sought a realistic depiction of everyday people in extreme dramatic situations. *Giacomo Puccini* (1858–1924) was an eclectic composer who combined realism and exoticism with intense emotion through a style focused on melody over spare accompaniment.

STUDY QUESTIONS

The German Tradition (HWM 654–65, NAWM 125–27)

1. What texts did Wolf choose for his songs, and what was his approach to the relationship of music and poetry?

Music to Study
NAWM 125: Hugo Wolf, *Kennst du das Land,* Lied (1888)
CD 10.30–37   Cassette 10.B

2. Diagram the form of Wolf's *Kennst du das Land* (NAWM 125).

3. Compare Wolf's vocal style in this song to that of Schubert's lieder (NAWM 115–16) and to that of Wagner's *Tristan und Isolde* (NAWM 124). What are the similarities and differences in each comparison? Which earlier composer does Wolf's style resemble most?

---

4. What is the relationship in Wolf's song between the voice and the piano? Which part carries the musical continuity?

5. How does the piano part in Wolf's song compare to the piano parts in Schubert's lieder? What aspects of Wagner's operatic style does it incorporate?

6. Describe the characteristics of Mahler's symphonies that distinguish them from other 19th-century symphonies. How are these characteristics exemplified in the Fourth Symphony, excerpted and discussed in HWM, pp. 656–58? How does he suggest a varied world in this work?

Music to Study

NAWM 126: Gustav Mahler, *Kindertotenlieder*, song cycle with orchestra
(1901–4), No. 1: *Nun will die Sonn' so hell aufgeh'n* (Now the sun
will rise again)
CD 10.38–39 (Concise 4.10–11)   Cassette 10.B (Concise 4.A)

NAWM 127: Richard Strauss, *Don Quixote*, symphonic poem (1897),
excerpts: Themes, and Variations 1 and 2
CD 10.40–45 (Concise 4.12–17)   Cassette 10.B (Concise 4.A)

7. Diagram the form of Mahler's *Nun will die Sonn' so hell aufgeh'n* (NAWM
126), using A for mm. 1–10, B for mm. 10–15, C for mm. 15–21, prime
signs (') for varied repetitions, and other letters for new material.

8. Mahler's setting highlights the irony in the poem. In the poem, the tragedy
that has befallen the speaker—the death of his child during the night—is
ignored by the sun, which rises as if nothing bad has happened. Mahler
heightens the irony by mismatching sad, lonely music to the bright, warm
images in the first line of the poem, and bright, warm music to the sadness
of the second line of the poem. Later repetition or reworking of these contrasting musical ideas is also ironic.

a. How is the effect of sadness and loneliness achieved in the music for the
first line? How does the contour of the vocal line negate the poetic image of
a rising sun?

b. How does the music of the second line suggest the rising sun and the
warming earth?

c. How does the varied repetition of this opening section in mm. 22–40 continue or expand upon the ironic setting of the first two lines of the poem?

d. How does the music in mm. 40–63 work against the apparently comforting message of the text?

e. What indication is there in the music at the end of the song that the protagonist utters the final line, "Blessed be the joyous light of the world," with irony rather than with sincerity?

9. How does Mahler use the orchestra in this song? How is it different from Wagner's use of the orchestra in the excerpt from *Tristan und Isolde* (NAWM 124)?

10. What two kinds of program did Richard Strauss use in his symphonic poems? Which does he use in *Don Quixote* (NAWM 127)?

11. How does Strauss depict Don Quixote? How does he depict Sancho Panza?

How are these themes treated and varied in the first two variations, given in NAWM 127?

12. What instrumental effects does Strauss use to suggest the bleating sheep and piping shepherds in the second variation? (Hint: The three strokes through the stems indicate tremolo on the strings or fluttertonguing on brass or wind instruments, a very rapid motion of the tongue that creates a blatty or buzzy sound; "mit Dämpfer" means "with a mute.")

13. Based on the descriptions of *Salome, Elektra, Der Rosenkavalier,* and *Ariadne auf Naxos* in HWM, pp. 663–64, what is distinctive about each of these operas?

Nationalism (HWM 665–77, NAWM 128–29)

14. What was the role of Glinka in the creation of a Russian national music?

15. What was *the Mighty Handful*? Who took part? What were their goals?

Music to Study

NAWM 128: Modest Musorgsky, *Bez solntsa* (Sunless), song cycle (1874), No. 3, *O konchen praedny* (The idle, noisy day is over)
CD 11.1–2 (Concise 4.18–19)   Cassette 11.A (Concise 4.A)

NAWM 129: Alexander Skryabin, *Vers la flamme* (Toward the flame), poem for piano, Op. 72 (1914)
CD 11.3–5   Cassette 11.A

16. What is unusual about the harmony in Musorgsky's song *O konchen praedny* (NAWM 128)? Describe some unusual progressions.

---

17. How does the vocal line in Musorgsky's song compare to that of the other 19th-century songs you have studied, by Schubert, Robert Schumann, Clara Schumann, and Hugo Wolf (NAWM 115–18 and 125)?

18. How does the vocal line in mm. 31–34 of Musorgsky's song show the influence of Russian folk melody (see HWM, pp. 668–69)? Are there folk influences elsewhere in the song, and if so, where?

19. What kinds of chords does Skryabin use in *Vers la flamme* (NAWM 129)?

20. *Vers la flamme* is not tonal in a traditional sense. How does Skryabin create a sense of tonal motion? What chord progressions (or root progressions) does he use most frequently?

21. What is the relationship between the opening passage of the piece and the closing passage (mm. 107–37) in terms of theme, rhythm, and harmony?

22. How does Skryabin establish the chord on the downbeat of m. 129 and its untransposed variants throughout the piece (that is, with *E* in the bass, *G♯* in the middle, and one or more of the notes *A♯ D, C♯ B*, and *F♯* in the chord) as a kind of tonic? Where else throughout the piece do untransposed versions of this chord appear?

23. Describe the rhythm of this piece. Does it suggest a strong forward motion, or a static hovering? How is the effect achieved?

24. Name nationalist composers active in Czech regions, Norway, Finland, and Spain in the late 19th and early 20th centuries and briefly describe what made their music nationalist.

New Currents in France (HWM 677–86, NAWM 130–32)

25. What was the National Society for French Music? When was it founded, what did it do, and what was its importance?

26. What are the three tendencies in French music in the late 19th and early 20th centuries? Describe the music of at least one composer associated with each.

Music to Study
> **NAWM 130:** Gabriel Fauré, *La bonne chanson* (The Good Song), Op. 61, song cycle (1891), excerpt: No. 6, *Avant que tu ne t'en ailles* (Before you depart)
> CD 11.6–10   Cassette 11.A
> **NAWM 131:** Claude Debussy, *Nocturnes,* tone poem suite (1899), No. 1: *Nuages* (Clouds)
> CD 11.11–16 (Concise 4.20–25)   Cassette 11.A (Concise 4.A)

27. What are the characteristics of Fauré's melodic and harmonic style, and how are they exemplified in this song (NAWM 130)?

28. How does Debussy use harmony in *Nuages* (NAWM 131) to create a sense of movement without direction, like clouds?

29. The motive in the English horn uses a fragment of an octatonic scale (alternating half and whole steps, here notated *C–B–A–G♯–F♯* and sounding a fifth below). It is never played by another instrument (while the English horn never plays anything else), it is never transposed, and it is changed only by omitting notes until all that remains is *B–A–F♯* (as notated). How does this treatment of a motive differ from motivic development as practiced in the 19th century? If motivic development suggests a drama or story, with the motives as characters, in what ways does Debussy's approach help to suggest a visual impression, rather than a plot?

30. How does the section at mm. 64–79 imitate a Javanese gamelan?

31. If the form is ABA', what is the relationship of the final A' (mm. 80–102) to the first A section (mm. 1–63)? What happened to the clouds?

32. How does Debussy use the orchestra? How does this reinforce the sense of a visual impression moving without direction, rather than a drama with conflict and resolution?

33. Briefly describe Satie's musical aesthetic and style.

Music to Study
    NAWM 132: Maurice Ravel, *Le Tombeau de Couperin,* suite (1917, orche-
        strated 1919), excerpt: Menuet
    CD 11.17–22   Cassette 11.A

34. Diagram the form of Ravel's minuet (NAWM 132), indicating the repetitions.

35. What does Ravel's minuet have in common with 18th-century music?

36.   Compare Ravel's minuet to Debussy's *Nuages* (NAWM 131). How are they similar? What is most different?

Italian Opera (HWM 678–87)

37. What is *verismo*? What are some notable examples of it?

TERMS TO KNOW

nationalism

whole-tone scale

octatonic scale

impressionism

verismo

NAMES TO KNOW

Names Related to the German Tradition

Hugo Wolf

Gustav Mahler

Kindertotenlieder

Das Lied von der Erde

Richard Strauss

Death and Transfiguration

Also sprach Zarathustra

Till Eulenspiegels lustige Streiche

Don Quixote

Salome

Elektra

Der Rosenkavalier

Ariadne auf Naxos

Hänsel und Gretel by Engelbert
  Humperdinck

Palestrina by Hans Pfitzner

Max Reger

Names Related to Nationalism in Eastern and Northern Europe and Spain

Mikhail Glinka

The Mighty Handful

Mily Balakirev

Alexander Borodin

Modest Musorgsky

Pictures at an Exhibition

Boris Godunov

Nikolay Rimsky-Korsakov

Sergei Rakhmaninov

Alexander Skryabin

Bedřich Smetana

Leoš Janáček

Edvard Grieg

Jean Sibelius

Edward Elgar

Felipe Pedrell

Isaac Albéniz

Manuel de Falla

Names Related to French and Italian Music

National Society for French
  Music

Vincent d'Indy

Camille Saint-Saëns

Jules Massenet

Gabriel Fauré

Nadia Boulanger

Claude Debussy

Nocturnes

Pelléas et Mélisande

Erik Satie

Socrate

Maurice Ravel

Le Tombeau de Couperin

Daphnis et Chloé

Bolero

Giacomo Puccini

REVIEW QUESTIONS

1. Add the composers and major works from the 19th century discussed in this chapter to the time-line you made for chapter 16. Make a new time-line for the entire 20th century, and place on it the 20th-century composers and major works discussed here. Leave plenty of space, as you will be adding to it in chapters 20–22.

2. How did Wolf, Mahler, and Strauss respond to the 19th-century German tradition from Beethoven through Wagner? What elements did they continue in their music, what aspects did they further intensify or develop, and what did they introduce that was new and individual?

3. What is nationalism, and how is it manifest in music of the 19th and early 20th centuries?

4. Beethoven's music conveys a sense of drama and forward motion toward a goal, as in the first movement of his *Eroica* Symphony (NAWM 106). Some of the music studied in this chapter conveys a different sense, of harmonic and rhythmic stasis, or of movement that is not directed toward a goal. Compare the works you have studied by Musorgsky, Skryabin, Fauré, and Debussy (NAWM 128–31) with Beethoven and with each other, seeking to show what musical techniques these later composers use to avoid tension, negate forward momentum, and create a musical experience of being present in the moment, rather than striving toward a goal.

5. For any of the following pairs of composers, compare and contrast their musical styles and aesthetics, showing what they have in common as composers from the same nation and what is individual about each: Mahler and Strauss; Musorgsky and Skryabin; Debussy and Ravel.

THE EUROPEAN MAINSTREAM IN THE TWENTIETH CENTURY

CHAPTER OBJECTIVES

After you complete the reading, study of the music, and study questions for this chapter, you should be able to:

1. identify some of the factors that have led to a greater diversity of style and technique in the 20th century than in any previous era;
2. name some of the most significant composers active after World War I in Hungary, the Soviet Union, England, Germany, and France and describe what makes their music individual;
3. describe the synthesis of folk and classical elements in the music of Bartók;
4. describe the music of Shostakovich and his circumstances under the Soviet regime;
5. summarize the careers and describe the musical styles of Hindemith and Stravinsky.

CHAPTER OUTLINE

I. Introduction (HWM 692–95)

After World War I, the division of the former Austro-Hungarian Empire, the rise of totalitarian regimes in Russia, Italy, Germany, and Spain, and a worldwide economic depression in the 1930s led to a greater cultural isolation between nations and thus a greater diversity in musical trends. Compositions without tonal centers or goal-directed harmony moved beyond common-practice tonality. Neo-Classical music evoked concepts, forms, and styles of the 18th century. Folk and traditional music from eastern Europe and Asia offered new possibilities in rhythm and pitch organization. Composers of film music and of *Gebrauchsmusik* (workaday music) for schools and amateurs sought a more accessible idiom. The Soviet and Nazi regimes controlled music in Russia and Germany and condemned most modern music. After World War II, many composers turned to aleatoric and serial music, which had little audience appeal; in reaction, the search for a more popular idiom led to new approaches after about 1970, such as minimalism and neo-Romanticism. Recordings, radio, and television created new audiences and furthered the spread of both popular music and art music around the world. The diversity of music in the 20th century is unprecedented, as composers sought individual solutions to the problem of how to write music for the permanent repertory of musical classics.

II. Ethnic Contexts (HWM 695–700, NAWM 133)

A. Collecting Ethnic Musics
New recording technologies aided the collection and study of the music of traditional peoples. Rather than changing this music to fit art music, as had been done in the 19th century, composers used folk elements to create new styles.

B. Bartók
Béla Bartók (1881–1945) collected and published folk tunes from his native Hungary, Romania, and elsewhere. Besides arranging folk tunes or incorporating them in his music, he synthesized a personal style that united folk and art music. He was also a pianist and a piano teacher, and his *Mikrokosmos* (1926–37) is a series of graded piano pieces that encapsulates his style. He worked in traditional forms, with a distinguished series of six string quartets, two violin concertos, a piano sonata and piano concerto, the Concerto for Orchestra (1943), and *Music for Strings, Percussion, and Celesta* (1936). From the Western tradition he took imitative and fugal techniques, sonata and other forms, and thematic development; from eastern Europe, modal and other scales, irregular meters, harmonic seconds and fourths, and certain kinds of melodic ornamentation; from both, the concepts of music with a tonal center, phrases, and motives that can be repeated and varied. He was also intrigued by symmetry, as in mirrors and retrogrades. **Music: NAWM 133**

C. Kodály
Zoltán Kodály (1882–1967) also collected Hungarian folk tunes and developed a strongly nationalist style. He was well known as a music educator.

III. The Soviet Orbit (HWM 701–5, NAWM 134–35)

A. Prokofiev
Sergey Prokofiev (1891–1953) left his native Russia after the 1917 Bolshevik Revolution, toured as a pianist, and composed on commission. He returned to the Soviet Union in 1934 and wrote some of his most popular music there, including the ballet *Romeo and Juliet* (1935–36) and *Peter and the Wolf* (1936) for narrator and orchestra. Soviet authorities demanded that composers adhere to the concept of *socialist realism* and attacked Prokofiev for *formalism.*

B. Shostakovich
Dmitri Shostakovich (1906–1985) was the most prominent composer to spend his entire career under the Soviet state, which both supported him and sought to control him. His opera *Lady Macbeth of Mtsensk* (1932) was an international success until it was condemned by the official newspaper *Pravda* in 1936. His popular Fifth Symphony was written in part to win back favor from the authorities. He is best known for his fifteen symphonies and eight string

quartets, some of which use his musical signature *D–Eb–C–B (D–Es–C–H* in German, for Dmitri SCHostakovich).   **Music: NAWM 135**

C. Post-Soviet Music
The relaxation of state control in the 1970s allowed younger composers to learn more about music in the West and to experiment with new ideas, and exchanges have intensified since the dissolution of the Soviet Union in 1991. *Alfred Schnittke* (b. 1934) often incorporates existing music or refers to Baroque and popular styles to produce music that is *polystylistic. Sofia Gubaidulina* (b. 1931) writes music with a spiritual dimension, often inspired by Christian themes. **Music: NAWM 134**

IV. England (HWM 705–10)

A. Vaughan Williams
Ralph Vaughan Williams (1872–1958), the leading English composer of the early 20th century, drew inspiration from English folksong, hymnody, and earlier English composers. (His first name is pronounced "Rafe," and his last name is Vaughan Williams, not Williams.) He wrote hymns, choral music for amateur singers, operas, and nine symphonies in a mixed tonal and modal style.

B. Holst and Walton
Gustav Holst (1874–1934) and *William Walton* (1902–1982) are also significant English composers.

C. Britten
Benjamin Britten (1913–1976), the most important English composer of the century, is known for his choral works, especially the *War Requiem* (1962), and his operas, inaugurated with *Peter Grimes* (1945). Marked by lyrical melodies often accompanied by drones or sustained chords and by mixtures of diatonic tonality with modal and chromatic effects, his music uses simple means to convey deep human emotions.

D. Tippett
Michael Tippett (b. 1905) has incorporated into his music elements of historical styles, African-American music, and Javanese gamelan music. Like the other English composers, Tippett frequently uses modal melodies in a diatonic setting.

V. Germany (HWM 710–15, NAWM 136)

A. The Nazi Regime
Nazi policies in the 1930s hindered modern music in Germany and led many musicians to leave.

B. Hindemith
Paul Hindemith (1895–1963) was important as a composer and as a teacher. His music from the 1920s is thoroughly modernist, but in the 1930s he began to compose *Gebrauchsmusik* in an accessible style and to give his art music a more Romantic quality. His best-known work is his symphony *Mathis der Maler*

(Matthias the Painter, 1934), drawn from his opera of the same name. Hindemith used a procedure he called *harmonic fluctuation,* in which phrases start with relative consonance, move toward greater dissonance, and return to consonance. **Music: NAWM 136**

C. Orff
Carl Orff (1895–1982) is best known for his choral work *Carmina burana* (1936) and for a method for teaching music to children in schools.

D. Weill
Kurt Weill (1900–1950) composed operas in Berlin on librettos by Bertolt Brecht, notably *The Rise and Fall of the City of Mahagonny* (1927–31) and the very successful *Die Dreigroschenoper* (The Threepenny Opera, 1928), adapted from John Gay's *The Beggar's Opera.* Brecht and Weill sought to promote a social ideology, and Weill used an easily understood musical language that parodied American popular music. After the Nazis rose to power in 1933, Weill emigrated to the United States and had a second career writing Broadway musical comedies.

VI. Latin America (HWM 716)

Major composers of Latin America include *Heitor Villa-Lobos* (1887–1959) of Brazil, *Carlos Chávez* (1899–1978) of Mexico, and *Alberto Ginastera* (1916–1983) of Argentina.

VII. Neo-Classicism in France (HWM 716–19)

A. Neo-Classicism
Composers in the first half of the 20th century frequently imitated styles, genres, and procedures from earlier periods. Music that referred directly to 18th-century models and deliberately avoided Romanticism was often called *neo-Classic.* (When the reference is to the early 18th century, some writers now prefer the term neo-Baroque, and neo-Renaissance and neo-medieval music was also written.)

B. Honegger
Arthur Honegger (1892–1955) is best known for *Pacific 231* (1923), an orchestral impression of a train, and for his opera-oratorio *King David* (1921).

C. Milhaud
Darius Milhaud (1892–1974) was extremely prolific in almost every genre. He absorbed a variety of influences, including earlier French composers, Brazilian music, ragtime, the blues, and jazz. He frequently used *polytonality,* in which two or more streams of music, each implying a different key, are superimposed.

D. Poulenc
Francis Poulenc (1899–1963) wrote in an engaging style influenced by French popular song and 18th-century French composers and, like them, light and witty more often than serious or ponderous.

VIII. Stravinsky (HWM 720–28, NAWM 137)

A. Career

Igor Stravinsky (1882–1971) took part in most major compositional trends during his lifetime. He made his reputation with three early ballets commissioned by Sergei Diaghilev for the Russian Ballet in Paris.

B. Early Works

All three ballets feature plots from Russian culture and use Russian folk melodies. *The Fire Bird* (1910) continues the exoticism and colorful orchestration of Rimsky-Korsakov, Stravinsky's teacher. Some of Stravinsky's distinctive stylistic traits emerge in the second ballet, *Petrushka* (1911), including octatonic and polytonal sonorities; ostinatos or repetitive melodies and rhythms over static harmony; blocks of sound that alternate without transitions; and independent layers of sound that are superimposed on one another. *Le Sacre du printemps* (The Rite of Spring, 1913) adds to this new orchestral effects; a greater level of dissonance (often octatonic or derived from superimposed triads); and rhythm that, through changing meters and unexpected accents and silences, negates regular meter and emphasizes instead the basic indivisible pulse, suggesting a musical *primitivism.* *Le Sacre* precipitated a riot at its premiere, but this apparently had more to do with the dance than with the music. All three ballets have since become Stravinsky's most popular works and among the most popular in the entire century. **Music: NAWM 137**

C. 1913–1923

Owing partly to the stringent wartime economy, Stravinsky's works during and just after World War I are for smaller ensembles.

D. Stravinsky's Neo-Classicism

From the 1920s to the opera *The Rake's Progress* (1951), Stravinsky adopted a neo-Classic approach that abandoned the Russian tunes and extramusical concerns of his earlier works and sought to create abstract, objective music based on historical models. This was inaugurated by his reworkings of 18th-century music by Pergolesi and others in the ballet *Pulcinella* (1919) and continued in a series of works that revived genres and alluded to (but never directly imitated) styles of previous eras from Machaut to Tchaikovsky. The most frequent target is the Classic era, as in the Symphony in C (1940, modeled after Haydn and Beethoven symphonies) and *The Rake's Progress* (modeled after Mozart operas). Despite Stravinsky's evocations of earlier styles, his music continued to show the personal characteristics listed above and exemplified in *Le Sacre du printemps.* In works of the 1950s and 1960s, he adapted the serial techniques of Schoenberg and Webern.

STUDY QUESTIONS

Introduction (HWM 692–95)

1. What were some of the factors leading to the diversity of style and procedure in the 20th century?

Ethnic Contexts (HWM 695–700, NAWM 133)

2. What were Bartók's activities in music, in addition to composing?

Music to Study

NAWM 133: Béla Bartók, *Music for Strings, Percussion, and Celesta,* suite (1936), third movement: Adagio
CD 11.23–28 (Concise 4.26–31) Cassette 11.A (Concise 4.A)

3. In the slow movement of *Music for Strings, Percussion, and Celesta* (NAWM 133) how does Bartók use mirrors, retrogrades, and palindromes? (A palindrome is its own retrograde, as in the palindrome about Napoleon, "Able was I ere I saw Elba.")

---

4. What elements of East European folk music are used in this movement?

5. This movement also uses techniques derived from Western art music, in addition to the use of traditional orchestral instruments and a complex arch form. Find instances of the following:

imitation _____

ostinato _____

inversion of melodic material _____

rhythmic diminution of material _____

stretto _____

canon _____

(Note also that the entire *Music for Strings, Percussion, and Celesta* uses cyclic recurrence of the fugue theme from the first movement. The four phrases of this theme occur in the third movement, in the original order and transposition but rhythmically altered, in mm. 18–19, 33–35, 60–64, and 73–74.)

6. How are pitch centers established in this movement? On what pitch does the movement close, and what is its opposite pole? How does this fit into the key scheme of the entire work? (Hint: See HWM, pp. 698–99.)

7. Bartók's synthesis of the folk and art music traditions creates something new within the realm of the orchestral repertory. List the ways in which this movement offers new sounds and ideas, in comparison with 19th-century symphonic music. (You may use NAWM 106, 108, 109, and 127 as points of comparison.)

The Soviet Orbit (HWM 701–5, NAWM 134–35)

8. As used by Soviet authorities, what is *socialist realism*? What is *formalism*? How did Prokofiev and Shostakovich attempt to conform to the demand for socialist realism?

Music to Study
> **NAWM 135:** Dmitri Shostakovich, *Lady Macbeth of Mtsensk,* opera (1932),
> Act IV, Scene 9, excerpt
> CD 11.33–37   Cassette 11.B

9. What characteristics of Shostakovich's *Lady Macbeth of Mtsensk* displeased
    the Soviet authorities? Once you translate the negative words of the *Pravda*
    article into neutral or positive ones, which of these traits, if any, appear in
    the excerpt in NAWM 135?

10. The *Pravda* critic accused Shostakovich of "naturalism." In what ways is
    the music in this excerpt from the final scene naturalistic? How does it
    capture the inflections and emotions of the characters?

11. Describe the main elements of Shostakovich's style in this excerpt. How does it compare to the operatic style of Wagner (see NAWM 124) and Verdi (see NAWM 122)? How does it differ from Bartók's style in *Music for Strings, Percussion, and Celesta* (NAWM 133), written around the same time?

12. What is characteristic of the music of Alfred Schnittke? Describe a typical example.

Music to Study
   NAWM 134: Sofia Gubaidulina, *Rejoice!* Sonata for violin and violoncello (1981), fifth movement, *Listen to the still small voice within*
   CD 11.29–32 (Concise 4.32–35)   Cassette 11.A (Concise 4.B)

13. What spiritual lesson does Gubaidulina seek to convey in this movement from *Rejoice!* (NAWM 134)? How is it conveyed in the music?

14. In what sense can this movement be said to have a tonal center? How is it established?

15. Measures 1–33 introduce a basic sequence of ideas, which is then varied and added to over the course of the movement. Chart the form of the violin part, using the following code, using the prime sign (') for variants, and introducing new letters as needed for new material. Start each repetition of the basic sequence on a new line.

Motive	A	B1	C1	B2	C2	B3	D	E
Measure	1	7	10	13	16	20	25	29

Motive	A
Measure	33

Motive	A
Measure	

Motive	A
Measure	

How does Gubaidulina use repetition, variation, and contrast in this movement? How is this like traditional 18th- and 19th-century procedures, and how is it different?

England (HWM 705–10)

16. Name three of the most significant English composers of this century and briefly describe their music. If their work is representative, how does English music contrast with that of Bartók (NAWM 133) in its relation to tonality and diatonicism?

Germany (HWM 710–15, NAWM 136)

17. Briefly summarize Hindemith's career.

Music to Study
> **NAWM 136:** Paul Hindemith, *Mathis der Maler* (Matthias the Painter), opera (1934–35), Sixth Scene, excerpt
> CD 11.38–42   Cassette 11.B

18. What is *harmonic fluctuation*? Describe how it works in the theme presented at mm. 198–213 of the sixth scene from Hindemith's *Mathis der Maler* (NAWM 136). Where do consonant chords occur? How do they help to delineate the phrases?

19. In mm. 320–29, Regina sings a chorale, *Es sungen drei Engel* (Three angels sang). How does the quotation of this chorale fit the dramatic moment, after Mathis has described a vision that he will paint as one panel of the Isenheim altarpiece?

    Where else in the excerpt in NAWM does this tune appear, in voices or instruments?

20. What other themes or motives appear prominently two or more times in the section from m. 198 to m. 418? (Indicate these by listing the measures in which they first appear and writing out the first several pitches.)

21. How does the orchestra relate to the voices in this section of the scene (mm. 198–418)? Which carries the main melodic material more often, the voices or the orchestra?

    How does Hindemith's practice in this respect compare to Wagner's (see NAWM 124) and to Verdi's (see NAWM 122)?

    How do orchestra and voices relate in the first section of the scene from *Mathis der Maler* (mm. 19–197)? How does this compare to Wagner and to Verdi?

22. What were Kurt Weill's "two careers"? What were his musical aims? Describe his musical style, and explain how it suited his aims and the types of music he composed.

Latin America (HWM 716)

23. Name three significant Latin American composers and their countries of origin.

_____ _____

_____ _____

_____ _____

Neo-Classicism in France (HWM 716–19)

24. If a work is *neo-Classic,* what are some characteristics one might expect to find in it?

25. Describe the music and musical style of Milhaud.

Stravinsky (HWM 720–28, NAWM 137)

Music to Study
   NAWM 137: Igor Stravinsky, *Le Sacre du printemps* (The Rite of Spring),
      ballet (1913), excerpt from Part I: *Danse des adolescentes* (Dance of
      the Adolescent Girls)
   CD 11.43–46 (Concise 4.36–39)   Cassette 11.B (Concise 4.B)

26. For each of the following characteristics of Stravinsky's style, find and de-
    scribe two or more passages in *Danse des adolescentes* from *Le Sacre du
    printemps* (NAWM 137) that offer examples of the characteristic.

    ostinatos

    repetitive melodies over static harmony

    blocks of sound that succeed each other without transitions

    independent layers of sound that are superimposed on one another

    unexpected accents or silences that negate regular meter and emphasize
    pulsation

    novel orchestral effects

    Note: Without a guide to orchestral markings, it may be hard to find the
    unusual orchestral effects Stravinsky calls for. Here are some of them:

• In m. 1 he indicates that the strings are to play each beat with a down-bow instead of bowing up and down; this will create a forceful, detached effect.

• "Con sord." in m. 18 means "with mute," which on the trumpet creates a thin, metallic sound.

• "Flttzg." on the chromatic scales in the winds in mm. 27–31 means fluttertonguing, which creates a sort of buzzy effect.

• The cellos in mm. 78–81 have a harmonic glissando, an effect Stravinsky invented; bowing the C string while moving the finger rapidly along it without touching the string to the fingerboard creates this effect by allowing only certain overtones to sound.

• "Col legno" at mm. 82ff. means to hit the string with the stick of the bow.

27. Within this essentially static texture of repeating figuration and almost constant pulsation, how does Stravinsky achieve variety?

28. How does Stravinsky create the effect of building intensity toward the end of the excerpt?

29. Summarize Stravinsky's career, including where he lived, his major compositions, and the main elements of his style in each period.

30. In what ways is Stravinsky's Symphony in C neo-Classic?

Which of the characteristics of Stravinsky's style listed above in question 26 are also true of the excerpt from the Symphony in C in Example 20.15 in HWM, p. 725?

31. In what ways is *Symphony of Psalms* neo-Classic and/or neo-Baroque?

Which of the characteristics of Stravinsky's style listed above in question 26 are also true of the excerpt from *Symphony of Psalms* in Example 20.17 in HWM, p. 728?

TERMS TO KNOW

Gebrauchsmusik   harmonic fluctuation
socialist realism   neo-Classic music
formalism   polytonality
D–S–C–H   primitivism
polystylistic music

NAMES TO KNOW

Names Related to Music in Eastern Europe and Russia

Béla Bartók   Sergey Prokofiev
Mikrokosmos   Dmitri Shostakovich
Music for Strings, Percussion,   *Lady Macbeth of Mtsensk*
  and Celesta   Alfred Schnittke
Zoltán Kodály   Sofia Gubaidulina

Names Related to Music in England and Germany

Ralph Vaughan Williams	*Mathis der Maler*
Gustav Holst	Carl Orff
William Walton	Kurt Weill
Benjamin Britten	*The Rise and Fall of the City of*
War Requiem	*Mahagonny*
Peter Grimes	*Die Dreigroschenoper* (The
Michael Tippett	Threepenny Opera)
Paul Hindemith	

Names Related to Music in Latin America and France

Heitor Villa-Lobos	*The Fire Bird*
Carlos Chávez	*Petrushka*
Alberto Ginastera	*Le Sacre du printemps* (The Rite
Arthur Honegger	of Spring)
Darius Milhaud	*Pulcinella*
Francis Poulenc	Symphony in C
Igor Stravinsky	*The Rake's Progress*

REVIEW QUESTIONS

1. Add the composers and major works discussed in this chapter to the 20th-century time-line you made for chapter 19.

2. Write an essay in which you summarize the major trends in European music between about 1915 and 1950 (excepting the atonal and twelve-tone music of Schoenberg and his associates, treated in chapter 21).

3. How does Bartók achieve an individual style within the Western art music tradition by integrating traditional procedures with elements abstracted from East European folk music? Describe how this synthesis works in *Music for Strings, Percussion, and Celesta*.

4. Compare the music of Shostakovich and Gubaidulina, using the excerpts in NAWM 134–35 as examples. What was each trying to achieve in these works, and what musical procedures or traditions did each find useful in achieving these aims? What did Soviet authorities ask of composers in the Soviet Union, and how did Shostakovich and Gubaidulina relate to the Soviet state?

5. Describe the musical style of Hindemith, using *Mathis der Maler* (NAWM 136) as an example. How does it compare to the styles of Beethoven, Brahms, Wagner, and Bartók (NAWM 106–7, 114, 124, and 133)?

6. Trace the career of Igor Stravinsky, naming major pieces and describing the changes in his style. What distinctive characteristics of his music, established in *Petrushka* and *The Rite of Spring,* continued throughout his career, and how are these traits embodied in his neo-Classical music?

ATONALITY, SERIALISM, AND RECENT DEVELOPMENTS IN TWENTIETH-CENTURY EUROPE

21

CHAPTER OBJECTIVES

After you complete the reading, study of the music, and study questions for this chapter, you should be able to:

1. describe the music and innovations of Schoenberg, Berg, and Webern;
2. describe in simple terms how twelve-tone music works and analyze brief passages;
3. describe the musical style of Messiaen and some of his characteristic devices; and
4. define expressionism, total serialism, electronic music, musique concrète, and indeterminacy, and name and describe at least one work representing each trend.

CHAPTER OUTLINE

I. Schoenberg and His Followers (HWM 732–44, NAWM 138–41)

A. Schoenberg's Development

Arnold Schoenberg (1874–1951) began as a late-Romantic composer writing in a style derived from Wagner, Mahler, and Strauss. Around 1905, he turned to smaller forms and a more concentrated language with complex rhythms and counterpoint and angular melodies.

B. Atonality

In about 1908, Schoenberg began to write music that was *atonal,* meaning that it avoided any sense of a tonal center (whether through traditional tonal harmony or any new way of establishing a central pitch). This extended the tendency among late-Romantic German composers to obscure the key through chromaticism and extensive modulation. Instead of treating each pitch and chord in terms of its function within a key and requiring dissonant notes and chords to resolve, all notes were equal and all sonorities possible; Schoenberg called this *"the emancipation of the dissonance,"* since dissonance was freed of its need to resolve to consonance. *Pierrot lunaire* (Moonstruck Pierrot), Op. 21 (1912), for female voice and chamber ensemble, is his best-known atonal piece. In addition to atonality, it uses *Sprechstimme* (speech-voice or speech-song) and creates unity through a variety of motivic devices.   **Music: NAWM 138**

C. Expressionism
Pierrot lunaire is an example of *expressionism,* which portrayed extreme inner feelings such as anxiety, fear, and despair through extreme musical means.

D. Twelve-Tone Method
Seeking a way to compose unified longer works without a tonal center and without depending on a text, Schoenberg by 1923 had devised the *twelve-tone method.* (This systematized two traits of his atonal style: accompanying melodic motives with harmonies derived from the same group of notes [often transposed or inverted], and using all twelve chromatic notes in almost every phrase or unit.) The twelve chromatic notes are ordered in a *series* or *row.* Tones from the series (or from a contiguous subset of the series, such as the first three or four notes) may be sounded in succession as a melody or simultaneously as a chord, in any octave and rhythm. (The order of notes in the row is not arbitrary, but is based on the motives and chords the composer plans to use in the piece, which are embedded in the row.) The series may be used in its original (*prime*) form, in *inversion* (upside down), in *retrograde* (backward), in *retrograde inversion* (upside down and backward), or in any *transposition* of these four forms. Each statement of a row includes all twelve notes, but different statements can appear simultaneously. Schoenberg first used twelve-tone methods in the last of five piano pieces, Op. 23 (1923), and the Piano Suite, Op. 25 (1921–23). He wrote many twelve-tone works in standard forms, including the Wind Quintet, Third and Fourth String Quartets, *Variations for Orchestra,* Violin Concerto, Piano Concerto, String Trio, and Fantasy for Violin and Piano.   **Music: NAWM 139**

E. *Moses und Aron*
In Schoenberg's unfinished twelve-tone opera *Moses und Aron* (1930–32), Moses speaks in Sprechstimme to symbolize his inability to communicate his vision of God.

F. Alban Berg
Alban Berg (1885–1935) was Schoenberg's student and used many of his techniques. Berg's expressionist opera *Wozzeck* (1917–21) is atonal (*not* twelve-tone) but looks back to earlier music in several ways: by using leitmotifs and continuous music, as did Wagner; by imitating in atonal style the rhythms and sounds of folk tunes, dances, marches, and other familiar musical types; and by casting each scene as a traditional form, such as suite, passacaglia, sonata, or rondo. In the opera *Lulu* (1928–35) and the Violin Concerto (1935), Berg used the twelve-tone method in a way that allowed him to introduce elements of tonal music, such as triads and quoted melodies. (The use of tonal effects and familiar types of music helped him to convey strong emotions in a language listeners could understand.)   **Music: NAWM 140**

G. Anton Webern

Anton Webern (1883–1945) also studied with Schoenberg and adopted his atonal and twelve-tone methods. But Webern's works are usually brief, extremely spare, often canonic, and without tonal references. He conceived of melodies that change tone color as well as pitch, so that a single line may pass from one instrument to others in turn. The effect of Webern's very spare texture is often one of individual points of sound, called *pointillism.* **Music: NAWM 141**

II. After Webern (HWM 744–48, NAWM 141)

A. The Spread of Twelve-Tone Methods

After World War II, several younger composers (as well as Stravinsky) took up the twelve-tone system, usually looking to Webern as a model.

B. Serialism

By 1950, composers at the *Darmstadt* summer courses and elsewhere began to apply the serial procedures of twelve-tone music to aspects other than pitch, such as duration and dynamics, resulting in *total serialism.* Such works can seem random, since pitch, rhythm, and other parameters are not being used to define and develop themes or to establish goals and create momentum, but instead produce a succession of unique and unpredictable events. *Pierre Boulez* (b. 1925), the most important European exponent of total serialism, moved beyond it to a more flexible but still pointillistic language in works such as *Le Marteau sans maître* (The Hammer without a Master, 1954).

C. Messiaen

Olivier Messiaen (1908–1992) was an organist, composer, and teacher (Boulez was his student). His music often has religious subjects, as in the *Quatuor pour la fin du temps* (Quartet for the End of Time, 1940–41), on the Apocalypse. He devised his own musical system, incorporating transcribed birdsongs, repeated rhythmic series (related to medieval isorhythm and music theory of India), *non-retrogradable rhythms* (durational patterns that are the same forward and backward), avoidance of regular meter, whole-tone and octatonic scales, and other devices designed to create music that suggests mystical contemplation rather than dramatic action or emotional expressivity. **Music: NAWM 142**

III. Recent Developments (HWM 748–57)

A. New Timbres

Composers after 1945 continued to introduce new sounds into music, as composers had done in the first half of the century.

B. Electronic Resources

Electronic music introduced new sonic resources through electronically generated sound. *Musique concrète* used recorded natural sounds that were manipulated through tape and electronic procedures. Both depended on the invention of tape recorders. Unlike music for live performers, music on tape allowed composers total control and an unlimited range of sounds.

C. New Technology

Technology developed quickly, from oscillators, to *synthesizers,* to computers and digital encoding of music. Since the invention of portable synthesizers, and especially since the rise of portable computers and the MIDI interface, it has become possible to create electronic music in real time, rather than solely on tape.

D. Influence of Electronic Music

Electronic music in turn suggested new sounds for traditional instruments and voices and a renewed interest in the spatial effects of locating performers in different places around a performing space. Edgard Varèse's *Poème électronique* was a tape piece created for the 1958 World's Fair in Brussels; played from 425 loudspeakers throughout the Philips Pavilion while colored lights and slides were projected against the walls, it gave a sense of sounds moving through space.

E. The Pitch Continuum

Partly influenced by electronic music, composers increasingly used the entire continuum of pitch, rather than only the discrete pitches of the chromatic scale. *Threnody for the Victims of Hiroshima* for string orchestra (1960) by *Krzysztof Penderecki* (b. 1933) uses traditional instruments to make electronic-sounding sounds through such means as glissandos, extremely high notes, and bands of pitch within which every quarter-tone is played simultaneously, and he created new notation for each of these novel effects. Penderecki's more recent music is written in standard notation and is more Romantic in style. *György Ligeti* (b. 1923) also used quasi-electronic sounds in such works as *Atmosphères* for orchestra (1961). Ligeti's work, like Penderecki's, has been stylistically diverse.

F. Indeterminacy

Throughout the history of notated music, performers have made choices or filled in what is not specified in the notation. Some 20th-century composers tried to exercise greater control over performance through very specific indications in the score. But composers have also explored *indeterminacy,* in which certain aspects of the music, such as the order of events or the precise coordination of parts, are not determined by the composer. *Karlheinz Stockhausen* (b. 1928) has used this in *Klavierstück XI* (Piano Piece No. 11, 1956) and other works. Several of his works use fragments of existing music. *Witold Lutosławski* (1913–1994) used indeterminacy to allow individual players to play at varying speeds or create a cadenza-like elaboration on a figure within controlled boundaries. New notations have evolved for these new playing techniques.

STUDY QUESTIONS

Schoenberg and His Followers (HWM 732–44, NAWM 138–41)

1. What was Schoenberg's early music like, and which composers most influenced it?

2. What is *atonal* music? What did Schoenberg mean by *"the emancipation of the dissonance"*?

Music to Study
> **NAWM 138:** Arnold Schoenberg, *Pierrot lunaire,* song cycle for female speech-song voice and chamber ensemble (1912), excerpts
> 138a: No. 8, *Nacht* (Night)
>   CD 11.47–48   Cassette 11.B
> 138b: No. 13, *Enthauptung* (Decapitation)
>   CD 11.49–52   Cassette 11.B

3. What is *Sprechstimme*? How is it notated, and how is it performed?

How is Sprechstimme used in the two numbers from *Pierrot lunaire* in NAWM 138? Where is it *not* used by the voice?

---

4. The first three-note sonority of *Nacht* (NAWM 138a) is *E♭-G-B♭*, an E♭-major chord (end of m. 1). If this is the case, what makes this movement atonal? That is, why is it not considered to be in a key?

5. In *Nacht* (NAWM 138a), how is the three-note motive *E–G–E♭* (presented in the piano in m. 1 and treated in imitation in all three instruments in mm. 4–7) used during the course of the piece? Where does it appear in original, transposed, or otherwise adapted form? Where does it *not* appear in some form?

6. In addition to this unifying motive, how else do *Nacht* and *Enthauptung* create a sense of unity and form, without tonality?

7. What musical gestures does Schoenberg use to express or illustrate the text in these two songs?

8. What is *expressionism*? What characteristics of these two songs mark them as expressionist works?

Music to Study

NAWM 139: Arnold Schoenberg, *Variations for Orchestra,* Op. 31 (1926–28), excerpts

139a: Theme

CD 11.53 (Concise 4.40)   Cassette 11.B (Concise 4.B)

139b: Variation VI

CD 11.54 (Concise 4.41)   Cassette 11.B (Concise 4.B)

(Note: This score is written at sounding pitch. Transposing instruments like the clarinet and horn are written here as they *sound,* and not according to the formerly standard practice of writing them in the score as they are notated for the player. In this score, **H** stands for "Hauptstimme," or principal voice, and **N** for "Nebenstimme," or countermelody.)

9. As shown in Example 21.1 in HWM, p. 737, the first half of the theme of Schoenberg's *Variations for Orchestra* (NAWM 139a) presents the row in the cello, in two forms: the untransposed prime form (P–0, meaning prime transposed up zero semitones), segmented into groups of five, four, and three notes; and the retrograde inversion transposed up nine semitones (RI–9), with the same groupings (presented backward, since it is a retrograde). These are accompanied by chords drawn from related forms of the row, using the same groupings of five, four, and three notes. (The rows are related because I–9, the inversion transposed up nine semitones, has as its first six notes the same notes, in a different order, as the last six notes of P–0, and vice versa. This means I–9 can accompany P–0 without duplicating notes; that is, a chord does not share any notes with the segment of melody that it accompanies. It was Schoenberg's standard practice to use rows that were related in this way. The same relationship holds between R–0 and RI–9.)

   With the first half of the theme as an example of Schoenberg's procedures, the following questions will help you figure out what happens in the second half of the theme (mm. 46–57).

   a. Before we begin, what does the harp do in the first half of the theme (mm. 34–45)? Where do its notes come from? (Hint: See the reduction in Example 21.1.)

   b. Now, what form of the row appears in the cello in mm. 46–50? _____
   (Hint: See the row forms in Example 21.1.)

   c. How is this statement of the row divided into groups?

   d. What form of the row is used for the accompanying chords? _____
   (Hint: Look at the three-note chord in m. 46. Which form of the row begins with those three notes, in some order?)

   e. How is this accompanying statement of the row divided into groups?

   f. Measures 46–47 include all twelve tones of the chromatic scale, half in the melody, and the other half in the accompaniment. How is this possible?

g. What form of the row appears in Violin I (marked "I. Gg"—for Geige—in the score) in mm. 51–57? How is it divided into groups?

h. What form of the row appears in the accompanying chords in the winds? How are the groupings in this statement of the row obscured?

i. A new transposition of the prime form of the row appears in the cello in mm. 52–57. By how many semitones up is it transposed, in comparison to P–0? If P–0 is the prime form transposed up zero semitones, what would you call this form of the row?

number of semitones by which it is transposed up: _____ name: _____

There, that wasn't so hard, was it? The point of Schoenberg's twelve-tone music is neither to be the musical equivalent of crossword puzzles nor to create completely arbitrary music, but to create logical, unified music based on motives that are developed and accompanied by harmonies derived from them. In that respect, twelve-tone pieces continue the 19th-century tradition of thematic development.

10. At the beginning of Variation VI (NAWM 139b), Schoenberg cleverly derives two new melodic ideas, a clarinet theme and its countermelody in other wind instruments, from alternating notes in a transposition of the inverted form of the row:

I–3:	D♭	G	F	A♭	F♯	D	A	B♭	E	E♭	C	B

Clarinet I:	D♭		F		F♯	A			E	E♭		
Flute I, English, Horn and Bassoon I		G		A♭		D		B♭			C	B

How are these melodic ideas treated in the rest of the variation?

11. In what sense is Variation VI a variation of the theme? What stays the same, and what is changed?

12. In what ways is Berg's *Wozzeck* similar to a Wagnerian opera? How does it use forms adapted from instrumental music?

Music to Study
   NAWM 140: Alban Berg, *Wozzeck,* opera (1917–21), Act III, Scene 3
      CD 11.55–57 (Concise 4.42–44)   Cassette 11.B (Concise 4.B)

13. What characteristics of Act III, Scene 3, from Berg's *Wozzeck* (NAWM 140) mark it as an expressionist work?

14. Berg called this scene "Invention on a Rhythm." The rhythmic idea is presented in the right hand of the piano at the beginning of the scene (mm. 122–25) and immediately repeated. Wozzeck then states it in augmentation and with a new melody (mm. 130–36). (Notice that the attacks are in the same rhythm, even though one note is sustained through what was originally a rest.) List below the appearances of this rhythm in mm. 138–54, by the measure in which each statement begins and the instrument(s) or voice that carries it.

Measure Instrument(s) or Voice   Measure Instrument(s) or Voice

1._____ _____   6._____ _____

2._____ _____   7._____ _____

3._____ _____   8._____ _____

4._____ _____   9._____ _____

5._____ _____   10._____ _____

How does the constant reiteration of this rhythm convey the dramatic situation?

15. Where does Berg imitate a polka? A folksong? How does he suggest these types of tonal music, despite using an atonal language?

16. Where do major and minor triads occur in the series for Berg's twelve-tone Violin Concerto (shown in Example 21.4 in HWM, p. 741)?

Music to Study

  NAWM 141: Anton Webern, Symphony, Op. 21, for nine solo instruments
    (1928), first movement
   CD 12.1–5   Cassette 12.A

(Note: This score is written at sounding pitch.)

17. Which characteristics of Webern's style, as described in HWM, pp. 741–42, are evident in the first movement of his Symphony (NAWM 141)?

18. What is *pointillism*? In what way is this movement pointillistic?

19. The opening section of this movement is a double canon. The leading voice of the first canon begins in horn 2, passes to the clarinet, and continues in the cello (see Example 21.5 in HWM, p. 743). The canonic answer is in inversion and begins in horn 1. In what instruments does the answer continue?

20. Looking through the exposition of this movement (mm. 1–25a), find all occurrences of the note *A*. In what octave(s) do they appear? On the grand staff below, write *A* in all the octaves in which it occurs in the exposition.

Next, do the same for *E♭/D♯*, writing those that occur in the treble clef to the left of the *A*(s), and those that occur in the bass clef to the right.

Now, do the same for *D, G, C, F,* and *B♭*, writing them as a chord vertically aligned with the *E♭* (s) in the treble clef.

Finally, do the same for *E, B, F♯, C♯,* and *G♯/A♭*, writing them as a chord vertically aligned with the *E♭*(s) in the bass clef. (Note: Harp harmonics, marked with a little circle above or below the note, sound an octave higher than written, and the viola harmonic in m. 19 sounds on *E* a tenth above middle *C*.)

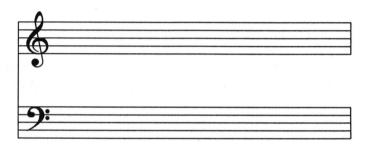

What do you discover? If all the notes played during the exposition sounded simultaneously, what would you have?

The collection of pitches you have discovered is symmetrical, in the sense that it can be inverted around a central pitch and the result will be precisely the same set of pitches, in precisely the same octaves.

What is that central pitch? _____

Where in the movement does it first appear? _____

21. From the listener's perspective, what is the effect of this type of harmonic structure?

After Webern (HWM 744–48, NAWM 141)

22. Which composer was the most influential on postwar twelve-tone composers?

23. What is the importance of Darmstadt for postwar composition?

24. What is *total serialism*?

Name a composer and a work influenced by total serialism.

Music to Study
> **NAWM 142:** Olivier Messiaen, *Quatuor pour la fin du temps* (Quartet for the End of Time) for violin, clarinet, cello, and piano (1940–41), first movement: *Liturgie de cristal* (Crystal Liturgy)
> CD 12.6 (Concise 4.45)   Cassette 12.A (Concise 4.B)

25. Messiaen's *Liturgie de cristal* (NAWM 142) features four mutually independent layers. The flute and clarinet lines are each based on birdsongs, but songs of different birds.

    According to NAWM, what bird's song is imitated in the clarinet? _____

    What bird's song is imitated in the flute? _____

    How is the opening material in each instrument treated in the rest of the movement?

    flute:

    clarinet:

26. The cello has a pitch series, analogous to the *color* of a 14th-century isorhythmic motet, and a durational series, analogous to the motet's *talea*. The entire cello line is in harmonics, which sound two octaves higher than the black note. (The notation tells the player to play the black note while touching the string at a spot a fourth higher, which creates the harmonic.)

    What is the pitch series? _____

    What mode or scale does this set of pitches belong to or suggest? _____

    How many times does it appear in the movement? _____

27. The durational series is given in Examples 21.6c and 21.6d in HWM, p. 747, in a form that shows it is a *non-retrogradable rhythm.* Such rhythms are the same forward as backward, which gives them a timeless quality Messiaen relished as a symbol of the eternal. In the piece, the last three durations always overlap the first three of the next statement of the series. Another way to think of this is that the series is actually one of 15 durations (rather than 18), and it becomes non-retrogradable when repeated again and again.

How does the durational series coordinate with the pitch series?

How many times does the durational series appear in the movement? _____

28. The piano also has a durational series and a pitch series, here a series of chords.

How many chords arc in the chord series? _____

How many times does the chord series appear in the movement? _____

How many durations are in the durational series? [Note: In an early printing of HWM, Examples 21.6a and b lack the final duration in the series, a half note (following the single quarter).] How does the durational series coordinate with the pitch series?

How many times does the durational series appear in the movement? _____

29. How are these four layers of music coordinated with each other?

30. What is the effect on the listener of this combination of bird calls, pitch series, and durational series? Is there a sense of a regular meter? Is there momentum toward a goal?

Recent Developments (HWM 748–57)

31. What have been some important developments in electronic and tape music since 1945?

32. What effects has electronic music had on music for traditional instruments and voices? Name two works that have been influenced by electronic sounds.

33. What is *indeterminacy*? How has it been used in composition? Name two European composers who have used it, and describe a piece by each.

TERMS TO KNOW

atonal music, atonality
"the emancipation of the dissonance "
Sprechstimme
expressionism
twelve-tone method
series, row
prime, inversion, retrograde,
    retrograde inversion

pointillism
total serialism
non-retrogradable rhythm
electronic music
musique concrète
synthesizer
indeterminacy

NAMES TO KNOW

Arnold Schoenberg
Pierrot lunaire
Moses und Aron
Alban Berg
Wozzeck
Lulu
Anton Webern
Darmstadt
Pierre Boulez
Le Marteau sans maître

Olivier Messiaen
Quatuor pour la fin du temps
Krzysztof Penderecki
*Threnody for the Victims of
    Hiroshima*
György Ligeti
Atmosphères
Karlheinz Stockhausen
Witold Lutosławski

REVIEW QUESTIONS

1. Add the composers and major works discussed in this chapter to the 20th-century time-line you made for chapter 19.

2. Compare the atonal music of Schoenberg's *Pierrot lunaire* (NAWM 138) to the music you know by Wagner, Wolf, Mahler, and Strauss (NAWM 124–27). How does Schoenberg continue the late-Romantic German tradition, and what does he introduce that is new?

3. How does Schoenberg's twelve-tone music, as exemplified in the *Variations for Orchestra* (NAWM 139), continue and extend 19th-century procedures?

4. How does Berg's music resemble that of Schoenberg, and how does it differ? How does it compare to the music you know by Wagner, Mahler, and Strauss?

5. How does Webern's twelve-tone music differ from that of Schoenberg?

6. List the predominant characteristics of Messiaen's style and explain how they are exemplified in *Liturgie de cristal* (NAWM 142).

7. What are some of the trends in European art music since 1945? Describe an example of each trend.

THE AMERICAN
TWENTIETH CENTURY

CHAPTER OBJECTIVES

After you complete the reading, study of the music, and study questions for this chapter, you should be able to:

1. summarize the historical background for art music in the United States;
2. outline the history of vernacular music in the United States from ragtime to rock; and
3. name the most significant composers of and trends in art music in the United States during the 20th century, explain what is individual about each one, and describe pieces by some of the major composers of the century.

CHAPTER OUTLINE

I. Introduction (HWM 759–60)

The United States became the center for new music in the classical tradition after World War II. American music grew out of the European tradition, as European composers emigrated to the United States, or lived there for a period, and many Americans studied with Nadia Boulanger in Paris or with other European teachers at summer festivals. But American music also drew from its many ethnic and popular traditions.

II. The Historical Background (HWM 760–65)

A. Music in the Colonies

The colonists in New England sang psalms, and singing schools were established in the 18th century to teach singing from notation. *William Billings* (1746–1800) is the best known of the *Yankee tunesmiths,* who wrote psalm and hymn settings and anthems. Most of his hymns were simple harmonizations, but many were *fuging tunes,* which include a middle section in imitation or free polyphony with staggered entrances. Billings did not follow the rules of "correct" counterpoint, but allowed parallel octaves and fifths and often used chords without thirds.

B. German Immigration

German-speaking immigrants brought their musical culture. The Moravians, Protestants from Czech and Slovak regions, encouraged music in church, including arias, motets, and anthems. Bohemian-born *Anthony Philip Heinrich*

(1781–1861) wrote program symphonies and became perhaps the first American composer with an international reputation. German immigrants were prominent as music teachers, conductors, and performers, and American composers often studied in Germany. *Lowell Mason* (1792–1872), trained by a German immigrant, introduced music into the public school curriculum and sought to replace the music of the Yankee tunesmiths with hymns harmonized in the "correct" European style; many of his hymns are still sung today. The Yankee tunes remained in use in the *shape-note hymnals* in the South. The folk tradition of slave *spirituals* was popularized after the Civil War by the *Fisk Jubilee Singers.*

C. Brass and Wind Bands

In the 19th century, almost every town and city had an amateur *wind* or *brass band,* and in the 20th century almost every high school and college had one. The 19th-century repertory included marches, dances, song arrangements, and solo display pieces. *John Philip Sousa* (1854–1932), leader of the U.S. Marine Band and later his own touring band, wrote more than 100 marches. Brass bands and dance orchestras played an important role in African-American social life and provided training for black musicians.

III. Vernacular Music (HWM 765–71)

A. Ragtime

Ragtime developed from a joining of the march with elements of African music. A typical *rag,* such as *Maple Leaf Rag* (1899) by *Scott Joplin* (1868–1917), used march form in duple meter and presented a syncopated melody over a steady bass.

B. Blues

Black laments evolved in the early 20th century into a style called *blues,* featuring a text in rhymed couplets, the first line repeated; a standard 12-bar harmonic framework; *blue notes,* lowering the third, fifth, or seventh degree of the major scale; and improvised "breaks" between lines.

C. Jazz

Jazz is a form of group or solo improvisation over a blues or popular tune. The basic procedures, from uneven rhythms and anticipated beats to trading solos, were developed by black musicians and imitated by white bands as early as 1915. A leading band was *King Oliver's Creole Jazz Band,* which used the typical instrumentation of cornet, clarinet, trombone, piano, banjo, and drums.

D. Big Bands

The popularity of jazz brought larger performing spaces, leading to the *big bands* of *Duke Ellington* (1899–1974) and others, which had trumpets, trombones, saxophones, and clarinets in sections and a *rhythm section* of string bass, piano, guitar, and drums. Big bands performed from an arrangement or *chart,* which still provided some opportunities for improvised solos. This style is also called *swing,* from the swinging uneven rhythms.

E. Modern Jazz

Bebop (or *bop*) of the 1940s and 1950s used smaller groups, more improvisation, and new techniques, some borrowed from modern classical music, to create a serious art music in the jazz tradition.

F. Country Music

Country-and-western or *country music* blended traditional music of the Appalachian and Ozark Mountain regions, derived from Anglo-American ballads and fiddle tunes, with cowboy music of the West and some elements of jazz and other African-American styles. Singers often accompanied themselves on guitar or were backed by a band of violins, guitars, and rhythm section.

G. Rhythm-and-Blues

Rhythm-and-blues was a black urban style combining blues with an unrelenting rhythm emphasizing the offbeats and often using electric guitar and bass.

H. Rock-and-Roll

Rock-and-roll, or *rock,* emerged in the mid-1950s from a blending of white country and black rhythm-and-blues styles. Like those two styles, it was promoted and virtually created by the recording industry and radio. The great success of *Elvis Presley* (1935–1977) in the 1950s and of *The Beatles* in the 1960s made rock the main style of popular music world-wide for the second half of the 20th century.

I. Musical Comedy

The *Broadway musical* (or *musical comedy*) has been the main genre of musical theater in the United States throughout the 20th century. Many popular songs by Cole Porter, Jerome Kern, Irving Berlin, and *George Gershwin* (1898–1937) were written for Broadway shows. Gershwin also wrote works that blend popular with classical traditions, such as his blend of jazz with the Romantic piano concerto in *Rhapsody in Blue* (1924) and his folk opera *Porgy and Bess* (1935).

IV. Foundations for an American Art Music (HWM 772–82, NAWM 143–46)

A. Charles Ives

Charles Ives (1874–1954) had an unusual career, making his living in insurance while composing in a number of very diverse styles from Romanticism to radical experiments. Trained in American band and church music and in European art music, he blended these diverse traditions in his symphonies, symphonic poems, chamber music, and art songs, evoking 19th-century America through modernist techniques. He often used existing music, especially American tunes, as a basis for his own, reworking borrowed material in a variety of ways and with various meanings. His music was not published or performed until 1920 and later, starting with his *Second Piano Sonata, "Concord, Mass., 1840–60"* (known as the *Concord Sonata*). When his music became widely known, his independence of mind, innovations, use of popular materials, and multilayered textures inspired many younger composers to seek their own paths. **Music: NAWM 143**

B. Carl Ruggles
Carl Ruggles (1876–1971) wrote a small number of atonal, very original works, of which the best known is *Sun-Treader* (1926–31).

C. Henry Cowell
Henry Cowell (1897–1965) explored new effects on the piano, including *tone clusters* in *The Tides of Manaunaun* (1912) and other works and strumming or playing directly on the strings in *The Aeolian Harp* (1923) and *The Banshee* (1925). His later music uses elements of folk and non-Western music. Cowell was also important as a promoter and publisher of new music.

D. Ruth Crawford Seeger
Ruth Crawford Seeger (1901–1953) composed in a modern atonal style, creating a series of very individual works, before changing her interests to transcribing and arranging American folksongs. **Music: NAWM 144**

E. Edgard Varèse
Edgard Varèse (1883–1965) was born and trained in France and moved to New York in 1915. Rather than using themes, harmony, or conventional rhythm, *Intégrales* (1925) and other works use pitch, duration, dynamics, and timbre (including many percussion instruments) to create *sound masses* that move and interact in musical space.

F. Aaron Copland
Aaron Copland (1900–1990) studied in France with Nadia Boulanger, who helped him gain a polished technique. His early works use jazz elements and dissonance, but in the mid-1930s he turned to a more popular style marked by thin, simple textures, diatonic writing, and folk tunes, as in *Appalachian Spring* (1944). In the 1950s, his music again became more abstract, and he adopted some twelve-tone methods. **Music: NAWM 145**

G. Other National Idioms
Roy Harris (1898–1979) is best known for symphonic music that evokes the American West through modal themes and open textures, as in his Third Symphony (1939). Critic and composer *Virgil Thomson* (1896–1989) studied with Boulanger but was attracted to the playful, simple music of Satie. He is best known for two operas on texts by Gertrude Stein, *Four Saints in Three Acts* (1928) and *The Mother of Us All* (1947), in a diatonic style that drew on the styles of 19th-century American hymns, patriotic songs, and dance music. *William Grant Still* (1895–1978), composer of the *Afro-American Symphony* (1931), *Florence Price* (1888–1953), and Ulysses Kay (b. 1917) were among the best-known African-American composers of art music. Other prominent American composers were William Schuman (1910–1992), Howard Hanson (1896–1981), and Walter Piston (1894–1976). **Music: NAWM 146**

V. Since 1945 (HWM 782–802, NAWM 147–52)

A. Abstract Idioms

Roger Sessions (1896–1985) wrote dissonant, complex music in an individual style based on continuous development. *Elliott Carter* (b. 1908) is noted for using *metric modulation* (or *tempo modulation*), in which the meter and tempo change in such a way that a fraction of the beat in the old meter becomes the beat in the new meter (for example, a dotted eighth in 4/4 becomes a quarter note in 4/4 at a proportionally faster tempo). Inspired by Ives's layered textures, Carter often gives each instrument a different rhythmic and melodic character to create a counterpoint of thoroughly independent lines, as in his String Quartet No. 2 (1959). **Music: NAWM 147**

B. The University as Patron

In the United States and Canada, composers of music in the classical tradition have been supported during the 20th century largely through teaching positions in universities and colleges. This has isolated composers from the public and has sometimes encouraged avant-garde experimentation, but it has also been the major way younger composers have been trained. Important universities for composers have included Harvard (where Piston taught), Yale (Hindemith), the University of California at Berkeley (Ingolf Dahl), Mills College (Milhaud), UCLA (Schoenberg), Princeton (Sessions and Milton Babbitt), the University of Illinois (Gordon Binkerd and Ben Johnston), the University of Michigan (Ross Lee Finney), and the Eastman School (Hanson).

C. The Post-Webern Vogue

Webern exercised a strong influence on composers in the universities who sought an objective approach free from Americanism and the influence of popular music. *Milton Babbitt* (b. 1916) extended twelve-tone music in new directions, applying serial principles to duration and other parameters before the Europeans did so and devising ways to derive new series from the basic row.

D. New Sounds and Textures

Conlon Nancarrow (b. 1912) anticipated the precision of electronic and computer music by using player-piano rolls to create pieces whose complex rhythmic relationships and rapid gestures were beyond the capacity of human performers. *Harry Partch* (1901–1974) rejected equal temperament as untrue, formulated a 43-note scale of unequal steps using only the pure harmonic ratios of just intonation, and built new instruments that used this scale. His works typically use these instruments to accompany dancing and singing; because his music cannot be played on standard instruments, it is seldom performed. *Ben Johnston* (b. 1926) applies just intonation to traditional instruments, such as piano or string quartet. *George Crumb* (b. 1929) draws unusual sounds from traditional instruments to create emotionally powerful music in an eclectic style, as in *Black Angels* (1970) for amplified string quartet. **Music: NAWM 148**

E. Electronic Music

Lacking performers, electronic music is less often played in concert than heard on recordings. But several composers have combined live performers with electronic music, as in Babbitt's moving *Philomel* (1964) for soprano and a tape with electronic and electronically altered vocal sounds. Recent developments include computer-driven synthesizers and pianos. **Music: NAWM 149**

F. Third Stream

Many 20th-century composers have used jazz elements in their classical works, and Duke Ellington used symphonic techniques in extended jazz compositions such as *Black, Brown, and Beige*. *Gunther Schuller* (b. 1925) merged jazz and classical elements in music he called *third stream*. Other composers have also joined classic and jazz styles in various ways. **Music: NAWM 150**

G. John Cage and Indeterminacy

In his music after 1950, *John Cage* (1912-1992) used both *indeterminacy,* in which some aspect of the music is left undetermined by the composer (as in the totally silent piece *4'33"*, 1952, where the sounds one hears are those that happen during the duration of the piece), and *chance,* in which some aspect of the music is determined, not by the composer's will or intentions, but by chance operations such as flipping coins (as pitches were determined in *Music of Changes,* 1951). (These two are often confused, and must be kept distinct. If something is determined by chance operations, it is not indeterminate.) Cage's purpose, inspired by Zen Buddhism, was to allow listeners to hear sounds as sounds in themselves, not as means by which a composer communicates a feeling or idea.

H. Minimalism

Minimalism is a term used for an approach which uses a deliberately restricted set of notes or sounds and an enormous amount of repetition. It was inspired in part by repetitive music of Asia and Africa and in part by a desire to make musical processes audible to listeners, in contrast to serial music. *Steve Reich* (b. 1936) used small repeated units that began in unison and gradually moved out of phase with each other, as in *Violin Phase* (1967, rev. 1979). *Philip Glass* (b. 1937) has written operas and works for his own ensemble using a very repetitive style. *John Adams* (b. 1947) has written operas and orchestral music using repeated ideas that evolve and shift in alignment with each other. **Music: NAWM 151**

I. The Mainstream

Many American composers continue to write music accessible to a wide public. Three composers are particularly noted for their vocal music: *Ned Rorem* (b. 1923) for his songs, *Gian Carlo Menotti* (b. 1911) for his operas, and *Samuel Barber* (1910–1981) for both. *Joan Tower* (b. 1938) and *Ellen Taaffe Zwilich* (b. 1939) are younger composers who have found a middle road.

J. Post-Modern Styles

Recent post-modernist architects have incorporated elements of earlier styles into their designs, and so do a number of post-avant-garde composers. *George Rochberg* (b. 1918) revisits and deconstructs the style of J. S. Bach in *Nach Bach* (After Bach, 1966). *Sinfonia* (1968) by *Luciano Berio* (b. 1925) quotes virtually an entire Mahler symphony movement and superimposes upon it more than 100 quotations from other works and verbal commentary from eight speakers. *David Del Tredici* (b. 1937) has written a number of works based on parts of *Alice in Wonderland* and *Through the Looking Glass,* using a style derived from Wagner and Strauss in order to communicate with an audience and match the innocence and whimsy of the stories.   **Music: NAWM 152**

VI. Conclusions (HWM 803)

The four characteristics that have defined Western music since the Middle Ages have been challenged in the 20th century. *Composition* has been augmented in some music by chance procedures or improvisation. *Notation* has expanded to include graphic and other notation. *Principles of order* do not always rule in chance or indeterminate music and are not always perceptible in serial music. *Polyphony* and *harmony* continue in novel forms. "Serious" music has found only a small audience, and radical experimentation a still smaller one. Recent composers have sought ways to please a broader public, often by incorporating ideas from popular music, non-Western music, or music of the past.

STUDY QUESTIONS

Introduction (HWM 759–60)

1. What were some of the ways in which 20th-century European composers interacted with and influenced American composers of art music?

The Historical Background (HWM 760–65)

2. When did William Billings live? _____

   What kinds of music did he write? What was his significance for American music?

3. What violations of "the normal rules of counterpoint" are there in *Washington-Street* (HWM, p. 763)?

4. What is a *fuging tune*? Explain what characteristics make *Washington-Street* a fuging tune.

5. What were Lowell Mason's contributions to music in the United States?

6. What was the importance of brass and wind bands in the United States? What was their repertory? What was their significance for African-Americans?

Vernacular Music (HWM 765–71)

7. What is *ragtime*? From what traditions did it derive?

8. Describe the style and form of the *blues*.

9. Describe the style of early *jazz*, and briefly trace its evolution through big bands to modern jazz.

10. Describe the characteristics of *country music*. From what traditions did it derive?

11. Describe the origins and style of *rhythm-and-blues*.

12. Describe the origins and style of *rock-and-roll*.

Foundations for an American Art Music (HWM 772–82, NAWM 143–46)

13. What was Charles Ives's musical background and training? What are some prominent characteristics of his music? What was his significance for American music?

Music to Study

NAWM 143: Charles Ives, *"They Are There!"*: A War Song March, for unison chorus and orchestra (adapted in 1942 from Ives's 1917 song *He Is There!*)

CD 12.7–9 (Concise 4.46–48)   Cassette 12.A (Concise 4.B)

Most of Ives's mature works are in the genres of European art music, includ-ing symphonies, symphonic poems, sonatas, and art songs, and use modernist techniques to evoke 19th-century America. *They Are There!* (NAWM 143) is not entirely typical, for it uses the verse-chorus format and melodic style of a Tin Pan Alley tune, including ragtime-like syncopations (compare George M. Cohan's 1917 song *Over There*, his earlier *Yankee Doodle Dandy*, or Irving Berlin's 1911 song *Alexander's Ragtime Band*). But it illustrates several characteristic features of Ives's music.

Tin Pan Alley composers often quoted existing tunes (for instance, *Yankee Doodle Dandy* strings together parts of four patriotic songs interspersed with Cohan's own melody). Ives continues and intensifies this practice, quoting or paraphrasing fragments of the following tunes. Most are Civil War tunes, used here to link what Ives considered the idealism of that war for the Union and the end of slavery with the ideal of ending tyranny in World War I and II and creating a "People's World Union."

Measures	Parts	Tune
1–2	brass, piano, clarinets	*Country Band March,* by Ives
8–9	voices, trumpets, violin 1 & 2	*Country Band March*
12–14	voices, trumpets, violin 1 & 2	*Marching through Georgia*
18–19	voices, trumpets, violin 1	*Tenting on the Old Camp Ground*
19–21	voices, trumpets, violin 1	*Columbia, the Gem of the Ocean*
20–23	trombones	*The Battle Hymn of the Republic*
21–22	winds	*Dixie*
23	winds	*Marching through Georgia*
23–25	voices, trumpets, trombones, violin 1	*Tramp, Tramp, Tramp*
24	winds	*Yankee Doodle*
25–26	winds	*Marching through Georgia*
27–30	voices, trumpet 1, viola 1	*Columbia, the Gem of the Ocean*
29–30	winds	*Maryland, My Maryland*
31–35	winds	*La Marseillaise*
32–33	voices, brass, viola 1	*Columbia, the Gem of the Ocean*
34–38	voices and brass	*Tenting on the Old Camp Ground*
40–44	voices and brass	*Tenting on the Old Camp Ground*
43–47	winds	*The Battle Cry of Freedom*
44–48	voices, trumpet 1, violin 1	*The Battle Cry of Freedom*
48–50	winds and brass	*The Star-Spangled Banner*
51–53	flutes and trumpets	*Reveille*

14. How does Ives connect these fragments of tunes into a coherent melody? Look at the voice part throughout and the upper winds from m. 21 to the end. How does Ives join his borrowed tunes together?

15. Ives harmonizes his vocal melody with the expected tonal harmonies, in most cases. But he also adds many elements that one would not expect to find in a Tin Pan Alley song, or in a traditional tonal work. What are some of these added elements?

16. How do these added elements affect your own experience of the work? In your opinion, how do they affect your sense of the work's meaning?

17. Ives often superimposed layers of music, each with its own rhythm, melodic or harmonic character, and instrumental timbre. In mm. 28–29, what rhythmically independent layers are sounding simultaneously? For each layer, name the instruments or voices that are performing it and describe its rhythmic and melodic character.

18. What new musical resources did Henry Cowell introduce in his piano music? For each one, name at least one piece that uses it.

Music to Study

NAWM 144: Ruth Crawford Seeger, Violin Sonata (1926), second movement
  CD 12.10–12   Cassette 12.A

(Note: In this work, accidentals apply only to the note to which they are affixed. For example, the fifth note of the piece is *A-natural,* not *A-flat.*)

19. The second movement of Ruth Crawford Seeger's Violin Sonata (NAWM 144) is built on a bass ostinato. How is this figure treated during this movement? Where is it repeated, where and how is it varied, and where (if ever) does it not appear?

20. How is the theme introduced by the violin varied and developed over the course of the movement?

---

21. Describe the music of Edgard Varèse. What resources does he use, and how does he deploy them? (Note: In addition to HWM, pp. 776–77, Varèse is also discussed on pp. 748 and 750 in chapter 21.)

22. Outline Aaron Copland's career, indicating distinctive aspects of his style in each period.

Music to Study
    NAWM 145a: *'Tis the gift to be simple*, Shaker hymn (not on recordings)
    NAWM 145b: Aaron Copland, *Appalachian Spring,* ballet (1944), excerpt
        (variations on *'Tis the gift to be simple*)
      CD 12.13–17 (Concise 4.49–53)   Cassette 12.A (Concise 4.B)

23. How does Copland vary the Shaker tune *'Tis the gift to be simple* in the excerpt from *Appalachian Spring* in NAWM 145b?

24.   What kinds of harmonies does Copland use in this excerpt?

25. Name two operas by Virgil Thomson on librettos by Gertrude Stein.

_____   -   _____

What are the characteristics of Thomson's music for these operas? How are they exemplified in the passage in Example 22.4 in HWM, p. 780?

Music to Study
> **NAWM 146:** William Grant Still, *Afro-American Symphony* (1931), third
> movement
> CD 12.18–20   Cassette 12.A

26. William Grant Still's *Afro-American Symphony* unites the symphonic and African-American traditions. What elements from the African-American traditions (including spirituals, ragtime, blues, and jazz) does Still incorporate in the third movement (NAWM 146)? Refer back to pp. 764–69 in HWM for a discussion of these types of music. (Two elements not mentioned there, both from jazz, are the trumpets with Harmon mutes, starting at m. 58, and the wire brush used to play the drum, starting at m. 69.)

27. What does this movement draw from the symphonic tradition? What does it have in common with symphonic works such as Beethoven's *Eroica* Symphony, first movement (NAWM 106), or the scherzo from Mendelssohn's *Midsummer Night's Dream* (NAWM 109)?

Since 1945 (HWM 782–802, NAWM 147–52)

Music to Study
> **NAWM 147:** Elliott Carter, String Quartet No. 2 (1959), excerpt: Introduction
> and Allegro fantastico
>   CD 12.21–23   Cassette 12.A

28. What means does Elliott Carter use to give the cello a distinctive rhythmic
     character in his String Quartet No. 2 (NAWM 147)?

29. What are some of the ways in which Carter gives each of the other players a
     distinctive character?

30. What is *metric modulation,* and how does Carter use it in mm. 57–61 of this
     work?

31. What has been the role of North American colleges and universities in supporting composition of new music? How does this differ from the situation in Europe?

32. Briefly describe the distinctive approach to music of each of the following composers:

Milton Babbitt

Conlon Nancarrow

Harry Partch

Ben Johnston

Music to Study
   NAWM 148: George Crumb, *Black Angels: Thirteen Images from the Dark Land,* for electric string quartet (1970), excerpts

148a: 4. *Devil-music*	CD 12.24	Cassette 12.A
148b: 5. *Danse macabre*	CD 12.25	Cassette 12.A
148c: 6. *Pavana lachrymae*	CD 12.26	Cassette 12.A
148d: 7. *Threnody*	CD 12.27	Cassette 12.A
148e: 8. *Sarabanda de*	CD 12.28	Cassette 12.A
la muerte oscura		
148f: 9. *Lost Bells*	CD 12.29	Cassette 12.A

NAWM 149: Milton Babbitt, *Philomel* for soprano and tape (1964), opening
  section
  CD 12.30–34 (Concise 4.54–58) Cassette 12.B (Concise 4.B)
NAWM 150: Gunther Schuller, *Seven Studies on Themes of Paul Klee* for
  orchestra (1959), excerpts
  150a: 3. *Kleiner blauer Teufel* (Little Blue Devil)
   CD 12.35–36   Cassette 12.B
  150b: 5. *Arabische Stadt* (Arab Village)
   CD 12.37–39   Cassette 12.B

33. What new playing techniques for string instruments does George Crumb use
in these six movements from *Black Angels* (NAWM 148)? (Hint: Check the
footnotes that explain how to perform certain effects; these footnotes
sometimes appear on a different page.) What additional instruments and
sounds does he call for, beyond the four instruments of the string quartet?
List all the new playing techniques, instruments, and other sounds you can
find. For each one, put down one word or a few words that describe how
the device sounds and what emotional effect it conveys.

34. Crumb quotes or refers to earlier music several times. *Danse macabre* (NAWM 148b) refers to the piece of the same name by Camille Saint-Saëns and—like Saint-Saëns—quotes the famous chant *Dies irae* from the Gregorian Mass for the Dead. *Pavana lachrymae* (NAWM 148c) is the title of a William Byrd keyboard transcription of a John Dowland song (see NAWM 45 and 47), but Crumb instead quotes Schubert's song *Death and the Maiden,* which Schubert himself had quoted in a string quartet. *Sarabanda de la muerte oscura* (NAWM 148e) presents a sarabande that is apparently not borrowed but written in 15th-century style, with double-leading-tone cadences, a Landini cadence, and appropriate ornamentation. What is the effect of these references to earlier music within the context of Crumb's music? In your opinion, what might these references mean?

35. How does music like this compare to earlier program music?

36. How does Milton Babbitt use the singer, taped vocal sounds, and electronic sounds in *Philomel* (NAWM 149)? What is each component like? How do they relate? And how do they work together to suggest the story and the feelings of Philomel?

37. What is *third stream*? How is it exemplified in *Kleiner blauer Teufel,* the third movement of Gunther Schuller's *Seven Studies on Themes of Paul Klee* (NAWM 150a)?

38. How does this movement compare to the third movement of Still's *Afro-American Symphony* (NAWM 146) in its use of jazz elements?

39. How does Schuller evoke Arab music in *Arabische Stadt,* the fifth movement of his *Seven Studies on Themes of Paul Klee* (NAWM 150b)?

40. Why did John Cage use indeterminacy and chance operations in his music? How did he use them?

Music to Study
> **NAWM 151:** Steve Reich, *Violin Phase* for four violins or violin and tape (1967, rev. 1979), opening section
> CD 12.40–43 (Concise 4.59–62)   Cassette 12.B (Concise 4.B)

In the opening section of Steve Reich's *Violin Phase* (NAWM 151), we hear the following series of events, numbered by the measure numbers in the score. Each measure is repeated a number of times, as marked at the beginning of the measure.

1. Violin 1 (or tape track 1) plays a repeated figure.
2. Violin 2 (or solo violin) imperceptibly fades in, playing the same figure in unison through several repetitions. It then plays just slightly faster, so that it gradually pulls ahead of Violin 1, playing out of phase. (The easiest way to follow this process may be to listen for the low C♯'s, which stick out of the texture.)
3. When Violin 2 is exactly an eighth note ahead of Violin 1, it returns to the opening tempo. It is now in phase with Violin 1 in terms of rhythmic pulse, but still out of phase in respect to the musical figure, as the two parts play a sort of canon. After several repetitions, Violin 2 again plays slightly faster and gradually pulls further ahead of Violin 1.
4. Violin 2 is now exactly two eighth notes ahead of Violin 1, and repeats the process in measure 3.
5. Violin 2 is now three eighth notes ahead of Violin 1, and again repeats the process.
6. Violin 2 is now four eighth notes ahead of Violin 1, returns to the opening tempo, and repeats the figure several times in this relationship with Violin 1.
7. Violin 3 (or tape track 2) gradually fades in playing the same figuration as Violin 2, which gradually fades out.
8. Violin 1 and 3 continue the pattern.
9. Over Violin 1 and 3, Violin 2 picks out some notes of the composite pattern they form, fading in (m. 9), repeating several times (m. 9a), and fading out (m. 9b).
10. The same, with Violin 2 picking out a different pattern.
11. The same, with Violin 2 picking out a two-measure-long pattern.

In the next section of the piece (mm. 12–16), Violin 2 moves gradually ahead of Violin 3, in the same manner as in mm. 1–6, until it is another four eighth notes ahead. In m. 17, it is gradually replaced by Violin 4, and from then on Violin 1 plays against the composite of the three other parts, using procedures already established in new combinations.

41.   What is *minimalism*?

In what sense is this piece minimalist? In what sense is it complex?

42. What is the effect when the parts get out of phase with each other? Can you still hear the original repeated figure?   Do other things become more prominent?

43. How can you follow this music? In your opinion, what should you listen for?

44. What does *Violin Phase* have in common with a piece by Beethoven (such as NAWM 104, 106, or 107) or any other 19th-century composer, and what is different?

45. How are the minimalist works of Philip Glass and John Adams different from Reich's *Violin Phase* and from each other?

Music to Study
    NAWM 152: George Rochberg, *Nach Bach* (After Bach), fantasy for
        harpischord or piano (1966)
      CD 12.44–46   Cassette 12.B

46. In *Nach Bach* (NAWM 152), where does Rochberg quote Bach or invoke the Baroque style directly?

47. How do these references to Bach or Baroque style contrast with the other music in the piece? How do the different kinds of music fit together, and what is the overall effect?

---

48. What is David Del Tredici's attitude toward communication with the audience, as summarized in his statement on p. 802 of HWM? How does his music reflect his concerns?

Conclusions (HWM 803)

49. How have the four characteristics that have defined Western music since the Middle Ages (composition, notation, principles of order, and polyphony) fared in the 20th century?

TERMS TO KNOW

Terms Related to American Music before 1900 and to Vernacular Music

Yankee tunesmiths	rhythm section
fuging tunes	chart
shape-note hymnals	swing
spirituals	bebop (bop)
wind band, brass band	country music (country-and-
ragtime	western music)
rag	rhythm-and-blues
blues	rock-and-roll (rock)
blue notes	Broadway musical (musical
jazz	comedy)
big bands	

Terms Related to 20th-Century American Art Music

tone clusters	indeterminacy
sound masses	chance
metric modulation	minimalism
third stream	

NAMES TO KNOW

Names Related to American Music before 1900 and to Vernacular Music

William Billings	King Oliver's Creole Jazz Band
Anthony Philip Heinrich	Duke Ellington
Lowell Mason	Elvis Presley
Fisk Jubilee Singers	The Beatles
John Philip Sousa	George Gershwin
Scott Joplin	*Rhapsody in Blue*
Maple Leaf Rag	*Porgy and Bess*

Names Related to American Art Music Before 1945

Charles Ives	*Appalachian Spring*
Concord Sonata	Roy Harris
Carl Ruggles	Virgil Thomson
Henry Cowell	*Four Saints in Three Acts*
Ruth Crawford Seeger	*The Mother of Us All*
Edgard Varèse	William Grant Still
Intégrales	*Afro-American Symphony*
Aaron Copland	Florence Price

Names Related to American Art Music Since 1945

Roger Sessions	Steve Reich
Elliott Carter	*Violin Phase*
Milton Babbitt	Philip Glass
Conlon Nancarrow	John Adams
Harry Partch	Samuel Barber
Ben Johnston	Ned Rorem
George Crumb	Gian Carlo Menotti
Black Angels	Joan Tower
Philomel	Ellen Taaffe Zwilich
Gunther Schuller	George Rochberg
John Cage	*Nach Bach*
4'33"	Luciano Berio
Music of Changes	David Del Tredici

REVIEW QUESTIONS

1. Add the composers and major works discussed in this chapter to the 20th-century time-line you made for chapter 19, or to the earlier time-lines you made for chapters 13 and 16, as appropriate.

2. Summarize the 18th- and 19th-century historical background for music in the United States.

3. What are the major forms of popular music in 20th-century America? Describe each kind, and explain how each relates to the others in historical succession.

4. Trace the history of American art music in the first half of the 20th century, naming the most important composers and describing their music.

5. What are some of the main trends in American art music since World War II? Define each trend, and describe at least one composer and piece associated with each.

6. Write a brief essay in which you defend or reject the position Milton Babbitt articulates in his statement on p. 789 of HWM. Whichever position you take, use examples from at least two 20th-century works in NAWM to support your point of view about the relationship between composers and their listeners.

7. Of the seven pieces in NAWM composed since 1950 (NAWM 134 and 147–52), which one or two do you like the best? Which one or two do you like the least? Write an essay in which you explain what is especially good about the piece(s) you like and what is unappealing about the piece(s) you like less, as if you were writing a review or trying to persuade a friend about which CD to purchase. Explain what it is you find most valuable in music and how your judgments are based on those values.